CLIMATE CHANGED

Climate Changed is an honest and humane account about the rapid downsizing of the world's natural resources and the consequences this has for millions of people who, year after year, are displaced from their home countries because of politically instigated and economically justified war and conflict.

Based on interviews with 110 refugees who arrived into Europe from 2015 to 2018 and observations of refugee camps, border crossings, inner-city slums, social housing projects, NGO and related refugee associations, it offers a moving insight into the refugee experience of leaving home, crossing borders and settling in Europe, and sets this against the geopolitical and commercial enterprise that dismantled their countries in the international chase for wilting quantities of the world's natural resources. Yet at every point of their journey to their new lives and in the resettlement process, the refugees are on the end of more perpetual victimisation and exploitation as there is always money to be made from them.

Even if their labour is in demand, all this is further exacerbated by a European social climate of intolerance and stigma which jeopardises integration and counters their well-being and safety. The climate has changed. Students, lecturers and professors and other similar academic workers, policymakers, various practitioners and voluntary workers within the sector of refugee front lines as well as aid workers, town planners and welfare support staff would find relevance in this book.

Daniel Briggs is an experienced ethnographer and social researcher who has studied some of the most disturbing and challenging social realities of the 21st century. He is currently a part-time lecturer in criminology at the Universidad Europea. His previous book, *Dead End Lives: Drugs and Violence in the City Shadows*, won the Outstanding Book Award 2018 at the Division of International Criminology, awarded by the American Society of Criminology.

CLIMATE CHANGED

Refugee Border Stories and the Business of Misery

Daniel Briggs

Routledge
Taylor & Francis Group

LONDON AND NEW YORK

First published 2021
by Routledge
2 Park Square, Milton Park, Abingdon, Oxon OX14 4RN

and by Routledge
52 Vanderbilt Avenue, New York, NY 10017

Routledge is an imprint of the Taylor & Francis Group, an informa business

© 2021 Daniel Briggs

British Library Cataloguing-in-Publication Data
A catalogue record for this book is available from the British Library

Library of Congress Cataloging-in-Publication Data
Names: Briggs, Daniel (Criminologist), author.
Title: Climate changed : refugee border stories and the business of
misery / Daniel Briggs.
Description: First Edition. | New York : Routledge, 2020. | Includes
bibliographical references and index.
Identifiers: LCCN 2020026801 (print) | LCCN 2020026802 (ebook) |
ISBN 9780367436728 (hardback) | ISBN 9780367436735 (paperback) |
ISBN 9781003004929 (ebook)
Subjects: LCSH: Immigrants—European Union countries—
History—21st century. | European Union countries—Emigration and
immigration—Social aspects—21st century. | Conflict management—
European Union countries.| European Union countries—Social
policy—21st century.
Classification: LCC JV7590 .B754 2020 (print) | LCC JV7590 (ebook) |
DDC 305.9/06912094—dc23
LC record available at https://lccn.loc.gov/2020026801
LC ebook record available at https://lccn.loc.gov/2020026802

ISBN: 978-0-367-43672-8 (hbk)
ISBN: 978-0-367-43673-5 (pbk)
ISBN: 978-1-003-00492-9 (ebk)

Typeset in Bembo
by codeMantra

For Lucy, Freddy, Lily, Nadia and Charlie. I love you all.

CONTENTS

FIGURES

FOREWORD

Christian Parenti

This very fine book is harrowing and brutal to read. The reality it portrays is so horrible you will wonder how on earth it is not front-page news everywhere all the time. Travelling the length and breadth of Europe, sociologist Daniel Briggs portrays the searing pain and humiliation that is the lived experience of so many of those who flee Africa and the Middle East in the hope of reaching Europe.

Using ethnographic participant observation, peppered where helpful with theory, Briggs takes readers behind the anonymizing statistics, into the cramped and fetid camps where refugees, fleeing hell, are revealed to be — just regular people who have been subject to extraordinary conditions. They are civilians whose lives are structured around the quotidian hopes and struggles that are universally recognizable: the love of family, the desire for education, the struggle to make ends meet economically, the battle with disability and illness and the struggle to be treated with dignity.

The only difference between the northern middle-class reader and the protagonists in these pages is that by misfortune of geography and history these immigrants have been plunged into a hell maze populated by sadistic religious fanatics, police torturers, abusive boarder guards, parasitic pimps, predatory nationalist thugs and maliciously incompetent welfare bureaucrats.

The "business of misery" described by Briggs is a pervasive criminality, the connective tissue in a world where the line between "licit" and "illicit" has dissolved. From the great wars for freedom arms like the US destruction of Iraq, to the ongoing arms trade that fuels the aftermath forever wars that drive the refugees forward, to the kidnapping, extortion, pimping, rape and labour exploitation of the refugees as they flee for safety, it becomes hard to distinguish the criminals from the law enforcers. Organized crime and the disorganized forces of the state start to appear not as opposites but rather as symbiotic components of a diffuse criminality. The police extort, mafia join ISIS, the Turkish coastguard coordinate with smugglers and European skinheads put on suits and get elected. Only one thing is clear: the vast bulk of immigrants are victims.

The least violent episodes in the book are sometimes the most painful to read. For example, a Syrian refugee recounting his attempts to enter Turkey:

> On one occasion, he had paid a smuggler to take him across but was told to wait by himself by a muddy river for a few hours to be collected. Aside from losing thousands of dollars, the only people who came were the Turkish Gendemarie who beat him up, arrested him and left his wheelchair in the mud. Such was the degrading nature of this for Mohamed that he then had to be carried around by his nephew for ten days. He says "they told me after they kicked me and put me in the car for arrest me" then said to him "why do you need your wheelchair, you get another one in Greece besides we don't want to get our car dirty and it has mud all over it."

Or, one traumatized survivor of torture in Syria describes his new life in Austria:

> They don't like the foreign people. When I go to spend my time in public, they watch me like I am scum or I am dirty. If they could kill me, they would. It gets stressful and I am afraid, I don't want to go out of the flat. I always try to stay in. People ask me to come out but I say no I want to stay here.

Finding himself trapped, badgered to learn German, unable to work until he does, but given few resources to do so, and on top of it all the man struggling with that seemingly most "first world" of problems: psychological and emotional pain.

Page after page of what follows are accounts of the most appalling cruelty, which the reader has to remind themselves that this is not the story of some medieval pillage. It is merely a deeper dive into today's news. Here you will meet police thugs and religious fanatics who are locked in mortal combat that from the point of view of civilians looks more like a sadistic romp of murder, mutilation, and enslavement. You also see Europe's ugly, racist, underbelly, its vicious unofficial welcome committee of xenophobic, right-wing populists and their infrastructure of aggressive policing, surveillance and border militarization. By one estimate, only 17% of EU spending on the refugee crisis was spent "to support asylum procedures, reception services and the resettlement and integration of refugees." The remaining 83% was spent on border militarization, detention, surveillance and deportation.

It is all so harrowing that one is tempted to turn away. But that is precisely why we need this book.

In the background of it all is climate change. Already climate change is displacing millions and will displace millions more. Estimates vary from 150 million to 330 million people displaced by the middle of the century by a rising global temperature. If robust emissions reductions are not achieved, historically unprecedented numbers of people will be on the move for the rest of the century.

The great irony in this horrible drama is that Europe needs immigrants. New migrants can help solve the demographic problem of a rapidly ageing Europe. The EU average "fertility rate" is about 1.6 per childbearing woman. To maintain current population levels – and thus maintain economies productive enough to fund welfare states – the fertility rate would need to be two per woman.

This "demographic transition" to fewer births per family is a normal pattern in developed economies. In industrial and service economies, families no longer need child labour. And when women have social and economic options, family sizes decrease. But as lifespans extend, this pattern becomes economically problematic. For a society to maintain a large dependent and ageing population, it needs a youthful workforce. In other words, Europe needs immigrants!

Just beyond Europe's borders, there are now 9 million refugees in the Middle East and another 15 million in sub-Saharan Africa. Three majority Muslim countries host roughly 30% of the world's refugees; two of these are at the edge of Europe, Turkey and Lebanon, and the third is Pakistan.

Alas the politics of this moment are misshaped by decades of neoliberal austerity and privatization. Cuts to social investment and deindustrialization that goes with laissez-faire economics leads to fear and inchoate resentment, and these are fertile ground for xenophobic populist reaction. And thus, the politics of this global-scale exodus is only just getting started. This painful but much needed book helps us seen the overlooked details, and it is these details that will help inform and shape a better politics.

PREFACE

This book is not an easy read, but it is a necessary one if we are to come to terms with the damage war and commerce have done to the climate, whole domestic economies and, as a consequence, everyday peoples' lives. Climate change is not something imminent which could shape our futures because it is already present and now is rapidly changing our political and social outlook. The current system is not working and we need to move forward from flimsy liberal policy recommendations which are made every few years and the big UN meetings where everyone has smiley photos taken as they shake hands and make tentative promises to reduce CO_2 emissions. We need to look directly at the gravity and severity of the kinds of social issues which neoliberal capitalism generates, which, in the context of this book, are climate change, war and arms trading, people displacement and refugees. To do this, we must be prepared to do research in a way that enables us to access and then report on disturbing stories and harsh realities, to feel the stymies of the people we study and use this to motivate us to look carefully at all the facets of their suffering. We need to go beyond undertaking feel-good and fluffy-sounding things like "needs analysis" or doing an evaluation of a course attended by refugees to allocate "success" to it and instead join these experiences up with larger, powerful processes which have an indiscriminate impact on the level of stigma, risk and danger refugees experience on an everyday basis.

Similarly, we can't just rely on periodic and temporary epiphanies which offer us a reflective space to recognise society's fragility and its systemic failures – such as those which arose with the advent of the coronavirus and the subsequent lockdown – and watch in wonder as "nature fights back," and we experience the brief motivation to change by doing things differently for a while. The history of the world shows that this in itself is not enough as, very soon after crises, the machinery of capitalism just fires up again with more ferocity. If we cannot bring to light investigations such as this in this book and act on them, then our only option is to plan quickly for life in a hostile future where more countries collapse and any partial law left descends into martial law, and the insecurity and danger prominent in the testimonies of the people in this book become the normality in other regions beyond the Middle East and Africa. We have been warned again.

ACKNOWLEDGEMENTS

Many people have been fundamental to this book – first and foremost, perhaps obviously, the refugees themselves. Abbas, thank you for chasing after me in the refugee camp in Melilla, for if you didn't, this book wouldn't exist. Mohammed, thank you for having patience with me in Paris during the long interviews and thereafter helping me expand the sample in France and Austria. I am also indebted to Mukhles who postponed everything he had on to take me around Istanbul and Ankara. Asim was pivotal in Brussels as was Wasif in Saarbrücken. Thank you Shizar for that text message after we met in Norway and for keeping me posted of your progress in Germany. Amir, wherever you are, I hope you are safe and well.

Andreia Bessa helped me with refugee contacts in the Netherlands and Italy as did Jeroen Vandekerckhove and David Lopez in France and Belgium and Ioanna Charalampous in Greece. Dag Rønning did the same in Norway and Sweden in the freezing −37° temperature, while Seve Sobrino did so in +37° temperature on the borders of Morocco. Thanks also to Davide Capecci and Mojca Kodela Lesemann at the Council of Europe who, after inviting me to speak at some meetings around Europe on youth inequality, turned a blind eye as I disappeared from the conferences into the dark corners of Strasbourg, Paris, Budapest, Izmir, Belgrade, Dusseldorf and London.

A great many thanks to my publishers, in particular Emily Briggs who was so enthusiastic about my work and Lakshita Joshi at Routledge. It means a lot to me that the three anonymous reviewers used by Routledge also give this project resounding and unequivocal support.

For their endorsement and support of my work, thanks to Dr Christian Parenti, Emeritus Professor Steve Hall, Professor Simon Winlow, Dr Anthony Lloyd, Professor Howard Williamson, Dr David Cairns, Professor Rowland Atkinson, Professor Theo Gavrielides, Dr Raili Nugin, Luke Telford, Dr Anthony

Ellis and Dr Valentina Cuzzocrea; in particular to Hanjo Schild, Mark Taylor, Professor Jeff Ross, Mark Bushell and Emeritus Professor Dick Hobbs for reading first drafts of the manuscript.

For their academic inspiration and friendship, thanks to Mariela Alvarez and Manuel Tejejro. My former tutor Professor Jock Young, Professor Geoff Pearson and Professor Roger Matthews, all three were fundamental to my career and all sadly have now passed away. Thanks to my colleagues at Universidad Europea such as Antonio Silva, Dr Rebeca Cordero Verdugo, Dr Jesus Soto Piñeda and Dr Jorge Ramiro Pérez Suárez.

Lastly but by no means least(ly), thanks to my mum and dad, Steve and Paulette, who showed me that humility and compassion should drive ambition to change peoples' lives and change the world. Thanks to my brother, Maurice, to who like me, does things unconventionally and to my friends Dave, Bob, Gabriel, Kev, and Ben who stand close to me as the best friends I could have.

ABBREVIATIONS

BIRN	Balkan Investigative Reporting Network
CEAS	Common European Asylum System
CETI	Centros de Estancia Temporal de Inmigrantes
CH_4	Methane
CO_2	Carbon dioxide
DNA	Deoxyribonucleic acid
DRC	Democratic Republic of Congo
EU	European Union
IOM	International Organization of Migration
ISIS	Islamic State of Iraq and Syria
NASA	National Aeronautics and Space Administration
NGO	National Governmental Organisation
NOAA	National Oceanic and Atmospheric Administration
NRC	National Research Council
OCCRP	Organized Crime and Corruption Reporting Project
OECD	Organisation for the Economic Co-operation of Development
O_2	Oxygen
PEGIDA	Patriotic Europeans against the Islamisation of the West
TEFL	Teaching English as a Foreign Language
UCCRN	Urban Climate Change Research Network
UAE	United Arab Emirates
UDI	Utlendings Direktoratet
UK	United Kingdom
UN	United Nations
UNDESA	United Nations Department of Economic and Social Affairs
UNHCR	United Nations High Commissioner for Refugees
UNODC	United Nations Office on Drugs and Crime
USA	United States of America

1

EXODUS

"Exodus," or the departure of a large number of people, is Chapter 10 in the Old Testament of the Bible. The chapter describes Moses's attempts to free the Israelites from slavery and the oppressive rule of the Pharaoh in Egypt and the subsequent journey to Canaan – a land "flowing with milk and honey" (3:8). Moses, along with the assistance of Aaron and through the power of God, bestows ten plagues on Egypt which include plagues of flies and mosquitos, locusts, disease and weather storms of thunder, hail and fire. After denying their freedom after each plague is inflicted, the Pharaoh puts the Israelites to work harder. Eventually, after Pharaoh's son is killed in one of the plagues, the people are freed and trudge towards the new sacred land, all the way deprived of food and water, and doubting their new "freedom." The symbolism of this story carries equal measure in the 21st century: a large exploited immigrant workforce living in slavery, the Pharaoh the manifestation of capitalism and its relentless subjugated work ethic and the plagues serving as a the loud-ringing alarm bells of climate change and war, conflict and social suffering.

Similarly, like today, there are hundreds of thousands of people who continue to risk life and limb to leave countries of war and oppressive governance and come to a continent like Europe which is constructed by many as a "promised land," a safe place to start again. Many leave with next to nothing, having sold all their belongings in their home country, and along the way they fight off hostile police, pay smugglers, and perhaps are humiliated and physically or sexually victimised – all the while clambering across European Union (EU) borders hoping that we would welcome them. However, Europe for millions of them is no such promised land. Their arrival in overcrowded, squalid camps and in city centres, often sleeping in streets, has since triggered a puerile nationalistic panic about their motivations to come like "who will pay for them" and "whether they are ISIS terrorists." Meanwhile, little serious, long-term strategic attention is being given to what this large-scale influx may mean for the social and cultural demography of Europe as there seems to be general misunderstanding related to *how* or *why* these people came in the first place.

My book is about their "stories" and the broader geo-political and ecological context which has led to their displacement. Everything you read in this book, even though many more refugee testimonies and notes have not made it to these pages, has been carefully collected to better understand how and why refugees leave their home countries, and what happens to them as they leave and when they arrive. Over the course of three years from August 2015 to August 2018, I met and interviewed 110 refugees in 14 different European countries. What you read in the chapters which follow is what they told me and how they experience life. The story starts one late summer evening in Madrid in 2014.

A (familiar) tale in two cities

It is about 11:30 p.m. in in the city centre, a Friday night in fact. The air is warm and in and out of the gloss and glamour of the touristic area of Sol, there is a bubbling ambience to the place. I walk into the main square where the lights illuminate the place and trawls of tourists pose for selfies between the weird sideshows of human-size cartoon characters and small groups of Spanish young people who start to congregate here for their night out. Suddenly, as I turn into a road south heading towards the Plaza de Santa Ana, I hear the pacey murmur of people running. I look behind me and up the street lightly jogging en mass are a small army of black African men with large white sacks on their backs. They are dark, lean and tall, which makes their steps look like giant leaps. As they pass, they look unnervingly yet cautiously behind them as they move quick in their beach gear and flip-flops. They turn left at the end of the road, only for the local police to follow in a half-hearted, sort-of-hot pursuit. The "manteros" – or people who sell goods from blankets as they are called – normally sell fake brand goods on the streets.

Then, just over a year later:

It is about midday in early August and people are enjoying their holidays around a beach near Cartagena, a city on the south Spanish coast. I sit on a beach which lines with people smoking, eating, reading, playing with their kids and generally relaxing in the sun. From time to time, tall, thin very dark men, and the occasional woman, trudge up and down the beach with trays of hats and sunglasses; they seem unmoved by the continual rejection they get from some people who wave them off as if they are pesky flies. Few seem interested. Over the course of several hours, these people filter through small spaces available on the beach and don't seem to tire. When I go to lunch in a nearby beach bar, I sit in the shade, necessary to escape the burdensome heat reflecting off the sand at the height of the day. Even in the beach hut though, the men continue to come through, almost in periodic waves, as if they comb each potential tourist site in twos and threes. They wear piles of hats, are laden with trays and bags, and back-packs and soldier on with such neutral determination to sell…then disappear.

And on the same holiday:

Another lean black man walks into the beach hut and puts down his tray of sunglasses on the plastic table which is about to collapse under the added weight. He looks around at all the people eating and drinking in comfort. It is, once again, a burning hot day with temperatures around 35 °C which are only mildly diluted by the sea breeze. The tall, dark man withdraws a towel to wipe his brow and fishes for his wallet in his back pocket. He looks in the part where there should be notes and there are none. He then tips out what he has available and taps it on the bar. It is busy and the waitresses who walk around in their beachwear seem to take no notice of him, yet he seems to be a regular; however, a few seconds later one appears to give him a 1.5-litre bottle of water. He starts to drink swiftly and within 30 seconds it is all gone. He picks up his tray and bags and leaves for the beach again. No one seems to notice his short stop. The beaches are white. The sea is warm. Everyone is having fun. And then there is this tall lean man who is selling something which doesn't seem to interest anyone. Still that is his job.

Where had these people come from? Where did they stay? How was it that they were plodding around these areas in Spain (as well as in France, Italy and Greece) selling these artefacts? No doubt, I am not the only person thinking about these questions, but it was these observations which formed the impetus for this book you have in your hands or, more likely, the pdf you read on your screen. While these experiences come from my own interests about refugees and immigrants, more importantly they also highlight the pressing need for us as a society, who should be responsible for everyone in it, to urgently reconfigure how we think about the problem of human displacement and its origin: we have to look closely at what is taking place which causes the conflict and generates the motivation for them to move.

Climate changed: a call for an urgent rethinking of the problem

I would like to think the public would be able to identify refugees' motivations for leaving their country, often leaving their homes or even dead family and friends behind, and that those immediate reasons didn't reflect their ambitions to take job opportunities from host populations or scavenge social security benefits. But the tide is turning in Europe as democratic societies across the continent increasingly drift towards a far right collective rejection of waves of economic migrants, immigrants and refugees. More than ever, there is increasing disinterest when it comes to their arrival to European borders and shores even if it is directly related to political turmoil, economic uncertainty and widespread violence and insecurity in their home countries. While it is therefore important to ask how these regimes are permitted to operate like this – resulting in significant people displacement – at the same time, increasingly it is related to the same process of climate change and studies are starting to show how and why this may be the case.

Take the Syrian conflict for example. Collin Kelley and his research team (2015) recently published their research which concluded that a devastating crop drought between 2007 and 2010 (before the 2011 Arab Spring uprising) was responsible for the desertification of large rural areas in the Fertile Crescent – the vast area which supports the bulk of agriculture in the Middle East. Incoherent and substandard agricultural and environmental policies were also partly to blame when millions of people flooded to the Syrian cities, of which were already suffering inequality and oppressive governance from the Assad regime, making city living conditions across the country even worse and thus being a factor in the subsequent uprising. They said in their study that

> ...the recent decrease in Syrian precipitation is a combination of natural variability and a long-term drying trend, and the unusual severity of the observed drought is here shown to be highly unlikely without this trend. Precipitation changes in Syria are linked to rising mean sea-level pressure in the Eastern Mediterranean, which also shows a long-term trend. There has been also a long-term warming trend in the Eastern Mediterranean, adding to the draw down of soil moisture. No natural cause is apparent for these trends, whereas the observed drying and warming are consistent with model studies of the response to increases in greenhouse gases.
>
> *(Kelley et al., 2015: 3241)*

Man-made climate change is therefore a prominent factor in people displacement, and this needs to be acknowledged. This makes the rationale for my book more pressing as these days people are critical of the consequences of climate change (populations like refugees flooding into Europe) and less so the cause of climate change (politicians, corporations, capitalism) so I hope that as you turn these pages you will be convinced otherwise.

Firstly, "climate changed" in the title of this book relates to the potential end game of humanity with regard to the advanced nature of climate change. "Climate change" often conjures up the idea that it has been either a continual part of history or something in motion, like an organic mechanism (if I can use those words parallel) which is possible to reverse. While this may be true in that by natural processes the world does change and evolve, I want to show how there is something more deliberate related to our actions that is responsible for sizeable people displacement, hence "climate changed" – it is something already done as never before have we seen so many people displaced in modern history as we do today.

Secondly, "climate changed" refers to how economic uncertainty is only accelerating a tendency to widen inequality. Despite the blatant facts relating to the deteriorating environment, I want to show how nation states are failing collectively – as well as individually – to kerb these changes: still, large-scale corporate companies and foreign investors move in on "new opportunities" to pillage minerals and other natural resources, thus also contributing to human displacement. Increased global instability resulting in the displacement and migration of millions of people is not simply something which is just happening as a result of processes like globalisation but how international political entities and companies are creating the rational to destabilise certain countries for their own political and economic interests.

For example, among the many exploited African countries – places from where originate many of the people in the my field notes in Spain at the beginning of the chapter – Chinese businesses have stepped up their quest in the Democratic Republic of Congo (DRC) to enable them to continue to secure a steady supply of metals, mainly copper, cobalt and gold. However, the use of Chinese labour and the continual lack of investment in DRC public agencies and infrastructure have starved the domestic economy and furthered its neglect even after millions died in regional wars related to power struggles. This has led to a substantive population exodus which continues to have social ramifications. Similarly, most of the political destabilisation of the Gulf region, which accelerated in 2011/2012, has been linked to the West's direct political pursuit of rich minerals and resources in the vacuum of "democratic governance." This is in the wake of having invaded those very same countries and notwithstanding the billions of dollars earned by countries like the United States of America ("USA" hereafter), the United Kingdom ("UK" hereafter), France and Russia, among others, which sell weapons to them, thus perpetuating war and violence (Sadowski, 2010). So,

> ...this produces the fateful miscalculation, mishap and calamitous military expeditions in Afghanistan and Iraq which culminated in the substitution of the old dictatorial regimes with a theatre of indiscipline, and frenetic violence, instigated and supported by the commercial global arms trade and inflated by the weapons industry, which are both thirsty for profit, notwithstanding the tacit support of governments obsessed with improving their GDP.
>
> *(Bauman, 2016: 13)*

Lastly, and related to the former, the term "climate changed" explains how in the disintegration of community and social cohesion, social feeling has been ideologically and politically channelled towards social groups such as the refugees – among other denizen groups – as the responsible actors for this economic uncertainty (instead of the speculations of the banking sector). Consequently, political discourse and news media present them as unwanted outsiders who are "invading" the safe and secure confines of Europe. This has resulted in increased hate crime and negativity towards the refugees. We have to concede that the climate has changed.

This morally absent uprooting of around 70 million people is therefore implicated in business practices and political economic commercial enterprise. In the words and sentences and photos which make up this book, I want to show how all this is *passed down* to those 70 million and how it is *felt* by them: from geopolitical resource wars and conflict over strategic minerals to corporate elites and their webs of private enterprises, corrupt European institutions and nation states, and ineffective international helping entities down to the local functioning of the security industry and organised crime groups. In addition, in many instances, the lack of/bungled international protection/intervention, at numerous points in the lives of these refugees, results in their victimisation. It starts when they are uprooted from their homes, the loss and suffering they experience, their haphazard journeys which involve paying corrupt officials or smugglers and the way they are subject to various abuses along the way. Thereafter, it continues when they have to settle and start again somewhere else which, more often than not, makes it difficult for them to access formal economies and achieve cultural integration. This victimisation even extends down to some of the agencies who are charged with managing their "integration" and forging their futures in European countries. The refugees are unequivocal victims of this, and I call this process the *business of misery*.

The main threads of the book use refugee testimonies to draw this out as well as focussing on their experiences of war/conflict/social instability in their home countries, the decisions they took to leave, how and where they went and why and other related aspects of their journey. However, it doesn't end there. For many people I met didn't just arrive and settle and then start again, get jobs and move on from the traumas they have experienced. Many have their applications for asylum denied which keep them transient and stateless, some end up abandoning the settlement country and seeking out another to start there, while others return to their home countries. Their continual transience makes them almost nomadic and this I try to capture in the concept of *refugee border stories*: there is no real end point and no real settlement, and the threat of upheaval from European countries is ever constant and sadly real. Moreover, and as we will see, the new life is somewhat stale and depressing, and the past experiences never seem to go away.

What is the real reality?

If we are to stay close to following these issues, we need to get out of our offices, and speak and spend time with people such as refugees that appear on the news as "benefit scroungers," "illegal immigrants" or "criminals." News media, internet and social media limit how we see the world to dumbed-down sound bites and a set of scripted images that don't do justice to the complexities behind human displacement and its consequences. The fast and simplistic way reality is depicted for us through these mediums gives us little true insight into the everyday dilemmas of these people.

So, by the summer of 2015, and having made these observations you read in the opening part of this book, I was ready to start my study. My objectives were simple: (a) to examine how and why these people were leaving their home countries; (b) to follow and analyse what happens to them when they left and how to they arrived and (c) to evaluate how they settled in the new countries and what happened to them as a consequence. During August 2015, I spent a week with a friend who worked in the Spanish National Police in Melilla – a Spanish city wedged in a corner of North Africa which is on the front line of the continuous attempts refugees make to clamber to Europe. A base sample of 25 refugees were recruited from border crossings and the city's immigration centre. Melilla is also one of the world's most dangerous border crossings, and even the statistics don't favour the brave: in 2014, the International Organization for Migration (IOM) estimated that 3,500 people lost their lives between Melilla and mainland Spain which, at the time, was 70% of the number of deaths in the whole world (IOM, 2014).

Until recently, it was easy to cross the border. Before the turn of the 21st century, there existed no such wall that you see in the image below (see Figure 1). Then the first construction was built in 1998 which stood three metres high before it became two walls which were raised to six metres in height in 2005. Since then, it has

FIGURE 1 The wall or fence ("la valla") which separates Melilla, Spain and Morocco.

widened and been reinforced with further razor-sharp wiring before being augmented with spotlights, movement sensors and 24-hour video surveillance. It is said that this has cost €33 million – just to keep out fellow humans like us from trying to escape persecution and look for safety. As you can see, in 2020, it still stands intimidating and is no small feat to climb.

Over the last decade, there has been a rampant increase in border crossings and attempted boat crossings into Melilla and Ceuta, both of which nestle in the geographically advantageous peninsulas of Morocco. It was when I visited Melilla that I was confronted with the extent of the refugee exodus and a seemingly never-ending influx into Europe, perhaps most poignantly captured when I was shown around the immigration centre which was built for a capacity of 400 refugees. On the first day of my visit in August 2015, however, there were over 2,000 people staying there.

The reality of exodus

As we exit into the courtyard again, the guard leads me to the left and then left again towards the doctors, and I pass a large, shady area to my right, where people have set up their beds. Young families crouch and lie and smoke in the shade and new born babies are wrapped in whatever material possible; one father painstakingly changes his baby son's nappy revealing what looks like a serious rash across the baby's body; I count five other babies in a space of ten square metres. To my left, on the floor, are beds. I say beds but they are more like bits of material which have been woven into a kind of mattress. Next to them are plastic bags of clothes.

I am then led into the hospital which is a small hut. As I walk past a few children who have their medical cards in their hands, the medical staff greet me and show me the facilities. There is a small pharmacy, a consulting office and several rooms for treatment, where sits a boy of 15 years old from the Ivory Coast; he nurses numerous large cuts and bruises on his legs that have other significant scars on. He looks to be one of the lucky ones who scaled the fence. I ask him how he is in Spanish, then in English, but he only speaks French. Turning his back on me, he continues to watch TV and moans in pain as he touches intermittently the cream which has been applied to the large open wounds on his legs.

I am led across the yard to the dining room as the sun beats down and reflects aggressively off the ground and forces me to put my sunglasses on again. I walk into the dining room where sit about 150 people eating a chicken curry dish from small metal trays, each with a measured glass of orange juice. As I walk past, some look up in curiosity as I smile at them. As I near the back, I get talking to the cook who shows me the kitchen and the large vats where the food is prepared. Outside, the queue is long and impatient as people wait for their small portion of lunch. The guard stops and talks to us about the difficult task of managing people saying they have few resources to keep order. Fights regularly break out when the food runs out he tells me.

We are then shown some sleeping quarters which are made up of 20 rows of bunk beds, each with only a few centimetres between them. People literally sleep on top of each other and next to each other, the only thing separating them being long drapes of white cloth. I have visited better prison cells. The guard lets me wander in as I take this all in, and some men start to talk to me in Arabic. I can't understand but somehow get talking to a young 25-year-old man called Abbas who speaks good English. Born in Syria but living in Palestine, he left a month ago in July 2015 because his family were in danger of being killed, in fact some had already been murdered. He left his wife and his studies, paid $4,000 to leave and took a flight to Algeria where he illegally crossed two borders into Morocco and then Spain.

As he stands tall over me, others crowd round and from a group of five we are suddenly 15. Those who seem to speak English nod occasionally when Abbas talks about the political turmoil of his home country. He introduces me to his friends, and I clasp their hands and am embraced by them as Abbas explains I am collecting stories and accounts for a book; they too have had similar experiences having left their countries and paid large sums of money in the process. Abbas says he wants to settle in Germany (like most it seems) and then pay for his wife, who is a medical doctor, to leave the country. This is if she is still alive as they have not had contact for a week. At this point, the guard comes over and starts to get annoyed and blazes at me in Spanish:

> what these people don't understand is that it is a false dream. They won't get to Germany. The Syrian and Palestinian Embassies in Germany have closed. There is nothing there for them, it is a false dream. But they go because they have family, or they think there is lots of work.

I am then ushered away by the guard, and as I say goodbye, Abbas chases after me and gives me his phone number before I am marched off again past more sleeping quarters.

A few days later I re-enter the refugee camp having sent Abbas some WhatsApp messages. I meet Abbas outside with a few of his contacts (an old man he calls "grandfather" and a young woman with a baby – see Figure 2), and I walk in, once again, past the young families fanning their newborns in the shade, past the long lunch queue, past the open windows permanently open in the hope that it will relieve the humidity in the overcrowded tents and huts. I walk slowly with the grandfather and Abbas, who has interpreted everything for me, and am led into a doorway where inside stay the grandfather's family. On the left is a wall of makeshift cupboards and shelves where lie different families' belongings: water, clothes, antiques, toys, anything and everything humanly possible which could have been carried thousands of miles. Clothes hang like cobwebs from all possible angles and corners of the room. Two babies, no older than one, sit naked on the dirty floor, while another traverses a stained bed. The grandfather introduces me to his daughter; she has two young daughters, one of whom shies behind her

FIGURE 2 Abbas and I with "grandad" outside the refugee camp in Melilla, Spain, in August 2015.

mother's legs, while the other reaches out for me as I hold her in her full nappy. I take hold of her and try and entertain her in my arms as the mother wipes her brow and starts to communicate through Abbas.

The first thing she wants is for me to speed up her application for refugee status and, even though Abbas has explained to them what I'm doing, I reiterate again that I have no influence over the process. I try to ask Abbas to explain this as carefully as possible as I don't want to upset anyone. She then explains to me that the single bed against the wall is where her and her children sleep, while only centimetres away sleep a family of four in another single bed. Above them sleep the grandfather in a single bed and another family in the single bed next to him. Sandwiched next to them are a set of four single beds: two next to each other and two above them. As she starts to explain who occupies those beds, the feet at the end of one bed start to move and the woman behind the small white sheet peers out and speaks to Abbas. She sleeps with her two children and in the bed next to her sleep another family of three. Below them sleep two other families: a family of three (father, mother and son) and a woman with two small sons.

I would estimate that this bed space takes up 80% of the room. The rest is basically a kind of walk-in-dining-room-children's play area. Another woman emerges from behind another sheet with her son and shows me her cards asking me to help her speed up her medical tests. Each time I look her directly in the eyes, I find it even more difficult to fathom what is going on here. Outside the guard is getting impatient and I am told I have to leave. I hand the baby back to her mother, so moved to the point that I end up kissing her on the head, before leaving to be escorted to the entrance.

As I walk out, the grandfather follows me with his granddaughter in his arms. As we walk, Abbas says that there is another woman who wants to talk to me.

I don't know if it's because they think I can help or by talking to me I can do something. The woman seems to think so because when we get outside, she quickly explains her situation while her two-year-old daughter cries from the high fever she has. She travelled from Syria to Algeria, before travelling with her husband's brother and their family through Mauritania, Mali and Nigeria into Morocco and through the border into Spanish territory. She wants to tell me more but breaks down in tears and rushes to the medical centre to get her daughter medicine.

Once the refugee camp officials find out about my second visit, I am banned from entering. Indeed a few days later, when I approach security, I am told I can't enter the premises. Fortunately, Abbas continued to bring people out for me to interview. In one conversation, one of his friends tells me of how he came to Melilla through Algeria having left Syria. In Algeria, he worked selling furniture for some months before paying someone €1,000, including the rent of an illegal passport to try and get to European territory: the going rate can be between €500 and €3,000. In the camp he says that there are regular thefts and threats from the young Moroccan men on the outside who, as he says, "know who has the money."

As we talk, however, there is a commotion and one of the male residents from the refugee camp starts shouting at some of the young Moroccan boys outside who are next to us. The man runs out, rips off his shirt and starts pushing one of the boys who I am to later learn are under licence at the Young Offenders Institution a little further up the hill. Suddenly, everyone around us scatters and the guards close the gates to the camp and we are left next to some of these men and the young Moroccan boys. There is a small scuffle before the man's brother appears and persuades him to come inside, and helps him put on his shirt again. There are shouts in Arabic from women inside the camp at the boys who then shout insults back, and as the women dissipate to their camps, the boys spread out around the periphery shouting insults at the women, throwing stones at them and pointing at them through the gaps in the fence. Abbas's friend then says that these boys often carry knives and mug people as they leave during the night. "They hate us Syrians," he says.

Word gets round about my study to some of the friendlier staff in the camp, and a French translator brings out to me a mixed group of young Syrians aged between 18 and 21 for me to interview. As we start talking, there is yet another small skirmish as one of the Moroccan boys who linger behind them sneers insults at one of the young men I am interviewing:

RAHEEM: It is not a problem to find someone. From Nador [which neighbours Melilla] to Melilla it is €1,000, the whole thing. No, €2,000. It depends as they charge different. If you lucky, you pay €1,000 if you not lucky, you pay €2,000. We go by car across the countries, they leave us in Nador and some of us get false passports. When we first tried, the Moroccan police caught us. We were beaten. Some women are caught and raped by the Moroccan police. In the end, many have to pay the police as well so this is more money.

ABDUL: Living in CETI [immigration centre] is a disaster, you share with 11 people in your same room, there are babies crying, diseases, it is not clean, people just get ill. Sometimes the police are there, but there are Moroccan guys outside the camp who work in drug gangs. One day they were throwing stones.

[There is a scuffle as one of the interviewees is pushed.]

DAN: Calm down. [I go over and pull back the man to our group]. So those are the boys who cause the trouble here.

RAHEEM: Yes, they are always walking around the camp, circling it. This is the life here.

There is a stand-off as the two go face to face, before I go over and separate them. We continue our discussions in the humid heat in which they reveal the true suffering of living in the immigration centre:

RAHEEM: A lot of families, its sad to see as they really struggle. Some sleep all on one bed, a whole family. Others sleep on the floor. But if we all want to leave to get to places like Germany so we are refugees and we have to put up with it. There is no choice.

ABDUL: The main problem is the communication, we don't speak Spanish and there is only one translator and we can't get hold of them sometimes and we sign things which we don't understand or have to do things which are not explained to us.

WASIF: We don't really talk to many people so we don't really trust them. We keep our money and passport and things on us at all times, there is a lot of stealing. I sow spare money in my clothes and emergency money in my shoes.

ABBAS: There are people who wait outside the immigration centre to rob us, they wait in groups, mostly young men. The look at us as we leave. We have had friends who have been robbed. Some young women also kidnapped. No one can do anything, no one comes from the Spanish police to do it. We are afraid to call them as we don't want to be a problem for them.

After that, the grandfather turns up with one of his other friends and we start another interview. The grandfather has family dotted all over the place: Algeria, Belgium, some still in Syria and some attempting to go through Turkey. He and his friend both left Syria because of the war and denounce the violence. The grandfather stands in the shade next to me while the other man, dark in complexion, answers my questions between adoring looks he makes at his young daughter who waves at him from the entrance of the immigration centre. Both men, and their families, have been here several months and await DNA tests: something which has to be done to determine that the people they entered with are their family. They don't understand what is taking so long given that by comparison their medical health check-ups were done quite quickly. I have no answers for them but they seem to look to me for an explanation to what is going on.

Meanwhile at the border: on the right side of la valla (the fence)

It's not long before a National Police officer asks us why we have spent the last few minutes watching people crossing the borders before Flavio says that he is also an undercover officer and that I am his colleague. The other officer retreats and goes back to his position next to the swarm of people crossing the border. Another empty car pulls up, battered on the outside, hollowed out on the inside; the cars are gutted out like this so as many goods, contraband and indeed people can be transported as possible across the border. The police officer asks him to open his boot and takes a step back before looking around under the guise of his sunglasses. He then asks for his documentation before placing a red scanner on the bonnet to detect for people underneath. There are none and the car thereafter passes into Spanish territory ready to load contraband and return to Morocco.

As I am to learn in conversation with Flavio, there are some innovative ways to traffic people into Spanish territory. He relays the story of a man hidden in a lorry's wheel and how three people were found in the bonnet of one car, almost dead from dehydration. A teenager died a few weeks ago because he couldn't swim having jumped out of a boat at night which was transporting him from the Moroccan port to the Spanish port. Only last Thursday, a Nigerian man was arrested for trying to transport his brother in a suitcase across the border; he might have made it but for the four-hour queue to cross which meant that his brother dehydrated in the heat and died.

To Flavio's amusement and my astonishment, he recalls an incident a few months ago where he was present at a car inspection because the man driving the car seemed nervous as he crossed the border. They pulled him over for closer inspection and, on pulling back the seat between the boot and the rear seats, found an exhausted but revealed in Flavio's words "a little black face" (a man fleeing from Nigeria). Then then asked the man for his "official documentation," and when he didn't answer, they went to check the glove compartment and, on opening it, found another, as Flavio says again "black face peeping out" (another fleeing from Mali). But these are common everyday stories and experiences for the border police in Melilla.

The scramble for Europe

More than ever in the history of our planet, people who appear in Flavio's memories are being displaced. This has continued to gather momentum since 2011 and seemingly shows little sign of ceasing. According to the United Nations (UN), that since 2013, year after year, record levels of people were being forced from their home countries and that the main refugee source countries were

Sudan, Somalia, Afghanistan and the Syrian and Gulf regions (UNHCR, 2016a). Equally, as we saw from the previous anecdotes, those countries are not the only ones which exclusively experience social unrest to the point that thousands evacuate their own homes.

The men Flavio talked about come from countries where there is little choice for people but to leave. For example, Nigeria now fosters substantial disorder and unrest and the increasing violent terrorist presence of Boko Haram. This has caused political instability and violence which made worse by other links to Al-Qaeda terrorist networks (Human Rights Watch, 2017). The origin of part of this political and social chaos has also been directly linked to man-made climate change. Rising temperatures in the region have extended floods and droughts which undermines food production. When thousands of herders and farmers across the Sahel belt – which stretches across countries such as Burkina Faso, Chad, Mali, Mauritania, Niger and Nigeria – struggled, they abandoned local customary agreements which would otherwise assist in the fair distribution of resources such as cattle and cropland. Conflict and violence broke out. With less to compete for, there is only more insecurity and political instability. The government struggled to manage the discontent and jihadi insurgencies and terrorist presence evolved in no-go zones (World Economic Forum, 2019).

So people have to move on, and for these displaced masses crossing borders in whichever way possible, the obvious destination is somewhere else within their country, but in some countries internally ravaged in the collapse of oppressive regimes, there is simply nowhere else to go. For this reason, since 2015 many more sought – or tried to seek – refuge within strong and stable European economies. This has led to the widespread opening of refugee routes, many of which traverse numerous countries, and requires them to endure inhuman conditions in transit and makes them vulnerable to exploitation (UNICEF, 2018). Indeed, the arrival of thousands of people is unsurprisingly reflected in asylum applications which, across all 28 EU member states, tripled from 259,395 in 2010 to 1,117,330 in 2015 (EY, 2016).

Europe has struggled to manage such an influx. The reasons for this are complex and political. Firstly, various EU countries simply cannot accommodate the number of people crossing their borders, and priorities on asylum are made vis-à-vis country of origin (some refugees told me that some EU countries classify countries like Iraq as "safe"), which means that their applications are more likely to be rejected and priority is given to someone from, for example, Syria. Secondly, other EU countries don't want to have the financial and social responsibility of more people at a time when austerity politics still prevails, social welfare and public healthcare spending has been squeezed, and investment in social housing is diminishing. For this reason, the most deserving are those who are more/most qualified so they will be those most ready to compete in a meritocratic system which requires them to work their selves into their own stability (Bansak et al., 2016). And, like anytime in the history of migration and the arrival of new social groups, political fear is whipped up to mask the growing inequality created by neoliberal capitalism. Blame mechanisms frame the new arrivals as "invaders" or even "terrorists" (Winlow et al., 2017).

Even the most "accommodating countries" such as Germany simply can't help everyone. For example, even though around 750,000 people presented applications for asylum in Germany in 2016, only 631,000 were accepted (CEAR, 2016). Equally, some countries develop a reputation for rejecting applications such as the UK and Hungary which in the same year only accepted 32% and 8% of asylum applications, respectively (ibid.). This problematises the refugees' situation further as they neither return home for obvious reasons nor are able to stay in their new host country, leaving many bereft from support and provision. They are just stateless (Chapter 8).

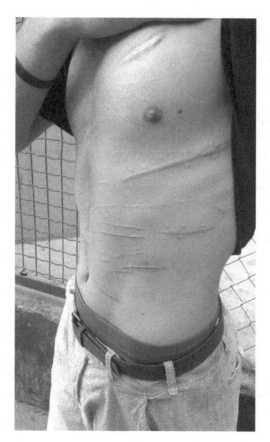

FIGURE 3 A young Syrian man shows his injuries from attempting to climb the fence seven times.

Meanwhile at the border: On the wrong side of La valla (The fence)

I pass the other police officers who sit looking bored as they check the occasional passport. He asks me, "Do you want to go to Morocco?" We go through the gate into Morocco. The noticeable difference is the amount of rubbish which sits at the foot of the fence, and torn clothes and shredded, broken shoes hang from parts of it. Failed efforts or successful scaling? The police officer points to a blue rope with a hook attached, explaining how it is used to throw over the fence so someone can climb up. As we look back at the terminal, he explains how last year 150 sub-Saharan men climbed over some nearby houses, jumped on top of the border control hanger and down into Spanish territory.

As I walk back into the hanger, he shows me how sharp the barbed wire is and then summons a young man across and asks him to lift up his shirt, revealing numerous scars where he had attempted to climb over. The young man has unsuccessfully tried seven times to climb this very wall (see Figure 3). We step into Spanish territory and look across the fence once again. He reflects how recently the local government received millions of Euros to fortify the fence, half of which was given to the Moroccan authorities. He shows me the barbed wire on their side and a moat which goes around the Moroccan side and turns to me, "Do you think this is worth million Euros? Everything in their pockets of the politicians, favours, etc" He thinks the same happened for the Spanish side as the government only invested in a smaller mesh to prevent people from digging in their fingers to climb and shows me a white pipe which supposedly releases gas to prevent people from climbing over, but it is "all a lie" he tells me.

View from the UN (United Negations)

Finally, Maria arrives and I greet her; she sort of swans around in an official jacket as if she is an expert in authority. She agrees to my interview and the police accommodate me by finding me a room for us to talk. She seems to give me a very official view on things saying how the UN intervention has persuaded people to seek asylum. She says the UN have been helping people since 1998 in Spain in response to growing concern about protection of people. She tells me the point of people requiring protection is when they enter borders. In 2013, she says that the concern got to a point where it couldn't be ignored and people were clearly in need when fleeing countries like Somali, Syria, Yemen and Mali. One of the main problems they had was that people were not applying for asylum which meant, in her eyes, they were not being documented and could not access their rights or services. Such was the concern that the UN sent two people to work out of Melilla and one from Ceuta (one stopped working in Melilla for reasons she didn't explain). One reason why they weren't applying for asylum was the length of time it took to process the applications, months and, in some cases, years. This was an immediate disincentive for the refugees. Why would you apply for asylum wait so long and perhaps be denied anyway when you could risk an illegal crossing? If you have already lost everything, what else is there left to lose?

She reflects on the problems Spain had with the Schengen agreement in 1990 so a pact was agreed with Morocco to continue to allow people from the nearby area of Nador to come and go by the day, but they were not allowed to stay overnight. This explains why the black market in borrowed passports is in operation, which allows Syrians to cross from Morocco (Nador) to Spain (Melilla). The asylum process is normally done through an application before being sent to Madrid for a decision to be made. With asylum applications, the refugees get a red card and are accommodated in the overpopulated immigration centre. While those who have no documentation are also accommodated there, instead they await an answer from the Spanish police on where they will go. Many times they are "expulsado" or sent home to their country of origin. These people are called "irregulares" or quite simply "irregulars," a term loaded with stigma. The other problems they have had, which were related to the lack of people applying for asylum, were that people required extra documentation to go to the mainland or the Spanish peninsula.

When we approach the subject of the immigration centre, she seems to downplay the problems which take place. When I say that it is built for a little over 400 people yet has 2,000 staying, she then seems to admit it is a problem but shrugs her shoulders when I ask her about the solution. She then reflects on how much of a success their intervention has been by making reference to July 2014 when there were no asylum applications, but by November that same year, they started to receive a regular flow of applicants. By October 2014, the police started better to understand the process and began to put other services and support in place such as an interviewing office, lawyer, translators and people trained to deal with the situations. It has taken some time given that numbers trying to get into Europe have been high for well over a decade previously.

Reflecting on the current situation, she says people don't really try to jump the fence anymore, even though only a few days earlier 400 sub-Saharan men tried to storm it as I am later shown on security camera footage from the Civil Guard. More common now are Syrians and Libyans, and the numbers of Sub Saharans have declined substantially. When I ask where they have gone, all she can say is that they looked for another way to come in perhaps through "la ruta clasica" or the classic route through Libya up to the sea to Italy.

Welcome to Europe and its social and political landscape

The large numbers of undocumented people flooding into Europe year after year are causing continual challenges for the continent as well as its respective nation states at a time when its democratic legitimacy has started to stutter. This, in part, is related to its failure to offer security to ordinary working people and society's most vulnerable, who are now becoming increasingly restless and discontent (Allsopp and Chase, 2017; Heldt, 2018). The growth in nationalistic rhetoric therefore pertains to this "supposed" crisis of European values (Tassinari, 2016) – even though the same Europe is responsible for leaving its own citizens behind in the wake of the financial crisis having imposed austerity measures on the working population in exchange for allowing inequality to continue to expand at a rate never before witnessed in history (Fisher, 2009).

This has all been provoked by the recent spate of increased terrorist attacks across Europe over the past few years which some say have been carefully exploited by political factions to increase social alarm of ISIS as the pseudo enemy and the "Islamic terrorist" (Žižek, 2016). Curiously, the concern has continued to be exercised about the "refugee" even though in numerous cases the attackers/perpetrators of these very same attacks have almost all been European-born citizens (Briggs, 2017). Hence, a sort of self-punishing rhetoric has evolved in which Europe blames its own free movement approach for the installation of radicalisation and related problems to the seemingly never-ending influx of people from outside its borders. This has translated into a kind of warped social fact which has since evolved into increased nationalistic policies and social attitudes, and has resulted in increased hate crimes across Europe, particularly against those of Islamic faith (EUAFR, 2016).

Refugee protests in Melilla

We get a taxi from the immigration centre to Melilla city centre in an illegal cab – a Moroccan man who charges us just €5 to go to the main town. We get out at the Plaza de España and walk around to a Western Union office where I help Abbas translate with the office staff so he can receive an international transfer. We then eventually sit down and drink coffee and smoke before they start to consult their phones for Spanish translations before drawing up large placards for their protest (see Figure 4). As we walk to the local government buildings, their cause is underlined

FIGURE 4 Refugee protests in Melilla, late in 2015.

to me: the motivation for leaving Syria as much as the demand for humane living conditions in the immigration centre:

WASIF: We are afraid if we reach Europe, they will say "no" to us and send us back to the war.

RAHEEM: If the free army still exists, I will never go back.

ABDUL: We will not go back I am afraid from the free army as I am from the government army. They are as bad.

RAHEEM: I was living with the free army. I saw what they did to people. There was a family who were connected in some way to the government army and they killed them, all of them, including the young boy who was only four years old. I have seen the death they bring. Now I fear for my family in Syria because the free army could easily attack my family because I left.

ABBAS: The death is everywhere, there are dead people in the streets.

HASSAN: People have been kidnapped for their organs. How can this happen? We are crossing borders, we pays smugglers and mafia, and they may kidnap us, demand ransom as they will hurt us, steal money from us and in some cases, they are killed for their organs.

RAHEEM: I was travelling to Damascus once in a convey and then suddenly a plane came over and bombed us. One bomb hit a truck with a woman and child in and they were killed. When I went over to see if there was anyone alive, there were just people screaming at the sight of half a dead girl. A girl. She was in half.

2

SOME NOTES ON THE METHODOLOGY

Introduction

Although Abbas was eventually given asylum in Spain, two years later he was in Germany:

> When I finish the interview with the second Iraqi family, Abbas and I come out of the block it is dark and Ahmad [Abbas friend] is waiting for us; he is talking to an older man who has a daughter who has started to go to the same school where Abbas now works. Next to them is a small, thin young man called Farhad who speaks to me in perfect English; it transpires he has two weeks to leave Germany as his asylum case was rejected. I promise to speak to him via skype through Abbas as my time in Germany is fast running out. As I get on my bike, he sort of runs alongside me and says "sir, I would be happy to tell you my situation, I look forward to talking to you."

I never got to talk to Farhad in the end because Abbas lost contact with him when he left the camp where he had been placed in Oelde, Germany. Where he went, no one knows. I don't know his story and nor did Abbas, but he was one of the millions of refugees across Europe placed in a precarious position of starting a new life somewhere else. Only for Farhad, the problem was, having got to Europe, he had to look for somewhere else to go because his case was rejected. This kind of transiency which was commonly experienced by refugees was the main barrier to my longitudinal study which ran over three years from August 2015 to August 2018: such was the unpredictable impermanence of many refugees that quite simply contact could be lost at any point for any number of reasons.

As it stands, I am convinced that the way social-science research studies are conceived, configured and funded prohibits us from actually learning about people like Farhad which is why, in this chapter, I want to make clear some important points about *how and why* I did this study *in this particular way*. Firstly, I completely ignored the demands made on me by my institution to generate research funding to do this work and was even more disinterested to undertake it just to raise my academic status by publishing in high-impact factor journals and thereafter wait to collect article citations as a measure of my "excellence." Generating new knowledge and awareness to the *direct benefit of society* should be our aim as social-science researchers, and this is jeopardized as more bureaucratic roles are imposed on us and our freedom to roam into deep, dark social realities swiftly becomes improbable (Briggs and Monge, 2017).

Why ethnography?

> We face grave global problems. One might think universities are doing all they can to help solve these problems. But universities, in successfully pursuing scientific knowledge and technological know-how in a way that is dissociated from a more fundamental concern with problems of living, have actually made possible the genesis of all our current global problems. Modern science and technology have led to modern industry and agriculture, modern medicine and hygiene, modern armaments, which in turn have led to much that is good, but also to habitat destruction, extinction of species, population growth, the lethal character of modern war, and the impending disasters of climate change. We urgently need to bring about a revolution in universities so that they put problems of living at the heart of the academic enterprise and take, as their basic task, to help humanity learn how to make progress towards as good a world as possible.
>
> *(Maxwell, 2017: 115)*

This book is written at a time when the social sciences are diminishing into bureaucratic and administrative control of the neoliberalisation of university education systems. The commodification of higher education and the integration of ideologies of entrepreneurialism and innovation were perhaps never intended to be a means of working towards participation in knowledge economies for all, but rather a means to turn the process of imparting knowledge into profit, with students as both client and commodity. Higher education has become so debased by the profit motive that it has made universities inefficacious for students seeking work and academic staff charged with the production of knowledge, but this is what happens when marketing and branding take precedence over pastoral care of students and useful research activity (Jones and Cunliffe, 2020).

Universities have instead become outcome-focussed institutions, losing quality in their teaching practices and rendering impotent previous research freedoms in order to provide service to a passive student body, lacking critical thinking and competitively conditioned to believe that "hard work" will create access to opportunities regardless of prevailing economic climate – something which, as we will see, is demanded of refugees as part of their "integration" (Chapter 8). It is the increased participation in this process that is the very undoing for people who are highly qualified, when their degree status does little to advance or even maintain their socio-economic position, since when, in reality as we will see with the refugees, human capital alone cannot counter structural economic problems such as widespread unemployment and job precariousness.

Our time as social-science academics is more one of course management, "improving" course content and dissemination, never-ending reporting and evaluation, mentoring as well as playing "friend, parent and personal counsellor" to students, having business competencies "installed" in our teaching practices as a means of "training" and of course, most painfully of all, the sale of what we produce – knowledge. To get that knowledge, we must undertake research studies and publish in the best journals with the most impressive impact factor, tweet live updates of our activities as evidence of our "excellence" and its impact on the community and attend conferences where similar other academics take battle in public-ego contests to see who knows more and who has received more citations. All this gives the university "kudos" and is how it is measured in national and international league tables.

But getting that "knowledge" is not that easy as it is not just a case of going out to do a research study: there is pressure on us to generate *research funding*. Doesn't sound like a problem, does it? However, when the main funders of the research calls stipulate how they want the research done or already outline the main focus of a study, then already this confines research approaches. A social study then is adopting pre-prepared research tools which immediately affect the reality that is studied. Similarly, funding bodies may confide on already-established academics in the research area to – on account of their "expertise" – take a study forward. Those very same academics may, however, already have their theoretical lens already set up to study the social reality; it's to say they may have decided what they are looking for before going out to get it. Theoretical preconceptions are epistemologically hazardous, particularly when combined with empirical short-sightedness. Because of this it is difficult for them to ignite a bit of ingenuity or innovation into doing something a bit different or thinking about how to overcome a problem – without breaking rigid ethical procedures bestowed upon them prior to the commencement of the study (Winlow and Hall, 2012; Briggs et al., 2018). This has been happening for some time:

> Such policy-oriented research within University settings has implied a constant battle to maintain academic independence and intellectual rigor, while simultaneously producing research of relevance to policy concerns, which is capable of attracting funding from major government and private donors.
>
> *(Black, 2001: 61)*

Can't bite the hand that feeds you or, in this case, *can't say the things no one wants to hear* and *can't write what no one wants to read*. In the field of *Refugee Studies*, for example, this is also historically apparent (Zetter, 1988; Chimni, 1998). Refugee and asylum-related studies have already been shown to be inadequately funded compared with mainstream-related research (Renzaho et al., 2016) which says something about the "significance" of the issue among governments. Much research also tends to narrow the lens of investigation. However, while there exist both sociological (see Lee, 2009) and psychological (Hernandez, 2009) theories of immigration into the assimilation, integration and well-being during the settlement process, they do not offer much in regard to explaining macro-level phenomenon – for example, the political economic and ideological context of displacement (Jacobsen and Landau, 2003). The uncritical nature of earlier pre-1990 literature largely oriented itself around the study of policy (Zetter, 1988: 3–4) where the "clientelist relationship" with agencies often meant that "the controversies which independent critical research may raise were not welcomed" (Zetter, 1988: 3, 4). Though completely political, studies on refugees were essentially depoliticized:

> International refugee law has long occupied centre stage in refugee studies. Its scholarship has been dominated by a positivist tradition which limits the possibility of engagement with politics.
>
> *(Chimni, 1998: 352)*

Undoubtedly then with the growth of journals and academic centres devoted to the study of refugees, scholarship has maintained close ties with government and policy makers, thus reproducing little more than- wait for it (drum roll) - nothing new (Thomas Cameron, 2014; Tombs, 2018). Indeed, we have to question the extent to which such research may even be explicitly or implicitly supporting the hegemonic or power-monopolising policies of developed powerful states (Hillyard and Tombs, 2004; Tombs, 2018). In the case of Europe, an abundance of critical studies in the name of refugee policy (for example, see Baines, 2016; Allsopp and Chase, 2017; Crawley et al., 2017; della Porta, 2018) have made little impact on reducing European countries' exclusionist and securitised approach to refugees and people seeking asylum (Žižek, 2016).

But even then, many "critical" social-science researchers studying refugees struggle for their critical edge. They can't be blamed in a way. Each job specification written for a post in a university is done so now attached with the expectancy that the new employee will consistently strive for funding from a recognised research body. Because of this there is rampant competition between university institutions for money to spend on "overheads," and this is once again amplified by the emergence of internal and external corporate enterprises which compete against the universities in commodifying knowledge around social problems. These "expert companies" are often favoured for their business approach to social research and win over funding committees with their well-versed outcome-focussed proposals (Briggs et al., 2018). After all, a funder wants evidence that the research was disseminated widely even if it results in- wait for it (drum roll) – very little social change (Thomas Cameron, 2014): unless the results are already in line with established policy and political agendas (Springer, 2008; Reale et al., 2018).

There is a general tendency for such studies to produce statistical reports because it is easy to digest for the funders and they want their findings to be cited in the most prominent high-impact factor journals – almost all of which favour quantitative methods and frown on studies which are unfunded or fail to achieve ethical approval from a recognised body (Winlow and Hall, 2012). This results in the continuous reproduction of misleading conceptions about how social problems occur because the research is not grounded in peoples' experiences. This has negative implications for the development of critical knowledge which should equip us to reconceptualise how and why social problems occur.

My study has tried to adapt itself to the lives and circumstances of the refugees (Thomas Cameron, 2014), which is why the way it was conceived was deliberately haphazard. My longitudinal analysis reflects the way in which data collection has followed as many of the refugees as possible on their journey into Europe and beyond. I am concerned with providing a critical account so I am interested in exposing the limitations of policy design and implementation as well as intergovernmental coordination and how combined this influences refugees' movements and decision-making. For this reason, I am interested in considering the political economy, power and corruption and the oscillating relationship between agent and social structure (see Fontanari, 2019).

Where qualitative researchers have failed to dip into ethnography, investigative journalistic accounts (Parenti, 2011; Andersson, 2014; Trilling, 2018; Miller, 2018) as well as theoretical narratives (Bauman, 2016; Zizek, 2016; Latour, 2018) make up the bulk of such critical approaches in the context of refugees, capitalism and climate change. Reece Jones (2016) and McDonald-Gibson (2017) document different border crossings across the world in their careful ethnographic depictions of the spatial and political suppression of the poor in the battle for the world's natural resources. Kingsley (2017) is concerned with offering a critical social and historical perspective to the refugee crisis. Using case studies, his main target is the failure of migration policies in the reasonable management of people and their livelihoods. From within Europe, we have Carr's (2015) moving account of illegal immigrants across the continent. Set within a context of a general documentation with police, border agents and policy officials, Carr gives good voice to the people who are subject to the political suffering internal to Europe (also see King (2016) for her ethnographic work in Calais, France, and Athens, Greece).

My work builds on these texts by offering a more sound empirical base from a wider pool of refugee participants across different countries. I have also tried to link the social climate of the respective country with its political economic and ideological context, thus focussing on how the macro (political powers, commercial interests) impact on the micro (refugee subjectivity and decision-making) – something also generally ignored in some current studies (for example, see Brekke and Brochmann, 2014; Alisic and Letschert, 2016; Crawley et al., 2017). My work is equally concerned with the refugees' country of origin as much as their reception country and country of (temporary) stay where I may have met them briefly or followed them over the research period. The three years over which my study was achieved is also important for such in-depth refugee analysis (for example, see Botfield et al., 2016; Lichtenstein and Puma, 2018; Ghaziri et al., 2019).

Objectives and methods of my study

As you can see from these field notes with Abbas two years on from having met him, I undertook observations and interviews so I was practicing ethnography. I did my observations in refugee camps, at border crossing points, in housing projects and immigration centres, with NGO associations and in general city centre spaces and poor suburban peripheries. To augment the observations, I undertook face-to-face, unstructured interviews with 110 refugees, almost all of whom were but not exclusively from Syria, Iraq and Afghanistan: no doubt this was to do with the mass exodus of people from those countries during this period of the study.

The research fieldwork was undertaken in 14 European countries of which were a mix between reception countries such as Turkey, Greece and Italy, and settlement countries which included France, Belgium and Germany. The main project's objectives were to (1) examine how and why refugees were leaving their home countries; (2) follow and analyse what happens to them, and find out when they left and how they arrived; and (3) evaluate how they settled in the new countries and what happened to them as a consequence.

The research was conceived into three main phases (Figure 5). A largest pool of participants were gathered in the first phase when visiting six different countries and had connected with it the first of the study's objectives – to examine how and why the refugees came (Phase 1). As contact was maintained with some of these refugees, it was then possible to see how and where they settled (Phase 2); where possible these very same refugees were visited and follow-up interviews were undertaken. More refugees were recruited at the same time when visiting contacts in these camps/housing complexes. The final phase (3) made use of contacts made from both Phases 1 and 2 to follow as best as possible what happened to them.

The term "refugee" here loosely to describe people I came to talk to who had been granted asylum, and therefore had access to protection, as well as those who had not qualified for it and consequently been rejected and/or those who had not applied for it. I was interested in speaking to anyone at any point in their journey from country of origin to settlement country, regardless of their age, gender and ethnic orientation. In this respect, there were no particular criteria to participate

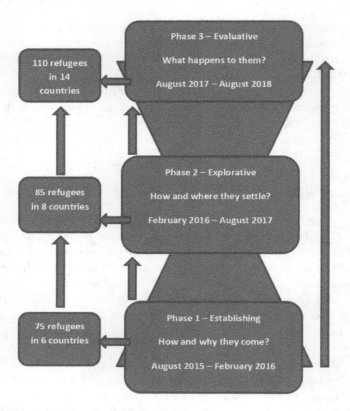

FIGURE 5 The different phases of the study.

in the study other than my participants were in circumstances of vulnerability and need. Contrary to a tendency in the social sciences to fetishise sampling strategies, and reliability and validity (Wright Mills, 1959; Bartolome, 1994; Carlon et al., 2006; Enticotte et al., 2018; Lindgren, 2019), I was simply concerned with doing justice to the people under study, getting to know them, their dilemmas and challenges. I knew that if I wanted to undertake a longitudinal study which measured the experiences of refugees' journeys from their homelands to Europe, I needed to be focussed on developing good relationships with as many people as possible and maintaining those bonds. This was my priority over anything else.

Ethnographic research normally adapts itself to particular fields of study and the contexts of the participants and the circumstances in which they live and the various social pressures around them. So any study interested in looking at how refugees move, what they decide to do, where they go and how they experience "integration" or otherwise requires the sampling strategy to adapt itself to the precarious circumstances of the refugees. There have been little cross-country comparisons or even studies which have shown how policy initiatives have front-line implications for refugees' everyday lives and decisions.

The study started in a Spanish city called Melilla in the north of Africa where a base sample of 25 refugees were recruited from border crossings and the city's immigration centre. After the interviews, participants were asked if they wished to remain in contact via phone, Whatsapp or Facebook and five consented. Contact was maintained as they settled in countries like France, Belgium and Germany. Even though many had sought asylum in Spain, many simply left for countries where the economy was perceived to be stronger and/or where they already had family/friends. When they arrived and started to settle, I visited them and recruited people they had come to know in the same area via the snowballing sampling method. The new participants were then asked if they knew anyone in other countries and whom might be interested in participating. Consequently, refugees were then recruited from countries such as Turkey, Norway, Hungary and the Netherlands. Where possible these people in these other countries were visited and interviewed, and in the absence of this, telephone, Skype or WhatsApp interviews were undertaken.

When interviewing, I used open-ended questions which related to the research aims so the approach was inductive. Participants were informed about what the study aims were and gave verbal consent to talk about their perceptions and experiences. As a researcher studying vulnerable people, care was taken to reduce the automatic power imbalance this generates by avoiding formalisms associated with the research process; for example, border crossings or refugee camps are not the sort of place to start producing pieces of paper for signed consent. As I have learnt over the years from other studies with similar groups, people do not appreciate these kinds of formal procedures as they associate me with authorities and can be an impediment to building trust. At the beginning of all the recordings, I explained either in English/Spanish or through a translator the purpose of my study and the nature of the questions and did not have to answer if they were not comfortable. The open-ended interviews lasted between 30 minutes and an hour. Once the interviews were transcribed, the recordings were destroyed. All participants were then given fictitious names.

At all times, I was sensitive to the refugees' needs and feelings since many had been significantly traumatised. I avoided just taking information from them and, as commonly undertaken in ethnographic research of this nature, demonstrated empathy and helped them by translating papers and to understand legal processes. Over the years, I have found most social research to fail in reciprocating the help the people under investigation offer. These kinds of studies should not be something which we – the academy – undertake so we can extract information from a group of suffering people and then withdraw from the study with our data, wiping our brows in relief at the misery we witnessed. It should not be a one-way process in this respect but should be second nature to people in fortunate and clearly advantaged circumstances such as ours so helping is something which all researchers should do when they are studying vulnerable populations (see Briggs, 2012; Briggs and Monge, 2017).

Getting to know refugees and following their movements

In the opening section of the chapter, I alluded to the main challenge related to the realisation of this study. After meeting as many refugees as possible in different countries, how do you continue contact with them and build a relationship? In a short answer, it relied completely on digital technology such as WhatsApp and social media such as Facebook – the former being the vehicle for contact and the latter acting as a sort of "reference point" as well as verification of who I was, what I did and my research intentions.[1]

After having met people and getting their contact details, the real challenges about how to continue the contact became evident when I started to message my respondents shortly after. For various reasons outside the control, many of the people I met in Melilla desisted from contact. Some changed numbers, others saw little value in my contact, while some were undoubtedly worried that continued contact with me might jeopardise their asylum applications. I can't account completely for all this, but in exchanges I always tried to make clear my research intentions and offer genuine interest in their lives so that our contact could continue for the greater good of telling the refugees' story. WhatsApp was firstly useful because refugees are transient as my field notes suggested. I met Ahmed in Paris in November 2015 where he had already been waiting for four months on his asylum application. By the new year, he was somewhere else:

WhatsApp conversation with Ahmed, November 2015

DAN: Happy New Year Ahmed. Hope all well in Paris or wherever you are. Will contact you in January.

AHMED: Hii 🖐 Happy new year… I wish you the best…And am in Bordeaux.

DAN: How is it?

AHMED: Good. Nice place.

DAN: How did you get it and have you started to learn French?

AHMED: Not yet, but we will start after short time.

DAN: Ok I will call in January to get an update on things. Say hello to your brother…Kasim wasn't it?

AHMED: Yes my brother is here come to visit my in holiday and after he will back to Paris.

I updated all my participants with my research progress as a means to show them the value they contributed to my study so they could see the small fruits of my labour. Some months later,

DAN: Dear friend. You kindly agreed to help in my research. Today I received an invitation to speak at a conference in Germany next year. I will do my best to tell your stories. Daniel

AHMED: Bonjour Welcome 🖐 Thank you very much, and I wish you success and hope you deliver the word of truth for all the world.

Shortly after, I had no contact with Ahmed, a man who had witnessed bombing and death on civilian communities in Syria and saved his brother's life twice when they dodged ISIS detention and the border crossing shooting target practice that the Turkish gendarmerie frequently undertake (see Chapter 7). As we saw in Chapter 1, Abbas escaped a country in total political and social turmoil. He had spent some months waiting in the refugee immigration centre in Melilla trying to decide which country to try to target to find work. Everyone around him told him that Spain had a weaker economy and fewer work opportunities, so he set his heart on Germany. When I visited him in Madrid six months later after our first meeting, he was planning to travel illegally to France and then to Germany. He paid hundreds of Euros to cross into France, but he was dumped on the streets of Brussels in Belgium where he slept and begged for money until he had enough to get a train into Germany. There the volume of people presented for asylum was high at the time, and the system was under significant pressure to carefully process/reject refugees accordingly. In our early WhatsApp exchanges, his worry was evident:

WhatsApp conversation with Abbas, April 2016

DAN: Abbas what's happening?

ABBAS: Hello my friend. I am very, very sorry because I don't contact with you but every day I wake up at 5am and go to school at 8am in another city after that I take a train to my work because I make a "practicum" in school for kids finally I reach my home at 7pm. And the court will send me back to Spain this month or the next. Please forgive me that I don't call you.

DAN: Its ok… you working now, that's great…is it paid in any way? Will you stay or come to Spain?

ABBAS: They will send me back within the next two months.

Abbas then received an order to return to Spain which further complicated the potential for our contact. He had already been pivotal in translating interviews for me in Spain, and when I went to visit him in Germany, he helped me interview more refugees. So, when he asked me for a favour, I obliged:

ABBAS: Hello Daniel. This is Abbas, here is my new number. I wanna ask you my friend Ibrahim you know him and he still in Madrid but and he is a professional in metal works. [He was part of a focus group I undertook with Abbas]. Some people told him that there is no job in Spain and he asked me to asked you if that's true.

DANIEL: Abbas…You are alive!

ABBAS: Yes am still alive – you know Syria, Algeria, Morocco, Spain, France, Belgium, and Germany and am still alive so I will not die now its so early!

DANIEL: Haha. Ok I need to look into this. Is Ibrahim in Madrid now? And if so can he meet and speak English or Spanish?

ABBAS: No, in place near Madrid.

Ibrahim

As it turned out, Ibrahim was in Salamanca, a smaller city 200 kilometres from Madrid. Ibrahim had found it difficult to learn Spanish and spoke no English, and the few refugees who had been housed there had started to lose hope about their future (Chapter 8). I created a WhatsApp group called "Help for Ibrahim" with another participant, Osama, who I had met through Abbas in Madrid who spoke good English, and together we started to converse through the app about supporting Ibrahim in his search for work:

Group WhatsApp conversation with Ibrahim and Osama, July 2017

Daniel created "Help for Ibrahim"

DAN: Hello Ibrahim. This is so you can contact us if you have problems.

IBRAHIM: تحياتي. 🦾"

DAN: 💪

IBRAHIM: Muchas gracias [Thank you].

OSAMA: براهيم هذا الغروب مشان نتابع الوضع معك

DAN: ¡Muy bien! [Very good]

OSAMA: و نضل على تواصل

IBRAHIM: انشالله

IBRAHIM: Poco a poco [Little by Little].

DAN: Eso es [That's it]

DAN: Ibrahim. Osama will translate everything I say though I cannot write every day, the idea is you have support. Do not doubt your decision. You made it for a reason. Now it is time to build your future. Osama and I will help as we can. We start with papers and learning Spanish.

OSAMA: براهيم. انا انشالله حر ترجم لك شي بيحكي الأستاذ دانيل، بس هو حرام نحن هون مشان نساندك. قله هو الوقت لازم تبني في مستقبلك او لك شي يقدر يكتبك بس الفكرة ان ال تشكت ال قرارات الاخذت، لأن يوم لك بس الفكرة الحمم خلي إيملي إيمانكن بالله كبير :) منبشلك بل وقارو و اللغة الاسبانية ثمل محامكين...و خلي إيملي إيمانكن بالله كبير :)

IBRAHIM: Daniel, muchas gracias y me animó mucho y voy a aprender Español Inshallah. [Thank you Daniel, it encourages me a lot and I will learn Spanish god willing].

Like many refugees I came to know over the three-year period, many were continually overwhelmed at what was demanded from them (adjustments to culture, language, housing, etc.). Very often, the people they shared accommodation with were sceptical over their chances of starting again often for good reason: many struggled in language classes and training, and only a handful of people I came to know got at best low-paid, low-grade jobs. Over the course of the next few months, our sporadic chats continued in the WhatsApp group as Ibrahim started to get around the bureaucratic nature of registering himself for work in Spain. Still I offered support and help with Curriculum Vitaes (CV):

IBRAHIM: شهر الخامس بعطوني إقامة مسموح فيها العمل

OSAMA: He gets the national identity in May and he takes the legal papers to work the same month.

DAN: That is excellent news! Tell him to ignore what people say and focus on himself and where he needs to go. Tell him to start working on a CV in Spanish or English and we can help.

OSAMA: Ok.

DAN: If I had listened to everyone who said I couldn't do something, I wouldn't have done anything because I wouldn't have tried.

Ten months later, again after more supportive messages and even some Arabic poetry:

DAN: Ibrahim. ¿Cómo estás? [How are you?]

IBRAHIM: ¡Muy bien! [Very good]

DAN: Esta mañana he visto a Osama. ¿Qué tal llevas con el español y la búsqueda del trabajo? [This morning I saw Osama and wondered how your Spanish was going and the search for work?]

IBRAHIM: ¡Estoy trabajando como soldador! [I am working as a welder]

DAN: ¡¡¡¡¡Enhorabuena!!!!!! [Congratulations!]

While at no point I can say this was down to me, the point is that there was a forum for Ibrahim to talk about his worries and at the same time receive support, and for this reason the WhatsApp group served its purpose. This, as I was to discover, paid off when I got back in touch with Asim – an Iraqi man I met in a homeless shelter in Brussels (Chapters 6 and 10).

In my WhatsApp conversations, I listened and showed support for complicated moments or troubles they were having, particularly with adjusting to language, culture and the demands of living in a new place while having to come to terms with leaving everything behind. Given that, as a westerner who has a comfortable life by comparison, there is no way that I could completely empathise with the kinds of things these people have seen/experienced. Instead in these situations I made neutral statements of shock/surprise mixed with general curiosity. The latter was particularly useful as it allowed me to delve deeper into how the refugees were feeling about things and permitted me to explore their inner anxieties.

I kept track of how my participants were progressing so that when I sent them messages, some weeks/months later I could follow on from what they had told me. While I had the conversation history to hand, my documentation was concerned with making links with milestones in their new life and correlating it with their feelings. Over time, as hopefully you will discover, I was fortunate to gain their trust from some as they opened up to reveal extremely personal feelings and experiences. As the light of the mobile screen is activated, prompts for the password are followed by a thumbprint on the green icon, and then on my profile photo "Professor of Happiness" (that is me by the way) there is no face to judge them nor is voice to moralise their decisions; however, there is a person that although may seem distant is actually close. It is this "closeness" I tried to cultivate: something between a respectful distance and personal support.

As someone outside official State channels who may decide their fate or has influence over their lives or equally someone related to family or friends, a WhatsApp message away, my neutrality was always there: the depth of contact evident in the cases of Ibrahim (getting the job a year after meeting him) and Asim (declaring his depression three years on after meeting him). Life for most of these people has been difficult for some time, and almost all have faced frustrating processes relating to their legitimisation and settlement in Europe. I have been privy to their clandestine movements as well as their reasons and methods for crossing borders often as they happen or shortly after, insights which few researchers using surveys or even conventional snapshot data collection approaches will have had. The value of the data is "live"; it came to me at times "as it happened." In this way, as others have alluded to (Dekker et al., 2015), this makes me very much part of their new support networks in their new settings.

Ethical and practical reflections

One of the most difficult tasks was convincing people who had uncertain legal status in Europe about my credibility as a researcher. While showing my university ID was often enough, explaining the concept of social research is not easy. Some thought me to be a reporter or a detective and, on occasions, I had to explain the type of work an academic at a university may do. My questions revolved around illegal routes, trafficking and smuggling which in most instances were unproblematic once participants felt comfortable that what they told me would not implicate them or affect their asylum status (see Assaffron, 2017). I spoke English and Spanish and relied on translators who worked in refugee camps or people I had come to know throughout my study. Lack of English was not necessarily a barrier as many of those who I communicated used Google to make general translations, thus aiding the communication. However, when a participant did speak those languages, it made a big difference to discard as quickly as possible any formalities and helped later when personalising the relationships via WhatsApp.

As you can see thus far, it is clear that refugees are very much digitally connected so it means that they too – as most Europeans – send and exchange photos such as selfies. In the first fieldwork trip in Melilla, after the interviews, I posed with photos with the refugees. In peer reviews of my work, some have accused me of engaging in a form of "dark tourism,"[2] but these academics show their true distance from reality when they make such comments. It is not that I am exploiting the refugees – as they see it – because by having my picture taken I am actually doing what they do normally and consider to be normal. The selfie pictures were a way of solidifying a bond which we could thereafter return to when building a relationship. This enabled a platform for me to clarify data or transcripts such as this which I came across when doing my data analysis:

MUKHLES: A lot of friends have died, arrested it is normal to have your friend to have them killed or arrested. I was working in hospital, working for doctors with the wounded like an assistant and every night there was bombing, maybe 10–20 killed or wounded and they needed volunteers and I volunteered and doctors were teaching me what to do. A lot of people died in my arms, some with no parts of their body. I once went out to take a man who was in a bomb from the street to the hospital but we could do nothing for him, we were just with him as he died. I did that for six months. When I left, a few weeks later that hospital was bombed.

Even if contact was related to the project or such or even this book, it was just friendly and supportive contact like this with Mukhles in March 2020:

DAN: I am going through your interview again. You are a brave and honourable man. You do good for people. It is an honour to know you.
MUKHLES: Thank you professor 😊
DAN: You are welcome…I hope we can meet again one day so I can thank you for all your help.
MUKHLES: No, no need for that 😊. Don't you wanna come to Turkey again?
DAN: Yes of course, don't know when.
MUKHLES: Great! So let me know, there are some new Syrian restaurant I want you to test there food! Maybe you gonna like it!

Notes

1 This was because on many occasions I updated my Facebook status with progress of my study.
2 Defined as types of research that involve observing places/collecting testimonies where some of the darkest events of human history have unfolded.

3

GLOBAL CAPITALISM

Profit at whatever cost

It is a cold winter day in Istanbul, late in 2015. This is the first time I am to meet Mukhles having been put in contact with him by Abbas from Melilla. Mukhles is in his early 20s and left Syria about a year prior to our conversation as he was forced to join the army. "I didn't want to fight against my family or friends so I fled," he says. While our conversation is frequently interrupted by the load banging and drilling noises of roadworks in Istanbul, some young girls approach us, all three walking dirty barefoot. One of the girls I would say is about 12–13 years old, and the other two around 8 and 5, respectively. The state of the youngest is particularly alarming as she has both her two front teeth missing and appears to be in pain. They hold their hands out and moan out something I can't understand while Mukhles starts to wave them off. I reach out for some money and ask Mukhles to find out where they are from. They tell us they are from Syria and say they are homeless having fled the country six months ago: they currently sleep in a bus shelter. They return to the moaning phrase and look at me in desperation as the five-year-old pulls at my shirt. We ask how they got here and what it is like living on the streets, but the girl just repeats the same sentence, "I didn't ask to be poor, help me please." After I give them money, they disappear quickly into Starbucks, paying close attention to the staff who have already moved on other vagrant populations.

At the time of my meeting with Mukhles in November 2015, there were around three million Syrians in Turkey, but the political situation in Syria has since deteriorated as it is estimated that there are around four million (UNHCR, 2019a). The geopolitical free-for-all underway in Syria as I noted in Chapter 1 is related to how climate change impacts agricultural populations and the poor management of rural economies leads to internal displacement from rural to urban areas. The increased tension in inner-city areas, caused as the population grew and inequality increased, unhinged violent state mechanisms on the country's citizens. This, as we know, led to rebellion and war as the political powerhouses strategically moved in for the battle for precious natural resources.

It has been estimated that 80% of those that remain in Syria live below the poverty line: the "war economy" means that the unemployment rate is around 55% and work is increasingly hard to find (Makki, 2018). There is a business attached to this misery which I examine in Chapters 5–7, but for now it is important to show that these are not organic processes of social change. Like climate change, the refugee crisis is a symptom of a form of out-of-control global capitalism. Current political ideologies and geopolitical interests weakly hide more sinister political economic agendas that produce a very focussed, aggressive and hungry pursuit of profit, which now threatens to kill off the very planet we occupy. This chapter is therefore about making a summary of our transition into this "out-of-control" situation, which has seen the inequality gap widen drastically and poverty and unemployment increase. This is because neoliberal capitalism renders some of the world's regions and, in some cases, whole countries obsolete. As a result, swathes of people are both internally and externally displaced as we see from my field notes from Istanbul and their newfound poverty is just dumped elsewhere.

Neoliberalism and social harm

Neoliberalism or new liberalism is an economic ideology which exists in the functioning of advanced capitalism where a market economy must be allowed to operate without governance, thus providing the "stability" and "driving force" for a healthy society and the wellspring of human freedom. It evolved from the old liberalism termed "embedded liberalism," which had come about after the Second World War when emerging states committed their social vista to welfare for citizens and full employment; in it, state power substituted the market economy as a democracy ran society, thus establishing a web of regulation to prevent the carelessness of market.

That regulation was undone by the "market turn" of the 1970s and early 1980s which marked the advent of neoliberalism. Led by a group of politicians and leading economic experts, neoliberalism broke away from the shackles of embedded liberalism and sought to actively construct free markets in which profit was withheld from public investment and instead ploughed into the market to generate further growth, expansion, dominance and importantly profit. Neoliberalism relies on what Naomi Klein (2007) calls the simultaneous implementation of different methods of "economic shock treatment," which hinge on deep budget cuts to government spending, even those dedicated to welfare programmes or social support, and private ownership of state companies that could generate profit. The economic model combines domestic policies with transnational policies which liberate the way international regulations may impede multinational companies so private capital can invest and profit where it seems fit. To do this, the line between politicians and powerful businesspeople blurs as both merge into *power elite*. Spending is increased on military, policing and policies to protect the elite before they look for next global target for deregulation, investment and profit making. This occurs at any cost, hence global political and social insecurity, war, soaring inequality, devastating government meltdowns, deeper political corruption, increasing government authoritarianism, and amplification of problems associated with climate change (Briggs, 2015; Winlow et al., 2017).

Over the past 50 years, we have witnessed this expansion of a global, neoliberal agenda which has let loose free-market economics on the social system. In the process, it has also withdrawn much of the security of the past such as employment, social justice, welfare, stable family structures, and consensual norms and attitudes and instead leaving in its place market and economic instability, "risk," high unemployment, and increasing social inequality and ecological catastrophe (Parenti, 2011; Standing, 2011; Briggs, 2012). Downsizing of traditional industries and the dominance of global markets and the growth of low-paid work as new consumer-oriented economies, manual labour or domestic industries – evolving as a consequence of new technological advancement – require fewer employees and associated costs (Lloyd, 2018). Increasingly, the profiles of these workers are likely to be migrants who are at an even greater risk of exploitation (Briggs and Dobre, 2014). This then creates an automatic competition for work among its citizens. This, in turn, makes us increasingly competitive citizens.

Under neoliberalism, governments only see individual decision makers or consumers because the philosophy of such an economic system loosens the role of the state and increases the responsibility on the individual, heightens their ability to compete for work and kindles their preferences towards consumption. We experience this ideological consumer "freedom" because while we still experience ourselves as "fully free" more than ever, our lives are controlled and regulated. We feel liberated when we choose what we buy or for what to study or for which job to apply without questioning the field from which these choices are available. Moreover, increasingly our everyday experiences are mediated around our individuality – which makes us feel more "free" – and our existence is now governed more and more through commercial ideologies attached to the pressure/need for consumption.

Criminological studies identify how even now a large proportion of crime is now intrinsically structured around consumerism and consumption – from the exploited child labour in production companies to the modus operandi of "criminals" themselves in their consumer counterparts (Hall et al., 2008). However, rather than being conceived as problems which should generate political and social interest, they are simply accepted as a trade-off for our ideological "freedom": the people in some poor, faraway country work countless hours and are paid pittance only so we can swan around a shopping centre and buy their products on a whim before moving on to the next shop. This represents the Hall's (2012) concept of "fetishistic disavowal" in that although they know that their perpetual shopping and consumption are probably having an impact on the environment, they simply dispel this into their unconscious as an inconvenient truth. There is no motivation to change this status quo because these "risks" are at best managed rather than reduced. Politicians, policymakers, academics and researchers like you and I (hopefully) are tasked with getting funding from a government body only to do a study which involves us "thinking creatively" about how such social harms can be mitigated by using the restrictive mechanisms of existing social policy (Chapter 2; Rayman, 2019). We are put in positions whereby all we can do is gently massage away at the grave injury we produce on people down the social structure without disturbing the unrelenting thirst to produce profit.

For some years, commentators such as Hillyard and Tombs (2007) have called for us to consider the notion of "social harm" in the analysis of current social problems. They indicate that many events and incidents which cause serious harm are either not covered by criminal law or ignored or poorly managed: corporate crime and state crime are obvious, heterogeneous categories of offence that remain largely marginal to dominant legal, policy, enforcement and indeed academic agendas, while at the same time creating widespread harm, not least amongst already relatively disadvantaged and powerless peoples. At a state and institutional level, a reluctance to recognise these kinds of social harms essentially muffles the need for critical investigation into the underlying structural and processual defects that generate them. For instance, a flash flood is often reported as a "stand-alone event" (see Briggs et al., 2018) linked to "freak weather storms" rather than a wider problem constituted by global warming, fossil-fuel burning, industrialism and neoliberal consumer capitalism.

Notwithstanding, some of the most significant problems facing contemporary 21st-century society not only lie beyond the present scope of legal prohibition but are embedded in the operations of neoliberal-capitalist political economy: climate change, resource wars, the increasing prevalence of the far right, widening inequality and the lack of basic employment, housing and rights. This is because Hall et al. (2020) suggest that many harms are symptoms of complex underlying structures and processes which are *zemiogenic* – which comes from the word *zemiology*, meaning "the study of harm." For this reason, as Boukli and Kotzé (2018) note, there is a general tendency that current studies directed at crime and harm to fail to consider multiple layers of "hidden victimage."

As I noted in Chapter 2, neoliberalism and its attached political apparatus seek to make zemiological studies one dimensional and very much confine them to the field of social and state reaction to crime and harm. Having spent the early part of my career working within these confines, doing bland and meaningless tickbox bureaucratic UK government studies into homelessness, drug offending and mental health, I remember thinking as a young researcher that we were asking "the right people the wrong questions." In fact, from 2001 – when I first started as a researcher – to 2013 I saw the situation become progressively worse, and I became quickly disillusioned with the State's ability to really help vulnerable people and critical of my seniors who continually brown-nosed officials in the Home Office by submitting reports that seemed to conveniently align with their policies. Surprise, surprise they then received more money to do more of the same sort of studies.

For some time, I was involved with numerous pointless research studies funded by the UK State apparatus (Borrill et al., 2003; Fox et al., 2005; Matthews et al., 2007; Briggs, 2008, 2010; Matthews and Briggs, 2008; Briggs et al., 2009, to name a few) which did nothing other than serve to build evidence to punish the poor and vulnerable (Wacquant, 2009). In the wider scheme of things, this is how criminologists become "administrative" and fall in line with the demands imposed on them by "academic capitalism" (see Chapter 2; Briggs et al., 2018). However, at the same time, it became the motivation to undertake meaningful and in-depth investigations – such as this one – which take an unbiased and critical view of the injurious consequences of neoliberal capitalism's internal logic and harmful structures.

Inequality, unemployment and poverty

Neoliberals sideline talk of harms such as global warming, poverty and unemployment because they believe the required interventions in the underlying systemic contexts will jeopardise their global economic project (Hall et al., 2020). The remarkable universality of neoliberal discourse used across different nations and regions of the world shifted, at least prior to the current crisis, popular debate in the "west," away from issues related to the inner workings of the global monetary system and its impact on economies and populations, towards generalised ideas about applicable policies. Therefore, issues such as increased social and/or political inequality have been and are being transformed into matters related to individual or governmental choices (Afouxenidis, 2015). For example, patterns of social inequality and poverty are reduced to ideas about individuals helping themselves (Springer, 2008; Bourgois and Schonberg, 2009; Briggs and Monge Gamero, 2017).

This is why, in official documents published by bodies such as the World Bank, the Organisation for Economic Co-operation and Development (OECD) and the United Nations Department of Economic and Social Affairs (UNDESA), all they can do is essentially make limp calls on governments to act against challenges such as inequality, unemployment and poverty, and/or provide guidance on policies to enhance "human capital" – the skills, knowledge and experience possessed by an individual or population. In a neoliberal society, citizens are called upon for their "meritocratic initiative" (Young, 2007) to work themselves into security and stable wealth as much as they are expected to work themselves out of their own suffering and destitution (Briggs and Monge, 2017).

Economic inequality is largely driven by the unequal ownership of capital, which can be either privately or public owned. Since 1980, very large transfers of public to private wealth occurred in nearly all countries, whether rich or emerging. While national wealth has substantially increased, public wealth is now negative or close to zero in rich countries. Arguably, this limits the ability of governments to tackle inequality; certainly, it has important implications for wealth inequality among individuals (Alvaredo et al., 2018). This is because we are talking about "individuals." Over the years, Oxfam have continued to document the steep increase in inequality around the world, and their latest report shows that "the world's 2,153 billionaires have more wealth than the 4.6 billion people who make up 60 percent of the planet's population" (Oxfam, 2020: 6). No surprise then that 10% of the world's population live on less than $2 a day (World Poverty Report, 2019).

Governments are massively under-taxing the wealthiest individuals, companies and corporations, and because of this fail to collect revenues that could help lift the responsibility of poverty reduction and inequality. But because neoliberal capitalism's main goal is to search for new profitable markets, exhaust them and then seek out new markets, inevitably there is a human cost. Companies and corporations look to streamline their operations and services to maximise their profit, which results in making redundancies, new and precarious work contracts, lack of work rights, low pay and increased pressure to work more hours, to name a few (Cardoso et al., 2014; Lloyd, 2018; Farina et al., 2019). In a time of reduced human labour and increased meritocratic pressure to compete to work (Young, 2007), there are inevitably large numbers of people who cannot find it. According to the International Labour Organization (2019: 2),

> An estimated 172 million people worldwide were unemployed in 2018, which corresponds to an unemployment rate of 5.0 per cent – a further 140 million people were in the "potential labour force" in 2018, which means that they have to be classified as underutilized labour. This group of people who are looking for a job but are not available to take up employment, or who are available but are not looking for a job, includes far more women (85 million) than men (55 million).

In low-income countries, these pressures are far more pronounced as political regimes, social infrastructures and employment relationships drastically impede the possibility to escape poverty. Other variables also make for startling consideration such as the increasing poverty associated with rural areas, hence the growing populations in cities across the world. In particular, this distinction is important because, as I hinted at in Chapter 1 when I referred to the research by Kelley et al. (2015), when combined with botched domestic economic policies and the increasing presence of man-made climate change, we see increased social pressure in poor urban areas. For example, a report by the World Bank Group in 2018 found the bottom 40% of the world's poor disproportionately live in rural areas, making them vulnerable to disruptions caused by the climate. Changes in climate impact ways out of gross inequality. For example, Uganda suffered significant setbacks in poverty reduction and shared prosperity in recent years largely due to a series of damaging droughts and pests that affected harvests throughout 2016. Consequently, Uganda's poverty rate rose from *no dun*

35.9% in 2012 to 41.6% in 2016 (World Bank, 2018). Climate change therefore exacerbates inequality.

As a result, these regions of the world have experienced increased social tension and conflict. While many of these people have protested about these threats to their livelihoods (Winlow et al., 2015), little change is seen which is why political crises have become everyday occurrence for many nations (Žižek, 2016). This is why the concept of social harm is fitting. Tifft and Sullivan (2001: 198) define social harms as "actions or arrangements that physically and spiritually injure and/or thwart the needs, development, potentiality, health, and dignity of others"; in other words, the perpetuation of social conditions that facilitate the mass production of what Bauman (2003: 5) refers to as "human waste," or more correctly wasted lives.

Expect there to be more wasted lives after the advent of the coronavirus outbreak. Just watch the companies and corporations cull employees because of the lack of economic activity as the weak, poor and vulnerable experience the brunt of suffering because of the virus (Chapter 11). As I write, we are at the tip of the iceberg in terms of redundancies, but in the few months since the outbreak hundreds of thousands of people have been sacked worldwide. This is because today's neoliberal capitalists, benefitting from advanced technology, the mobility of capital and the precedence of finance capital, no longer need labour in numbers (Hall and Winlow, 2018).

Neoliberalism + new market opportunities = increased inequality, people displacement/migration and climate change

Poor social groups are therefore normally those on the front line of neoliberal policies and practices, but it is their spatial and structural disadvantage that authenticates their vulnerability in the context of climate change. While the elite have better adaptive capacities largely because of their wealth, status and political influence, conversely the poor are on the front line of altered environmental changes. Research already confirms that climate change exacerbates inequalities across the fault lines of gender, race and ethnicity (Wright and Nyberg, 2015; Hallegatte et al., 2015; Barbier and Hochard, 2017; UNDESA, 2020). Moreover, estimates suggest that even under a low-impact scenario where powerful mitigation and adaption strategies are successful, between 3 million and 16 million people will fall into poverty by 2030 because of climate change. Under a high-impact scenario, those figures could rise to between 35 million and 122 million (Hallegatte et al., 2015). Inadvertently what also occurs as a result of climate change is that the same social groups are forced into aggressive competition with each other for limited resources (Parenti, 2011). As we will see in Chapters 5–7, this form of "meritocracy gone wrong" (Briggs, 2018) not only invariably contributes to the communities and regional self-destruction but also manifests itself in rioting, uprisings, armed struggles (see Chapter 1), terrorism and outbursts of internal country violence or that between neighbouring countries.

For example, projections suggest that if climate change rates continue at their current trajectory, surface water levels will reduce and groundwater sources deplete in already mostly dry subtropical regions (IPCC, 2019). This essentially produces "water scarcity" and therefore competition for water. For some time, Egypt has been threatening war with Ethiopia over the Grand Ethiopian Renaissance Dam on the Blue Nile for this reason (Lawson, 2017). Jordan has been grappling with water shortages due to increased pressure put by Syrian refugees (Hussein et al., 2020). Such internal resource conflicts can result in civil wars like the Sudan's Darfur conflict which arose as a consequence of water scarcity (Chellaney, 2014). Water scarcity is exacerbated further, as Jonathan Crary (2013) argues, by pollution and privitisation and the accompanying "monetisation of bottled water": commodifying water, making it a product even if access to it is a human right.

In many cases, the only options for people experiencing these things are either to stay in a decaying community and compete over resources or leave, many choosing the latter and moving to cities. Indeed, there are no organic migratory processes behind the fact that, for the first time in history, more people now live in urban than in rural areas (UNDESA, 2020) because climate change impacts more rural areas, and in particular, agricultural and farming land (Daoud et al., 2016; Diwakar et al., 2019). They are, as Hallegatte et al. (2015) note, more exposed to all types of climate-related shocks – natural disasters that destroy assets and livelihoods; waterborne diseases and pests that become more prevalent during heat waves, floods or droughts; crop failure from reduced rainfall and spikes in food prices that follow extreme weather events. This is because climate change reduces agricultural and farming productivity, especially in tropical regions. And because many poorer countries have a greater dependence on agriculture and climate-sensitive natural resources, a slight increase or change in climate variability, including more frequent and erratic weather extremes, only exacerbates existing conditions of poverty in these very countries.

For example, rising sea levels caused by the melting of the polar caps could displace five million Pacific Islanders who occupy Tuvalu, Kiribati, Vanuatu and the Marshall islands. Research indicates that if water continues to rise at the same rate, these islands will be underwater by 2050 and the inhabitants may have to move to Australia and New Zealand (Adams, 2007). There, however, this influx undoubtedly presents the two countries with challenges of where they will be housed and how they will be economically supported in two countries already feeling the strain of increased competition for food, water, land, jobs, etc. Similar climate threats potentially await the Indian cities of Mumbai, Chennai and Kolkata should Bangladesh continue to lose costal land at its current rate because of rising sea levels stimulated by climate change (Roy et al., 2011); research estimates that as many as 20 million refugees could cross over the border from Bangladesh to India and seek sanctuary in these cities (Kulp and Strauss, 2019).

As a consequence of this, cities expand because they are catalysts for economic growth, innovation and potential employment. However, in most cities and towns, a population influx can put pressure on infrastructure and compound deprivation, making inequality more pronounced (UNDESA, 2020). Furthermore, in cities, the new migratory group normally form part of an urban precariat (Standing, 2011) – bereft of security, dignified work and socially excluded. In cities, skills such as herding and farming are not recognised and the new migratory group are not educated like the urban population. Rural workers are then reduced from self-sufficient farmers to labourers, cleaners and/or temporary daily wagers undertaking menial jobs in exploitative conditions (Standing, 2011; Briggs and Dobre, 2014). For example, the Gobi Desert in China expands more than 3,600 square kilometres every year because of drought caused by man-made climate change (Rueff and Middleton, 2015), and farmers and merchants are increasingly migrating to China's overcrowded urban areas as grassland becomes desert (Sternberg et al., 2015).

These kinds of climate changes which result in inequality, conflict and people displacement, however, are also compounded by neoliberal business interests. Over the past 30 years, powerful global food corporations and companies have been involved in acquisition, otherwise known as "landgrabbing" in the expansion of factory-farmed food (GRAIN, 2011). Like with other industries under the guise of neoliberalism, the "corporate food system" puts the profits of the few before the needs of people, hence the complications associated with food safety incidents, environmental destruction, labour exploitation and the cultural and social decimation of rural communities around the world (McMichael, 2012).

Billions of dollars are being invested by banks, corporations and pension funds in farming and land acquisition. While the precise data is difficult to obtain, current estimates are that 60–80 million hectares of land has fallen under the control of foreign investors for the production of food (GRAIN, 2011). Much of this is happening in Africa, where people's customary rights to land are being completely disregarded. These companies have extreme market power and can force their contract growers to agree to exploitative working conditions. As the farmers are not employed directly by the companies, there is no adherence to labour laws and no dealings with representative unions: the goal being to extract as much for the farmers as possible at an economical cost for the company.

One consequence of this trend towards vertical integration and tightly integrated supply chains is the emergence of "corporate farmers." These are companies, sometimes owned by families and often owned by a mix of investors and even shareholders, with large-scale operations, typically in different parts of a country and sometimes in more than one country. In Argentina, for instance, where the emergence of such companies is particularly striking, just 30 companies now control over 2.4 million hectares of farmland (Senesi et al., 2016). Similarly, only 25 companies control around three million hectares of farmland in the Ukraine, which is 10% of the country's total Gross Domestic Product (GDP) (Kuns and Visser, 2016). Most of these new "corporate farmers" have special supply arrangements with downstream corporations, as China's poultry producer DaChan has with McDonald's, and some of them have been taken over by their downstream clients, such as Hortifruiti, the biggest fresh-fruit and vegetable producer in Central America, which has recently been acquired by Walmart.

This vast machinery of corporate "agribusiness" has also become inseparable from the global financial sector. The past three decades of globalisation have, more than anything else, seen a consolidation of wealth and power in the hands of Wall Street and other financial centres. Access to this huge pool of capital is propelling the expansion of "agribusiness," giving companies the financial resources to take over smaller firms or to set up new operations, while also harnessing them to the logic of quick and high returns, which are made off the backs of workers, consumers and the environment.

Take meat production for example. The Food and Agriculture Organization of the United Nations indicates that, per capita, meat consumption in developing countries doubled between 1980 and 2005, while the consumption of eggs more than tripled. Agribusiness corporations, backed by substantial subsidies and government support, have ramped up global industrial meat production to substantial levels over recent decades, and this has had devastating consequences for poor, rural communities as well as animals and the environment. In the countries importing cheap meat, local farmers lose markets. In the countries where these companies set up operations, local farmers lose their livelihoods and are plunged into poverty. For example, the rise of China's industrial poultry production since the mid-1990s forced 70 million small farmers to abandon poultry production (Bingsheng and Yijun, 2007). In Romania, the opening of its markets to imports and the entry of corporations into pork production, by both foreign and domestic firms, resulted in the dramatic loss of 90% of its pig farmers between 2003 and 2007 – 480,000 farmers dwindled to 50,000 in just four years (Hoste, 2015).

Farmers who remain in the game have to sign contracts with the corporate conglomerates and thus the grip corporations have on the food market tightens. Companies, only interested in operating at minimal costs, employ migrant workers who are more than likely to be unprotected to exploit their labour and pay them poor wages (Briggs and Dobre, 2014). Meanwhile, the cattle are "harvested" in "factory farms" which release significant quantities of greenhouse gases. Indeed, the meat industry alone is responsible for 18% of the world's total greenhouse gas emissions, when considering that this encompasses not only the clearing of forests for cattle but also the clearing of more forest for the production of crops for animal feeds (GRAIN, 2011).

The subsequent emissions – produced by industrial farming practices – often rely on chemical (nitrogen) fertilisers, heavy machinery that operates on petrol and highly concentrated industrial livestock operations that pump out methane waste (Reay et al., 2010). Across the globe, agriculture is rapidly eating up savannahs, wetlands and forests, in the process of ploughing huge amounts of land. This expansion of the farming industry is the overriding contributor to deforestation which accounts for about 70%–90% of global deforestation (GRAIN, 2011). Forests, in particular, are important as they remove carbon – a harmful gas – from our atmosphere and replace it with oxygen – a friendly gas. Deforestation

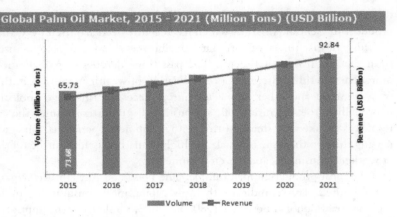

FIGURE 6 2018 Global projections of profit made from palm oil (see Zion Market Research, 2018).

is also occurring to make way for new market products such as palm oil (Greenpeace, 2019a, 2019b) – a key ingredient used in snack foods, cosmetics and cleaning products so is therefore found in many everyday products. The palm oil tree grows well in tropical environments and produces high-quality oil which is mostly used for cooking in developing countries, but it is also a very productive crop which offers a far greater yield at a lower cost of production than other vegetable oils. Palm oil has risen in global importance in the past several decades, with the world production of palm oil rising from 13.5 million tonnes in 1990 to 155.8 million tonnes in 2014 (FAOSTAT, 2016).

These days, global production of and demand for palm oil continue to increase rapidly and each year generate billions of dollars (Figure 6). Indeed, more recent estimates forecast that the same market could be worth 147.59 billion by 2026 (LLC, 2019). Naturally, these are all speculative market analyses which serve to propel investment on behalf of the most powerful food industry companies such as Nestle and Mars. Yet this comes at a price. Take Indonesia for example – these companies drain carbon-rich peatland forests to create vast palm oil plantations; this alone risks the tropical biodiversity that kills hundreds of different species of animals and insects. Such deforestation has therefore pushed Indonesia into the top tier emitters of global greenhouse gas emissions, alongside the United States and China (Petrenko et al., 2016).

When peatland forests are drained, however, they become flammable, and if ignited, such forests are thereafter hard to control. Notwithstanding, a flammable forest releases a staggering amount of carbon dioxide into the atmosphere. In July 2015, devastating blazes spread in Sumatra, Kalimantan and Papua. These fires produced a haze that affected millions of people across Southeast Asia. It is estimated that the smoke from 2015 Indonesian fires may have caused 100,000 premature deaths, and the World Bank calculated the cost of the disaster at

US$16 billion (World Bank, 2016). Research also shows that the palm oil expansion has increased inequality among local farmers (Bou Dib et al., 2018; Purnomo et al., 2020), and the national narrative of palm oil as a "force for good" is questionable given the conspicuous underinvestment in public services and infrastructure, uneven access to land, volatile pricing trends, problematic financing and loan schemes (Tyson et al., 2018). Displacement of local residents and the destruction of natural habitats have been issues, which have provoked international NGO criticism and local conflict. The resistance against displacement and deforestation for palm oil plantations has been violent and, in some cases, divided citizens along ethnic lines, reinforcing ethnic tension left from the colonial era (Colchester and Chao, 2014).

All in the name of capital, all in the name of profit. It's no wonder that these powerful corporations fund political campaigns and parties to assist in the grand denial that is man-made climate change: something that is not on the agenda of European politicians as Thierry, the manager of a volunteer-led Refugee Welcome Centre, said to me in Belgium:

> Increasing nationalism and it is worse among liberals. We just got out of a crisis [from 2008] and the country is a little better and people now say fuck refugees they are not important...like growth and economy are now important. That is now important. Ha, climate change and refugees? Nah. It is not important.

4

LET'S BE HONEST, WHAT IS THERE TO DEBATE ABOUT CLIMATE CHANGE?

It is just after 11:00 p.m., when I jog up the steps to meet Jeroen on a bitterly cold night outside the splendour of the North Station in Brussels, Belgium; this is the first time I am to meet him through a friend of an activist whom I interviewed in Paris. He immediately talks me through how the grand financial buildings support the refugees – although this was not the case at first. When the refugees initially arrived in their numbers early in the summer of 2015, citizen groups united to help house the refugees in the tents on the Parc du Maximillian, opposite the World Trade Centre. "The third world came to the first," I say to Jeroen. We come across a Syrian man walking alone in the darkness and start up a conversation:

SYRIAN MAN: There was a huge surge in August [2015] of Iraqi but many are returning to Turkey or Lebanon. I know a family they wait six months and then after one more week they go back to turkey as they have family. Wait five months for first interview, then two months for the second but they can't wait but it is not well organised.

As we walk down the deserted street in December 2015, we see two workers from a local NGO scour the area for rough-sleeping refugees. Though none apparently visible, last week in one night they found 200. We get talking to a smiley woman in a florescent jacket who says to us, "They [the government] keep it vague and chaotic to send out the message that you [the refugees] are not very welcome here, better off somewhere else" (see Chapter 8). It seems that when the Red Cross accommodation fills in the World Trade Centre, they filter into a nearby church. When the church fills, they sleep on the streets. We then walk around the corner to where the refugees queue to register a request to seek asylum seeker status – and this is just to register. Until they do, they are not entitled to any rights or benefits from the Belgian government. To ensure they can, they need an appointment which can take some weeks but very often months.

As we talk and approach the entrance, we meet six young Afghani men from Kunduz aged between 21 and 22 lying underneath donated covers and all the clothes possible to stay warm; they lean and huddle against each other like new-born puppies to stave off the cold. They have their appointment the next day but don't want to take their chances to lose it so are camping out until the doors open at 8:30 a.m.:

AMIR: We want to be first one, we arrive one month ago. We sleep Red Cross but we want to be first to register. When I came here, they gave me a date for the first interview.

JEROEN: Can I see the paper?

DAN: You will sleep here? Its December, where are your shoes and socks its freezing.

ABDUL: We wait 3 or 4 month then to another camp.

JEROEN: Once registered, they are entitled to food and things like that, the buses come and take them to those camps. But there are 1000s not registered as they only admit 150 people per day in the office.

AMIR: We need to come 8am so we stay overnight.

These young men are all agricultural farm workers from Kunduz – a province in Afghanistan which, over the past ten years, has suffered low crop yields, live-stock reduction, food insecurity and irrigation scarcity (Aich et al., 2019). Further, constraining factors include a lack of information, limited access to farm management instruments, lack of financial and credit facilities and limited connectivity of food products to the market and business (Hassanyar et al., 2019). Thousands of workers, like Amir and his five friends, have little choice but to find an alternative. That alternative perhaps should be some other area of the country, but with meaningless governmental action coupled by the presence of the Taliban, it is almost impossible. Amir said, "America has helped the Taliban, American soldiers I see with my eyes they sell weapons to Taliban. In my province" (see Chapter 5).

Indeed, Afghanistan is among the most highly vulnerable countries to climate change shocks because of weak economic foundations and poor social capital (Savage et al., 2009), and since 2012 it ha been ranked by the Global Adaptation Index among the most vulnerable countries in the world in terms of climate change (Eckstein et al., 2020). Thus, the aim of this chapter is to look at the vast evidence which indicates how man-made climate change impacts on human survival and people movement. In this respect, the thrust of the chapter is to move forward from the flimsy conservative as well as liberal arguments that climate change just marks an organic phase in the planets' history and makes a more real and urgent case to make the environment our pressing concern for the future.

What is man-made climate change?

Most people know now that global warming has been recognised as a significant issue for decades, but perhaps became more of a serious issue when the United Nations Framework Convention on Climate Change (UNFCCC) was established in the mid-1990s (Jackson, 2017). Up until then, it was not until the 1970s science and technology had not been sufficiently capable of measuring and modelling the global atmosphere (Askew, 1987). However, this development combined with increasing evidence and concern for the consequences for the atmosphere of man's activities started to produce new and troubling insights about the consequences of man's commercial and industrial expansion (Parry, 1990).

In the wider historical scheme of things, the relatively recent expansion of human populations and activities through industrialisation, agricultural development, deforestation and the burning of fossil fuels such as oil, gas and coal produced higher quantities of what science calls "greenhouse gases" at a much faster rate than they would otherwise be released through natural processes alone (Schellnhuber, 2006). While the air, water and land of the planet are all linked to its atmosphere through the exchange of gases such as clouds/water vapor (H_2O), oxygen (O_2) and carbon dioxide (CO_2) – and this is what produces Earth's climate or "average weather" – it is the greenhouse gases which are of concern because they produce a heat-trapping effect, hence the word "greenhouse" (Aizebeokhai, 2009). These gases, in particular CO_2, nitrous oxide (N_2O) and methane (CH_4), absorb radiation from Earth's surface, clouds and gas molecules and trap it as heat within the lower levels of the atmosphere (Newell and Paterson, 2010).

This is where the term "global warming" comes from. It is therefore a range of human activities, which include the plunderous burning of fossil fuels, widespread and unceasing industrial activities and the annihilation of forest for agricultural purposes and urbanisation, that are substantially increasing the concentrations of greenhouse gases in the atmosphere, thereby upsetting this atmospheric chemical balance (Chapter 3). Through these processes, this human activity has contributed to the increase in carbon dioxide in the air by 40% since the late 1700s, and when the gases warm the surface, evaporation increases as the atmosphere warms, which increases humidity and produces heavier rainfalls, and the frequency of heavy rainstorms in many places, while at the same time, contributes to drought in others (EPA, 2016).

Nowadays, there is a broad consensus within the scientific community, supported by agencies such as the National Aeronautics and Space Administration (NASA), the National Oceanic and Atmospheric Administration (NOAA) and the National Research Council (NRC), that climate change is real and that humans are contributing to it (Bonan, 2008; Newell and Paterson, 2010; IPCC, 2013). Such institutions have attempted to lobby countries and governments for change through agreements through the UNFCCC such as that in Kyoto (1997) – which took eight years to ratify – and Paris (2016) – which took three years to ratify. This is because the same evidence also suggests that if we do not act, then we endanger millions of the world's poor (Jackson, 2017) as well as the future of the human race (Hulme, 2019).

While many of the commitments made by countries that signed up to these treaties have struggled to reach them, even if they were reached, evidence suggests that CO_2 emissions will continue to rise. For example, King et al. (2015) indicate that by 2035 the concentration of carbon dioxide in the atmosphere will exceed the critical level for a 2 °C rise in temperature, and on current policies the temperature will eventually reach 4 °C above the pre-industrial level. This is the central forecast, implying a 50% chance of still higher temperatures. Yet, as it stands, business interests lie with the continuation of our current neoliberal status quo which has no let up, feels no need to rest.

The deniers

Despite the undeniable scientific evidence, one of the main reasons we continue to march down the pathway towards Earth's destruction is that powerful global corporations and companies – which have strong interests in industries and businesses that pollute the planet in various ways – buy political power. Such companies and corporations have gone and go to great lengths to minimise knowledge about the real harm of their operations as well as hiding scandals and denying the damage their business practices have on the wider community.

Take ExxonMobil – one of the world's largest international oil and gas companies – which went to great lengths to deny the significance of their activities with global warming and climate change. During the 1970s and 1980s, they "conveniently funded" their "own research" into their "own activities" as well as climate variation to "conveniently find" that what they were doing was nothing of major harm to the planet. In particular, they funded private institutions and pretty much bribed university departments to produce favourable reports of their operations as well as other studies which criticised treaties and agreements like the Kyoto in 1997 (see Burke et al., 2014; King et al., 2015). Research by Supran and Oreskes (2017) which examined 187 climate change communications by ExxonMobil Corporation found that, after discussing whether climate change was real and caused by humans as their documents become more public, they increasingly communicated doubt about global warming and climate change. Supran and Oreskes note that 80% of ExxonMobil's internal documents said that climate change was man-made and real, while in advertorials in newspapers and other media, only 12% of their communications took the same stance; instead, much of this space was reserved for expressing doubt (81%).

Naturally, ExxonMobil misled the public because of their business interests. Similar denial has taken place in the hotel and tourism industry which undoubtedly relies on international travel operators, the aviation industry and a sizeable number of tourists interested and motivated to travel and take holidays: this in itself generates significant pollution. Notwithstanding, the expansion of the industry into naturally protected areas not only contaminates but puts at risk endangered wildlife and fauna. So as with companies like ExxonMobil, there are similar underhand processes taking place. Writing as academics working in the hotel and tourism industry, Shani and Arad (2014: 82) draw into question the *real* impact of man-made climate change by suggesting that it is "exaggerated" and that any change to the climate "will be positive for humans, plants and wildlife" in their extremely extensively researched three-page article titled "Climate Change and Tourism: Time for Climate Scepticism" in the journal *Tourism Management*.

The problem with these types of communications is that they are also used by media institutions – that also have spurious business interests related to generating controversy via capturing audiences – which use other neoliberal puppets to reel off the message to the public. For example, in their analysis of 3,200 UK newspaper articles over three periods in (1) 2007, (2) 2009 and 2010 and (3) 2011, Painter and Gavin (2015) found that climate change "sceptics" increased their presence markedly across all newspapers and all types of articles in the second period and maintained a significant presence in many in the third. Importantly, there was a tendency that, in line with this increase, that sceptical voices or opinions were more likely to be included in pieces written by their own "in-house non-specialist columnists" rather than by environment editors, scientific experts or related correspondents.

This produces a kind of "climate change confusion" and is reflected in an increasingly divided electorate, which, in turn, splinters opposition and erodes collective action against heavy polluter companies while simultaneously permitting things to simply continue as they are. In their 2016 study, Dunlap et al. reviewed commendable yet futile efforts made by Al Gore, the US ex-vice president at the time, at the turn of the 21st century to create awareness and lobby the American establishment to change their thinking regarding man-made climate change. Gore's book *An Inconvenient Truth*, which was released in 2006 and published in book form the following year, received considerable attention, and its message was buttressed by the Intergovernmental Panel on Climate Change's (IPCC) 2007 Fourth Assessment Report, proclaiming that the evidence for global warming was "unequivocal" and that it was "very likely" due to human activities. Yet Gore's plea, however, was counter-attacked by powerfully backed business enterprises via right-wing media institutions like Fox News to rubbish his claim. As Dunlap et al. (2016) note, this essentially produced what they call "partisan polarization" where voters fell into more partisan voting camps, thus jeopardising homogeneous support for climate change (also see Dunlap, 2019).

More recent, high-profile attempts to lobby the market-led political establishment has been from Greta Thunberg – a young Swedish environmental activist who has gained international recognition for promoting the view that humanity is facing an existential crisis arising from climate change. She has famously given high-profile speeches openly criticising world leaders, such as Donald Trump, in their continued inaction on manmade climate change. In one speech, she famously said,

You have stolen my dreams and my childhood with your empty words. And yet I'm one of the lucky ones. People are suffering. People are dying. Entire ecosystems are collapsing. We are in the beginning of a mass extinction, and all you can talk about is money and fairy tales of eternal economic growth. How dare you! For more than 30 years, the science has been crystal clear. How dare you continue to look away and come here saying that you're doing enough, when the politics and solutions needed are still nowhere in sight.

(NPR, 2019)

Even though she herself – just like Al Gore – has been criticised for her "radical approach" which could jeopardise the slow progress environmental activists have made over the recent years and for campaigning for "environmentally friendly" electric cars – even if the lithium ion batteries rely on the mining of cobalt which are linked with exploitative working conditions. Given that half of the world's cobalt comes from the Democratic Republic of Congo – which is one of the world's poorest countries and suffers from endemic corruption and war – men, women and even children have almost had no choice but to join the ranks of the cobalt mining industry which has been condemned for its involvement in human suffering and environmental destruction (Dummett, 2016). Still, our planet continues to heat up. The seas continue to rise. The unpredictable weather becomes more and more unpredictable. And more and more people are displaced because of it.

Man-made climate change: its implications for humanity

There are countless ways in which human activity is shaping not only changes in the environment and climate but also the habitats and local businesses of millions of people across the planet. Perhaps the main threats are from extreme heat, rising sea levels and unpredictable weather changes (Sriver, 2011; Palmer, 2014) which produce floods (Artur and Hilhorst, 2012) and droughts. For example, it is projected that by the year 2070, three billion people will be living under extreme heat conditions (BBC, 2020a). In Chapter 1, I showed that the mass exodus we are now witnessing from rural areas to urban areas is related to this kind of climate change. Projections made by Gunerlap et al. (2015) suggest that should we continue along our current trajectory by 2030, five billion people will live in urban areas: this equates to 60% of the world's population. They also hypothesise that by 2030, the percentage of urban land lying in high-frequency flood zones[1] will rise to 40% – a 10% increase from what it was in the year 2000.

This means that while the exodus because of climate change continues to the cities, it is those very cities where people flee that will also in turn be affected by the very same processes (see Knippertz et al., 2015; Jackson, 2017): these people will leave and only find it difficult not to leave again. Research shows that many of these expanding cities such as Harare, Nairobi, Abuja, Cairo and Johannesburg are extremely vulnerable to corrupt procedures in the development of social, political and climate change infrastructure. The arriving rural migrants also bring with them their cultural and livelihood practices which facilitate their entry into the rapidly expanding informal sectors because their modes of life are unrecognised in developing cities where technological and digital industries increasingly predominate (Chirisa et al., 2016).

There will be further changes to urban land already exposed to floods and droughts which some researchers suggest will provoke increases of over 250% (Gunerlap et al., 2015). With regard to the former, it is estimated that over the past 30 years Earth's surface has gained 115,000 square kilometres of water −20,135 square kilometres of which is found in coastal areas (Donchyts et al., 2016). An elevation in sea levels and increased ocean temperature could see the disappearance of 17,500 islands and over 81,000 kilometres of coastline in Indonesia (Zikra and Lukijanto, 2015) as well as jeopardising fisheries on which such communities rely on for their sustenance (Sainsbury et al., 2018).

Regarding the latter, droughts not only produce water shortages but also jeopardise farming practices and livestock and, consequently, put at risk whole regions and communities. The local farmers in Ethiopia who, because of climate change, see higher temperatures and seasonal shifts in rainfall mixed with bouts of diseases, often blame god and/or loss of indigenous practices and values, but can't identify the causal factors of deforestation, increased CO_2 emissions and global warming (Hameso, 2017).

In droughts, crops fail, and this produces "food insecurity" as well as a battle for basic resources like water. Research from 20 years ago already indicated that a large proportion of the world's population experience "water stress", and rising water demands greatly outweigh greenhouse warming in defining the state of global water systems (Vorosmarty et al., 2000). Water availability looks set to decline as the prognosis for the total number of people living in cities where freshwater availability from stream flow will likely decline by at least 10% by the 2050s, compared to the present day (UCCRN, 2018). Evidence from various African countries indicates that climate change which produces droughts presents a high risk to food resources, their distribution and consumption, often resulting in famine (Simatele and Simatele, 2015; Masipa, 2017). Projections look dismal as well. The UCCRN (2018) forecast that the total number of people living in cities where their national yield of at least one of four major crops (maize, rice, soya or wheat) is projected to decline by at least 10% by the 2050s, compared to the present day. It's no wonder Amir and his friends who I met in the middle of the night in Brussels move on. Like them, people like Sadar who came from a village in another part of rural Afghanistan which experienced droughts have had to come a long way because of it and are now stuck in improvised oblivions such as the "Calais Jungle" in France.

Far from home: Sadar in the "Calais Jungle"

We pass a sign saying 28 kilometres to Calais in France as Jeroen tells me many parking laybys on the E40 have since been closed as they have been used by smuggling mafias to load lorries full of people to then hide them in the vehicles. Shortly after, we stop off in layby to find out the whereabouts to exit the "Calais Jungle." Next to us is an empty truck with the door open which within minutes attracts police attention. We manage to work out that we should take the next turning on the right towards the port area. As we take the bend, a police van sits on the corner with its lights flashing, and a policeman patrols up and down a pathway, looking out over the flat farmland which has in the background the port. Sections of the fence to the right are cut and broken in places, and as we negotiate a small slope which goes over a bridge, we see the sprawling camp on our right. Suddenly two large fences appear on each side of the road about five metres in height, and they trap us in the carriageway as we see police vans parked on either side. Within a few seconds we pass the camp and seem to be heading towards the port, seeing only to the left and right of us the large intimidating fence. We turn around at the port, passing dunes where police patrols monitor the stretch of beach which joins the harbour as the waves crash against the shore.

We pass the camp again now on the left and take a side road which leads us to a sports park, parallel to the refugee camp, and the road seems to reduce in quality from one of asphalt to one narrow, muddy gravelly potholed road. We pass broken fences and a police blockade. We get out and ask the police if we can pass and are waved on past. We enter into a main road where police vans surround us and take a right towards the camp entrance before parking up next to a mud bank. Perhaps as a poignant reminder of the past, we get out and see in front of us a Second World War Bunker which slowly gathers moss and history. Ironically, it sits as a timeless reminder of the consequences of conflict and war just as the "Calais Jungle" next to it where we are told informally about 3,500 people live.

We walk down the road in wellies, into another muddy road which leads to two of the rear camp entrances. Police wave us into the camp as we pass volunteers, more police and sizeable numbers of refugees – it seems there is an eviction plan in place for today or tomorrow which will see the site cleared and the residents moved to better conditions in shipping containers. Inside the camp, the mud is everywhere – on tents, wooden buildings, peoples' clothes and children's faces. There seems to be one main street which passes through the heart of the camp, and on either side are donated old and new caravans, and various tents of all shapes and sizes which wobble around in the wind and wooden constructions of all types.

Later that day, we amble around for a while before stumbling upon the hospital which is basically a wooden hut with three separate rooms with a few small beds and chairs. At least the medics have some clean spaces away from the mud and the patients have some privacy should they need it. As we speak, a mobile medical volunteer walks in with all his medical equipment attached to his body; he looks like a superhero. They explain how a baby was born last night in the "jungle" and the family had no clothes or food for them so they asked a local supermarket to deliver basic products they required. We are then shown inside the adult school which is split into two sides, one for where Afghani and Kurdish men learn English and the other for where some Africans learn French. Along the back of the wall are piles and piles of donated pens, papers, folders, books, all sorts.

We step outside and walk for a short while before seeing a bland wooden building covered with plastic tarpaulins with a small square hole into which someone leans in and out and then leaves. Another person follows after, leaning in and then leaving. We look at each other and move towards this square hole no larger than a computer screen. As we try and fit our faces in, we see on the floor a young Afghani man sitting cross-legged over a cigarette machine and a tub of Winston tobacco making Do-It-Yourself cigarettes. He looks up and smiles saying, "Jungle cigarettes?" and presents his hand forward with a batch of ten homemade cigarettes wrapped in a bit of silver foil; "ten for one Euro," he says. It is an offer we can't refuse and we dig around in our pockets for the cash.

Instead of dealing through the hole, we walk into the dark door into the room where his counter is. Inside it is poorly lit and damp, and there is a musty smell about the place. To the left are tables with rags and sheets on which are bed duvets, next to the post which props up the structure is an old bike caked in mud and to the right is a small kitchen with stove and a few bits of food lying around. Behind the young man, hanging from the ceiling and wall are washing packs (toothbrush, toothpaste, soap, etc.), biscuits, drinks, fruit and almost anything he can fit in the space to sell.

The plastic tarpaulins flap violently in the wind making it difficult to hear him while he continues to sit and make cigarettes on the floor: his name is Sadar and he is 24. He talks about droughts, war and unrest in Afghanistan and how he had left to find a place where he couldn't "hear bombs and firing." He says he hasn't heard from his brother for months and suspects he is dead and recalls how the Taliban came to his community to recruit one person per family to fight for their cause. Sadar then invites us to have some tea and delves under his wooden counter and in between another into a kitchen area where he fills an old kettle with water and lights up the gas stove. Though we try to inform him about the improved circumstances of applying for asylum in France and Belgium, he is not interested because he says the authorities are a "problem" for him and has his heart set on the UK. Each night, he makes his way down to the docks to try to board lorries or even boats, anyway he can. He hands us the tea in a plastic cup and we sip it welcomingly. Though it seems he has been here for some months, he has had no success – "even less so now because since five months they build a fence and now it is almost impossible." While he bemoans the lack of opportunity to leave, he is also bound to the camp by his business which makes him on average about €30 a day. It could, however, all be lost in an instant as there is talk that the whole camp will be evicted today or tomorrow. He says,

> The problem is that the world needs to know about the real situation, where the people are coming from and why are they here in this camp (Calais). You must listen to this if you are journalist, researcher, you must write this, you can tell the real story, our story.

Afghanistan, Amir and armed conflict

In a parallel world, Sadar would have been working in the farmland in Afghanistan but severe droughts across his region from 2008 to 2010 (Savage et al., 2009) – and more pressingly for him in the consecutive years of 2013 and 2014 (World Vision, 2019) – put his future in significant jeopardy. The most recent droughts in 2018 and 2019 in the Badghis Province led to widespread crop failure and the displacement of over 298,000 people in search of food and water (World Bank, 2019). Crop failures lead to conflict between communities for the scarce resources, and this is further exacerbated by population growth, inefficient irrigation practices and deforestation. It is perhaps unsurprising that Afghanistan is one of the most water-stressed countries in the world, ranking 31st out of 195 countries (World Vision, 2019).

As a consequence of climate change, Afghanistan also has seen a reduction of underground water and suffered the effects of extreme heat (UNEP, 2017). Temperature increases break records each year (Figure 7 – the darkest colour signifying a 0.7–1.2 °C increase), and projections of mean annual temperature for the future suggest an increase by 1.4–4.0 °C by the 2060s and 2.0–6.2 °C by the 2090s (Ghulami, 2017). Climate models indicate that these patterns will lead to drought being the norm by 2030 and that desertification and land degradation will accompany this (Aich et al., 2017). The poor working in this rural agricultural regions, suffer most (C-Adapt, 2016) even if the population and the economy are almost completely dependent on agricultural production, particularly subsistence farming. This poverty, lack of development and adaption-to-climate-change

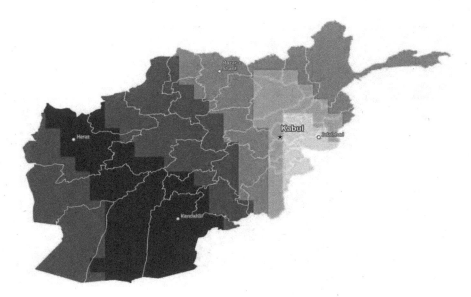

FIGURE 7 Afghanistan: change in annual average temperature (1981–2010).

strategies have been further hampered by armed conflict and internal war (Aich et al., 2017; Ghulami, 2017).

Amir's "big ship" to long queue

After a brief introductory conversation outside the registry centre, we sit down with Amir and his friends, and they talk about a long journey over "many months" from Afghanistan. They say they didn't know which country they were heading for, and even when they crossed in "big ship" from Turkey to

FIGURE 8 Playing "give" and "no" with Amir and his friends.

FIGURE 9 Queue to "register" to "register."

Greece, they still had little idea. One man, Amir, said his friend told him to go to Finland, but on arriving in Belgium his friend said it was "closed, don't come."

Suddenly Amir produces a deck of cards and invites us to sit down with them for a few games (see Figure 8). With nothing on the agenda at about midnight on a Monday night, we walk around the metal fences and sit down with them. I don't know what the games were called and I'm not even sure they did but for people who were taught how to play the game as it was being played, we did ok. We were taught on the basic instructions of "give" (as in play your card) and "no" (as in don't play your card), and at times we were helped. Jeroen wins the first game and I the second and then we play a sequence of a more familiar games. We talk and laugh, and in the company of our new friends, we forget the cold. It passes midnight and we say our goodbyes and shake hands, wishing them well. I say I will return to see them in the morning as they go in to get registered.

The next day, and after, skipping breakfast, I leave the hotel the next morning to find the ground grimly decorated with puddles: it has rained during the night. I walk swiftly towards the World Trade Centre. As I near, other refugees walk at a similar pace and I pass a queue of 50 outside the block where the interviews are done. However, when I arrive at where Amir and his friends were camped out, there are two solid queues of 400 plus; they gently graze against each other as if they were filtering out of a football game in which their team had just lost and relegation was imminently on the horizon. The few people with appointments furiously wave their hands with their papers to get the police attention and come towards the front of the queues (see Figure 9). Others queue hoping to get in before doors shut on their opportunity to register before then registering for asylum. In the queue, some people carry everything, trampling on the sheets which kept Amir and his friends warm last night. As I look up and down this line of people which expands each minute, a young family pass me, the mother carrying what can be a baby no older than two months wrapped in a blanket.

Note

1 Defined by the UCCRN (2018) as "coastal cities are defined as those within 10 kilometres from the coast and have an average elevation below 5 metres."

5

THE BUSINESS OF MISERY AND THE REFUGEE "CRISIS"

Later that day, I listen to the recorded conversation from the previous night when I played cards with Amir and his friends on the streets of Brussels:

AMIR: There is Taliban, ISIS, no security.
DAN: So a lot of people leaving? Where do you want to go?
AMIR: Any place we go we can improve our life?
JEROEN: Did you know of Belgium before you left?
ABDUL: No, but friends say come here. He say is better.

They talk among themselves, nod and agree that "Belgium good" they say before:

AMIR: When we come to Turkey, we ask and he say come Belgium.
ABDUL: Really we don't understand where to choose, we have friends on Face-
    book and they advice us on the Facebook. So we come here.
DAN: And Germany?
ABDUL: No we not have a good stay there.
AMIR: Hey friend [to Daniel], you look Syrian. [They all laugh]
Soon after, I meet Jeroen again, my contact:
JEROEN: The situation in Afghanistan has got worse, it has been gradual but last
    summer in 2015, a big city called Kunduz fell to the Taliban and this crushed
    the spirit of the Afghans. They fear now in Kabul that it will fall again. The
    economy has gone bad and international donors have retreated, with NGOs
    pulling out. There were huge queues at the passport centres, it just takes a
    few months but the reality that two thirds of those that fleed went to Iran.
    Same in Pakistan, they are now telling the refugees to go home. Iranians are
    recruiting Afghans to fight in Syria and they pick them in the street, saying

we send you back to Afghanistan or we pay your family 500 dollars and you fight in Syria. So the message is go and die or go and die and your family get some money.

Amir's story is complete: his displacement from his cultural heritage, life, work, relationships and homeland came as a consequence of a cruel mix of external elements. From a situational perspective, he had no influence over global warming and how it squeezed opportunity in his province nor did he have much control over the Taliban's resurgence across the region. Yet how is that the Taliban have made continued insurgency? Without revising the complete history of Afghanistan, it is possible to locate this political instability, failure of domestic economies and climate uncertainty to the initial liberalisation of the country, which marked a series of internal feuds that drifted into neighbouring Pakistan due to governance and ethnic territories (Siddique, 2012).

Initial American interest in Afghanistan stemmed from agricultural companies which developed hydroelectric and irrigation projects in the 1930s. This initiative triggered interest from the Soviet Union, and thereafter it has remained a "country of interest" between these two global powerhouses. The "interest," however, was then exacerbated by the Cold War in the 1960s, which essentially made the country a geopolitical plaything for the United States and the Soviet Union in the production and sale of arms and weaponry. The see-saw interest from both the United States and the Soviet Union, coupled with increasing internal ethnic tension because of the political vacuum, saw Arab and fundamentalist presence sponsored by Saudi Arabia and Iran emerge in the form of the Taliban. At the time, teachers, merchants and rural workers all said that the Taliban promised two things: security and an end to the conflict between rival mujahidin groups that continued to plague Afghanistan through the 1990s and, indeed, quell the influence from Russia and the United States (Roy, 2002).

Things changed again in 1996 when Osama bin Laden relocated from his refuge with the Sudanese government to the Taliban's quarters in Afghanistan. Bin Laden caused a seeming paradox for Afghanistan watchers. On the one hand, the Taliban, recognised as the government of Afghanistan by only Pakistan, Saudi Arabia and the United Arab Emirates, sought to break its isolation. On the other hand, the Taliban continued to shelter Osama bin Laden, even after his involvement in the 1998 bombings of the US embassies in Kenya and Tanzania.

Bin Laden brought with him to Afghanistan a well-equipped and fiercely loyal division of fighters – numbering as few as 2,000. While many of these men were trained in al-Qaeda camps in preparation for terrorist acts abroad or protected bin Laden and his associates at their various safe houses, bin Laden made available several hundred for duty on the Taliban's front line; his presence was enough to assure the Taliban continued balance. While the Taliban suffered a high international cost for hosting bin Laden, this was offset by the domestic benefits the regime gained. And those benefits were found restoring some sort of domestic stability even if it was through the cultivation of opium (Windle, 2016).

The persistent droughts over the past 40 years due to man-made climate change internally as well as externally displaced hundreds of thousands of Afghanis (Chapter 4). Those who didn't leave the country had to provide for themselves and were forced to look for lucrative alternatives. Opium is relatively drought tolerant and more valuable than other crops, and Afghani farmers earn approximately four times their annual income from the sale of opium. Because of long-term drought conditions and a weakened political system, many farmers turned to opium to support themselves. However, while the farmers earn a higher annual income with opium, they must share their earnings with the Taliban in exchange for protection and distribution of product. It is estimated that the Taliban funds 60% of their warfare through Afghanistan's illicit drug industry (Windle, 2016). Even though opium cultivation is illegal, the industry constitutes 7% of the nation's Gross Domestic Product (GDP), and while, at the time, many farmers may not want to support the Taliban in a country without alternatives, it was often their only option (UNODC, 2011). In essence, the Taliban, much like ISIS as we will see later in this chapter as well as Chapter 6, were operating a form of *exploitative entrepreneurialism* – establishing an innovative yet exploitative business to fill a gap in the market.

The Taliban rule was and still is notably violent, but it was a reluctant trade-off for many in Afghanistan. However, when Osama bin Laden and al-Qaeda were singled out as those responsible for the September 11th attacks on the twin towers, this was enough to motivate the United States into an all-out war to "eradicate"' the network. Experts and academics now contest this by suggesting that it was a strategic effort to quell Russian power and influence in Afghanistan and into Pakistan (Siddique, 2012). Others go further by suggesting that the war in Afghanistan was – and continues to be – part of a profit-driven agenda: a war of economic conquest and mineral plunder "a resource war". While Afghanistan is acknowledged as a strategic hub in Central Asia, bordering on the former Soviet Union, China and Iran, at the crossroads of pipeline routes and major oil and gas reserves, it has huge mineral wealth as well as its untapped natural gas reserves. For these reasons, American companies have been negotiating access in Taliban-controlled areas for the extraction of these minerals (Lakhani, 2013; Loewenstein, 2019).

This chapter mixes documentary analysis with the observations and refugee testimonies to challenge awkward questions about exactly who and how many are benefitting from human suffering and displacement. People like Sadar and Amir and thousands of others like them fall fodder to these processes because of the business attached to their operations. There is, if you like, *a business in their misery* and this chapter case studies Iraq. The Marxist critique of the *business of misery* is important because not enough people are talking openly about these issues as neoliberal capital steamrolls forward: creating wars, destroying the environment, uprooting people and crushing their livelihoods and homes.

The Gulf between resource wars and climate change

Take the three main current threats in Iraq: terrorism, corruption and climate change (Azooz and Talal, 2015), all the three of which are inextricably linked to one another (EWGCSR, 2018) and triggered in the main by competition for natural resources (Le Billion, 2018; Price, 2018). "Resource wars" as they have been termed (Klare, 2011) are either *international* or *territorial* conflicts which arise over the competition and control over natural resources which could be, for example, gold, silver, minerals, wood, oil, and water. In the case of Iraq, it is its vast desert areas which harbour expansive oil reserves. Research by the International Energy Agency (IEA, 2020) indicates that Iraq is capable of producing around 4,443,457 barrels of oil a day and has the potential to generate $5 trillion in oil revenues by the year 2035. This would make the country the second largest oil exporter and the provider of 45% of overall global production.

From an international perspective, it is unsurprising then that the potential wealth Iraq has to offer attracts attention from consumer countries such as those in the West. War fought over petrol and oil – often provoked by previous political grievances or historical disputes – has direct humanitarian consequences as it damages political infrastructures (such as the provision of food, water, electricity and communication), creates social unrest and displaces people and communities (Chapter 6). Everyday people who are the regular residents of these resource-rich areas often lose their mode of living, cultural heritage and well-being, and rural famers and their communities are rendered worthless: they become the victims of these wars and prone to bribery, slavery, kidnapping, rape and violence. A prime example of this is what took place in the Gulf 30 years ago.

The Gulf War (1990–1991)

There exist more detailed and dedicated accounts to the advent of the Gulf War which took place between 1990 and 1991. These works agree that Saddam Hussein's Iraqi regime broke international conditions in 1990 and forcefully invaded their oil-rich neighbour, Kuwait – a small country sandwiched between Iraq, Iran and the Persian Gulf. Sources indicate that the motive for the invasion was linked to clearing significant debt estimated to be between $50 billion and $60 billion accrued from Iraq's war with Iran as well as providing Iraq with strategic advantage in the distribution of oil (Kostiner, 2009). The United States along with the UK and a coalition of neighbouring Arab countries such as Saudi Arabia, Syria and Egypt mounted a response which culminated in what was called "Operation Desert Storm" in January 1991 which made use of 900,000 troops. The United States did this even having sold weapons to Iraq to aid its war against Iran (1980–1988), which was also stimulated by ethnic tension and political control over oil reserves McNaugher, 1990). America feared that should Saddam's invasion continue into Saudi Arabia, he would then govern the distribution of 20% of the world's oil reserves. At the time, President George Bush was famously quoted as saying,

> Our jobs, our way of life, our own freedom and the freedom of friendly countries around the world would all suffer if control of the world's great oil reserves fell into the hands of Saddam Hussein.
>
> *(Hoffman and Tyler, 1990)*

Even in the build-up to the Gulf War in 1990, classified documents confirm that British arms manufacturers scrambled into production to provide assistance to those countries keen to flex their political muscles and/or protect themselves. That market opportunity in 1990 paid dividends as it secured deals that continue to reap benefits which extend to this day. In 2016, for example, the UK won £6 billion of arms contracts, and half of that value was generated from weaponry sold to the Middle East (Doward, 2017): so much for the "impending humanitarian catastrophe." Yet we have to remember we are talking about a business from death and destruction: this is a *business of misery*.

The coalition forces then spent five weeks bombing the Iraqi bases from air and sea using 84,200 tonnes of munitions (Salvage, 2002) before mounting a ground assault in February in an effort to regain control of Kuwait. The whole operation, though months in the planning, was over in a matter of 100 hours as the coalition pushed back Iraqi forces to the border and a ceasefire was agreed. However, such was the damage to the country that the oil industry – on which the country relies as its main source of export – had to shut off 90% of imports and 97% of its exports, plunging the country into economic hardship (Alnasrawi, 2000).

While the coalition lost only a few hundred lives, the estimates of Iraqi deaths were up to 261,000 (Salvage, 2002). However, research also shows that a further 110,000 – including 70,000 children – in the first year suffered directly "war-induced adverse affects," and around two million children and one million pregnant women suffered malnutrition (Salvage, 2002). Further revolts ensued in Kurdish north area of the country which led to violent suppressions that killed 30,000 people and 5,000 soldiers (Daponte, 1993). All this was mostly as a consequence of the destruction of the country's infrastructure. Indeed, the political and social destabilisation meant that around 40% of the population could not access drinking water as the demand increased for medical supplies (Salvage, 2002). At the time, it was estimated that two million people were internally displaced and a further 900,000 sought refuge in other countries. One such family were Ahmed and Masri whom I met in Izmir in Turkey.

In a forgotten corner of Izmir, a forgotten family of eight teeter on the brink of survival

The taxi driver gets lost and stops to ask a passer-by for directions. It looks like even he doesn't come so far out of the centre into the suburbs. In the process of stopping, he causes a major traffic jam. Then three cars behind have to reverse so we can allow a large truck past – which somehow fits down the dark, narrow road – before continuing. In the night-market stalls are spices, medicines, fruit and vegetables, and I can almost wind down the window and reach out for what I want as we pass. We then drive quite fast up a hill, further into the shanty area of Izmir, and the light almost disappears from the roads. Soon the passers-by become shadowy figures in the streets. We continue up until we see a light and what looks like to be a main street in the shanty area, where cars bustle up and down and young kids loiter and play in the streets.

We turn the wrong way again and ask a local man where we need to go; we are trying to find the place where we are to interview an Iraqi family. We are directed back on ourselves, and, eventually, we come out into an open road, high in the hills which look down on Izmir – a beautiful sight at night. After five more minutes of driving, we stop outside a local market selling fruit and we wait. A young boy about ten years old runs up to us with a mobile phone in his hand and waves us into the darkness, and we turn right into an intimate alleyway with no lighting before turning left into another alleyway where the buildings look more ominous against the night.

At the doorstep is Ahmed who welcomes me into his home. I say "home" because half of it is falling down. Inside, I step on to a broken-tiled floor past a kitchen in which sit four of his children and into the living room/dining room/ bedroom/play area/conservatory. The walls are damp and the paint peels off between the sockets and the wires which hang off the wall. We are asked to sit on one of the three sofa/beds where five people sleep. Outside clothes and carpets hang to dry slowly in the humid temperatures. To me the rent of Turkish 1,000 or $150 a month seems expensive.

Arabic tea is brought in with a home-made cake. As we sit, Ahmed's wife Masri does most of the talking, while the older children patrol the younger ones who run riot around us – there are eight in total. As we start to talk, Masri sits forward on the chair and is heavy in her hand gestures when she explains what has happened to her family. Initially leaving Iraq after the Gulf War in the 1990s, they stowed away on a butcher's truck. At the time, she was pregnant and on the makeshift boat from Turkey to Greece, one of her sons drowned. The police eventually caught up with them in Istanbul and they were returned to Iraq. They stayed for a week before selling more land and goods and started a long journey paying for illegal transport, hitchhiking and walking towards the land border between Turkey and Greece. In total, they spent $17,000. When they arrived, they found difficulty in applying for asylum and with no official status. While they got by for some years, in the end they had to return to Iraq to sell more property and land.

The Iraq (2003–2011) war-occupation

Kostiner (2009) states that in the wake of the first Gulf War, the UN Security Council set the terms for the ceasefire which would supposedly

1. Recognise the adjusted Kuwait–Iraq border;
2. Accept a UN guarantee of the border;
3. Allow the UN to position a peace observer force in a zone along the Iraq–Kuwait border;
4. Acknowledge and reaffirm the Chemical Warfare and Nuclear Non-Proliferation Treaties;
5. Allow the UN to conduct weapons inspections and destroy all biological, chemical and nuclear weapons, and related equipment and supplies;
6. Return or free Kuwaiti prisoners;
7. Accept liability for Kuwait's losses;
8. Accept liability for pre-war debts; and
9. Renounce terrorism.

Many politicians and commentators in the West were hoping that there would be a military coup and Saddam would be toppled from power. However, despite attempts throughout the 1990s, no such successful coup evolved (Crawford, 2013). A "back-and-forth" tension persisted between the United States and Iraq because the former was concerned the latter would break the UN peace sanctions. The continued presence of US forces, however, seemed more about America asserting political and economic hegemony in the area as well as generating business from the sale of arms and weapons to fellow Gulf States. Indeed, it is estimated that collectively Gulf States spent $82 billion in the aftermath of the first Gulf War (al-Shayeji, 1997).

During this period, the combination of food shortages and hyperinflation meant that there were serious social problems developed. Theft, begging and prostitution increased as people were forced to look for alternative ways to survive. Deteriorating infrastructure caused the sanitation, sewage and water facilities to break down leading to widespread health risks. Healthcare deteriorated because basic medicines, vaccines and necessary supplies were not available (Hinnebusch, 2007). In April 1995, in response to growing international concern regarding the Iraqi humanitarian crisis, the UN established the "oil-for-food deal" which permitted Iraq to sell $2 billion in oil every six months to buy food, medicine, and other humanitarian supplies for the Iraqi people. Saddam rejected this program, which immediately plunged the economy into further uncertainty. When Saddam finally accepted the deal towards the end of the 1990s, many of the products which were thereafter imported fell into illegal networks and were sold on the black market. Still...

> ...even under the most benign conditions, Oil-For-Food only allows Iraq to be run as a relatively efficient refugee camp in which people get just about enough food to eat.
>
> *(Gazdar, 2002: 134)*

The September 11th, 2001 Twin Towers attacks in New York fuelled immediate American retribution on al-Qaeda and Osama bin Laden, who was hiding in

Afghanistan. In a speech the following year, however, President Bush also identified Iraq as a threat and as one of the countries part of the "axis of evil," thereafter making calls for its disarmament – even if Weapons of Mass Destruction had not been found (Bowen, 2003; Keegan, 2010). American intelligence made a case for a "preventative war" based on the fact that such an attack on the Twin Towers could easily occur again if action was not taken. Britain sided with America and even despite widespread public protests against the war at which I marched as a young man – it went ahead. War was declared in the name of "freeing the Iraqi people" and the suggestion that Weapons of Mass Destruction could be used by Saddam (Hinnebusch, 2007).

> And if intentions toward Iraq were benign, why did the US destroy the country in the process of "liberating" it; the sins of the occupation, notably the dissolution of the Iraqi state – the army, party and bureaucracy.
>
> *(Hinnebusch, 2007: 2011)*

Further evidence suggests that the 2003 war that turned into a botched-transfer-of-power job because it dragged out until 2011 was the result of several decades of strategic thinking and policymaking about oil in the region and Iraq. Seizing Iraq's oil was already part of the plan, even with the advent of war as a group of oil executives were contracted to advise American officials on the establishment of a new Iraqi oil policy. After the occupation of Iraq, the country became dependant on US security – another convenient business opportunity. Furthermore, the US military forces were the only power able to keep stability and security in the region. The new Iraqi political regime unsurprisingly favoured close partnerships with the powerful American petrol and oil firms (Mahdi, 2012).

While oil continued to be exported between 2000 and 2002, the import of goods was often disrupted because the United States and the UK withheld the approval of contracts, particularly relating to humanitarian goods. This highlights Naomi Klein's (2007) "disaster capitalism" thesis about how neoliberalism both precipitates disasters and makes use of these same disasters (and others) as an opportunity to facilitate its expansion (also see Fletcher, 2012). The "shock doctrine" employed by Western countries such as acting to exploit the disorientation and confusion of a country in political and social turmoil for the purpose of expanding free-market policies in the course of recovery efforts.

Masri's Iraq homecoming part II

When the work in the informal economies started to dry up as Greece's economy started to squeeze in 2007/2008 because of the financial crisis, the family then decided to return to Iraq in 2010, where they found their country in further turmoil in the aftermath of Saddam's death. ISIS terrorists controlled her home town. In the two years Masri was there with her family, her brother had his jewellery shop raided by bogus police and he had his finger cut off when he refused to hand over his gold ring. This happened before some months later he was eventually beheaded by "police":

> Nothing is there, no food, no doctor, no water, no infrastructure, when I leave the house I have to cover up, not like here in Istanbul where I can walk around and it didn't used to be like that. There are police, but they are not police. You can't be sure who is police and who is a thief, well they are the same. They put guns to your head and tell you to shut up and be quiet. They pretend to be police and kidnap people, all because there is no government.

Her son of 13 (at the time) was kidnapped for three weeks by people whom she suspects were ISIS and they demanded $25,000 in ransom. By selling more land and borrowing money from other relatives, they raised the money and he was released. It is a miracle he is alive and now sits next to his sister, playing nervously with his hands.

They managed to cope in Iraq until 2012 – the last straw being when her other brother was kidnapped and taken hostage. "ISIS terrorists," she says, demanded $60,000 and to raise that they sold another house to save him. They returned to Turkey, poor and in debt. Applying for asylum in America has been difficult, and she says the UN required fees to process their application. Every week, they have to sign on in the police station as they are refugees in Turkey. Being poor, it has been difficult to afford to bring the whole family down to the centre of the city because it takes her "five hours." Missed appointments have accrued fines from the police.

To pay that and to collect the meagre benefits, she needs to present herself at the police station. However, she can't afford to pay the fine so she has not collected the benefits. They are counting the days before the 90-day visa will expire, trying to raise the revenue to move on illegally somewhere else. While Ahmed earns 800 Lira a month from making wedding dresses in a factory which is just under $120, his son, only 15 years old, earns 400 Lira a month (about $60) from sewing shirts. Together, this just about covers the rent and food costs.

Now they have three weeks before they will be kicked out of the house as the owner has increased the rent from $100 to $300 because of the demand for rented accommodation. I look around and in the hallway, all the bags are packed, they are ready to leave. They have contemplated calling the smugglers but will need $1,200 per person to get into a boat full of 40 people (around $1,500 to be guaranteed more "leg space" and fewer people, say 35 people). As we finish, Masri sends her five-year-old to the main street to get the taxi. She apologises for crying and shakes and kisses my hand. Tearfully she admits that in the last month, she has tried to commit suicide three times. I give her all the money I can find in my pockets and leave wishing them well.

ISIS crisis

Unfortunately, the combined international "intervention" led in the main by the United States on Iraq over these past three decades only created a political vacuum and kind of social chaos-martial law, hence Masri's experiences on her return. Research suggests that the aftermath of the second Iraq war served to exacerbate the feelings of anger and frustration among Islamic nations about American foreign policy (Hegghammer, 2006). Indeed, evidence suggests that Iraq replaced Afghanistan as the main training ground for Islamic militants who were there prepared for combat (Priest, 2005). As a consequence, these kinds of territorial disputes, conflict and violence erupt in the places hit most hard by the effects of climate change, and the social discontent often melds with poor climate adaptive policies. While internal Iraq conflict has been more as a result of oppressive leadership of Saddam Hussein, corruption and exclusion of Arab Sunnis (EWGCSR, 2018), it has been further exacerbated by the effects and impact of climate change on the region.

Iraq is currently suffering its worst water shortage for 80 years and, because of this, is considered to be one of the worst countries in the world to be affected by climate change. It has witnessed rampant temperature increases (1°–2° from 1970 to 2004 – see Price, 2018), declining precipitation rates and altering rainfall distribution patterns with increasing evaporation. People in its rural regions in the West feel this in the form of increased sandstorms, land desertification and rain droughts (Ulloa, 2018). Moreover, most of its coast is vulnerable to sea-level rising, and it is thought that by 2050 it could be submerged below water (Adamo et al., 2018). The industry most affected by all these elements is agriculture: reduced water cannot farm arable lands, and water security instead relies on the diminishing Tigris and Euphrates rivers, both of which are quickly losing their source as dams built in Turkey and Iran – countries also in dire need of water – decrease supply to Iraq's regions (Hall, 2019). Furthermore, it is estimated that seven million people live up and down the Tigris and depend on it, but continued damage to its water quality will see those people uprooted (EWGCSR, 2018).

Further strain comes from pollution generated from the antiquated methods of oil extraction in the form of fertilisers and industrial waste/sewage without treatment. Water, rivers and streams become increasingly polluted, and this generates public health concerns. When crops fail because of drought and irregular rainfall, this increases food insecurity and all this boils up in social tension, unrest and violence as these mostly rural regions see their livelihoods and futures literally dry up (Ulloa, 2018). A destabilised and corrupt State – still recovering from the international body blows of two wars – is unable to respond and could only watch on as the unemployed youth and angry farmers took up rank in terrorist organisations like al-Qaeda and ISIS.

Indeed, it is thought that crop failures of 2006 and 2007 and the drought in 2008 were what principally laid the social and political foundations for al-Qaeda and ISIS (Ulloa, 2018) as tensions started to percolate in 2009 resulting in the increasing support for ISIS in rural areas (Oosterveld and Bloem, 2017). As I noted in Chapter 4, in the absence of work opportunities and general security, rural workers find refuge in insurgent and terrorist organisations. And the same happened here. While ISIS took control of depleted oil fields in much need of modernisation, they used them in the main to trade oil and petrol for weapons (Le Billion, 2018). They also took control of water resources, and infrastructure was a critical way for the terrorist group to turn the conflict in its favour, as they controlled large sections of the Tigris and Euphrates rivers that provide water downstream to Iraq's capital, Baghdad. They used these "crisis situations" to their favour, by providing food and money payments to families affected by extreme weather events in exchange for support. The severe economic vulnerability of rural farmers and young people in these regions combined with the environmental degradation created conditions for recruitment into ISIS (Ulloa, 2018) – a regime of oppression and violence under strict Sharia law. And as their governance expanded, minority groups such as the Yazidi people were decimated; they fled to nearby as well as faraway countries such as Germany for refuge.

Yazidi persecution

We dismount from our bikes and prop them into the concrete wedges, and I am led into one home where await me an Iraqi family of six who fled their country two years ago in 2015. They come from an area where ISIS were reported to have raped thousands of young girls before killing them and escaped from the town when it came under siege from them. This is because they are Yazidi, an ethnic group that faces now practical extinction as ISIS have pretty much gone about killing them off because they are non-Muslim. ISIS have also been known to undertake mass rapings and killing of Yazidi women. We sit and start talking. Generally a poor family, they had less than $2,000 to their name when they left. Within a matter of months, they had spent that money in Turkey so the father returned to Iraq and borrowed money from family and friends to make the journey by himself. "There are smugglers and mafia at every stage of the journey," he says to me as he claps his hands and points at me. When I ask him how he felt doing the journey alone, he says, "I went without food and drink for days but I would rather risk my life than lose it as well as my family to the carnage of ISIS."

His two young sons aged five and seven who are present just stare at me, while his wife makes yet more coffee. When he was granted asylum, he started saving money so he could pay for his family to make the journey. This took some months, but after the transfer was made, they followed after and were fairly quickly reunited. Now they are safe and the youngest children are quickly learning German. The father wants to work, but his German is extremely limited and he struggles with the language.

When we finish, we are led into another block to speak to another Yazidi family who serve up more coffee. Such is the curiosity that some of those from the first family come into the other block and cram into the limited seats. The meagre room there is for a family of six is quickly reduced by three more people, and Abbas and I. This family come from the same region of Iraq. They stayed in UN camps in Turkey after leaving three months before ISIS took their home town. There they stayed before paying €4,500 for the entire family to cross to Greece and make their way slowly towards Germany. The journey was made difficult by the poor health of the father and mother who look distinctly ragged even as we talk to them. As far as feeling integrated, the eldest son plays football with some local team and the two daughters aged 17 and 20 go to refugee-only education centres.

Kill or be killed

ISIS's main peak were 2014 and 2015, during the early period of my study, so it was common for me to meet Iraqis who had fled ISIS strongholds. At this time, it was reckoned that one-third of Iraq was loosely governed by ISIS (EWGCSR, 2018). Like the Yazidi families, young Iraqi men like Hussein, Asim and Younis were among thousands of others across the country who faced a choice: to be recruited and kill or to die. The other risk was to escape. Ali was one who made it after leaving Iraq on 7th August 2015 and arriving four months later in Belgium:

ALI: Iraq, no talk, no walk, no do anything, free army and ISIS is your enemy.
DAN: Why did you not leave last year?
ALI: I tried to go to Finland but my friend said best to try somewhere else as he
       failed there. So I will try anywhere.
DAN: How did you get from Iraq to Belgium?
ALI: The problem for me is I am a journalist and I was working in the militia,
       like the coverage. I was in a very bad situation, one person Kurdish tried to
       kill me. Because I am Shia and everybody in my city also Shia so they are
       hated. You know all of us have problem for work now in Iraq, we cannot
       get work and for this reason Iraq is bad…My boss in the Militia killed my
       brother, this is how bad it is. He was suspicious of his name. My two friends
       also killed, right in front of me. Militia are controlling everyone, and you
       must not say a thing to anyone or the militia will kill you. Dead. It maybe
       shot, it maybe car bomb.
[HE SHOWS ME PHOTOS FROM IRAQ]
ALI: I tell my boss my son is sick, I need to go to hospital and this was my excuse
       so I was able to leave the free army and escape to Turkey. In Turkey, my
       friend and I finally talk and he tells me Finland but I had no money because
       I spent it all to get out of Iraq, $10,000. I borrow money, take a boat, no
       sleeping, no eating, Greece, Macedonia…

Ali has been in Brussels for four months and attends the volunteer-led Refugee Welcome Centre run by Thierry where people "help each other." He attends to learn English and translate Farsi for Afghani refugees because "someone speak some language and we need to help each other." He then shows me a video of his city, Kirkuk, in rubble as a small musical celebration starts up in the Welcome Centre.

The Welcome Centre: a forgotten corner of Brussels tending to forgotten people

At the time of my visit to Brussels in Belgium, many of the Iraqis I meet are either mulling around pondering an asylum application or awaiting a long response from a blocked asylum application system. They spend their days in the Welcome Centre where, just outside, hangs a large banner which declares, "Modern Urban Buildings: 270 New Apartments Coming Soon." Below it is another smaller banner seemingly painted by children, which says, "School – Ecole." We walk into the entrance which is next to four large industrial-size bins. Inside it smells of creosote as around 150 refugees – the majority from Iraq, Afghanistan and Syria – congregate in small groups. The smell is musty, and from the building's construction it's difficult to work out how this was a former post office. Each room is separated by questionable and improvised Do-It-Yourself panels and between wires and cables hang from all places. No one seems to care though. The Centre supports around 500 refugees on a daily basis. A real shame that in February (2016) it will be knocked down so that plush flats can be built; an uncertain future awaits the Centre and its medical staff and volunteers.

Ali nor Amir, the translator seem to be around. Nor is Tierry, the manager who is supposedly on his way to the Centre with more donated clothes. I talk with two volunteers who wait for him, and within a few minutes he walks in with heavy bags. The two volunteers then disappear out of the door and I follow. Outside in the unloading area, where the post used to be shifted in, is a parked estate car and inside are bags and bags of clothes. They start to unload and so I start to help. We make numerous trips with our hands full, dumping the bags in the clothes depository.

In the main room, the refugees just sit around either in silence or in small groups making smaller talk. At the far end, there is another room where several old men sit asleep in sofas so worn they practically touch the floor. We walk around together and up the stairs to the "reception area" where volunteers include students from Mexico, France and, of course, Belgium. They each have t-shirts on with the Centre's name. To my right are more large sofas on which sprawl African men. To the far end is the clothes depository – separated by large boards and a wooden doorway with no real door. Inside this room, thousands of items of clothes await collection from shoes to luggage, hats to scarves, socks to shirts. It is all ordered by gender and size, and at the end of each day, the team of volunteers fold up all the clothes ready for the next day. "Its important for these people to retain their dignity, they need to get their self respect back so they come here every day to pick what they want" says one. There is even a rail with children's clothes on.

I leave and walk down the corridor, and to the left is the library, prayer room and children's play area. Further to the left is the medical centre which has consultancy rooms separated by hanging rags. At the far end to the right is the children's school which was initially the room with the banner I had seen from the outside. Inside, three young African children play with cars and teddy bears as the teacher tidies up the books. On the wall outside the school is a series of paintings made by the children. One image commands my attention, and it's not a painting but a photo of two children playing in rubble which I can only suppose was a school.

I return to the clothes depository to Tierry who has arrived: he tells me they have given nearly 500,000 items of donated clothing away to refugees in a little over three months. I sit down and watch as he calls numbers so refugees can enter in an orderly manner, try on clothes, and leave with one of each item – one pair of shoes, one trousers, one shirt or t-shirt. One refugee then emerges smiling as he leaves the depository with only a pair of shoes; his face seems to have been severely burnt, yet this does not hide his satisfaction at finding a pair of shoes that fit him. As he takes off his trainers and rams his bare and bruised feet into the shoes, he smiles. I look at him and raise a thumb saying, "ok?" He says, "yes I take."

I then find my way down the corridor towards the toilet. Around to the left and then to the right, the corridor winds and the strong odour of urine grows. At the end of the corridor and basically the end of the building it seems are the toilets where a man dressed in white clothes smokes a joint and leans over his mop; as he takes a draw, he screws up his face and blows it towards the window ajar. The puddles of urine and water combine in some places on the floor, and while two Afghani men wash their feet in the sinks, one of the urinal overflows.

I go to the toilet and then on my way out get talking to this lean man in white. His name is Fayez and he is from Iraq. He has no papers and he says he awaits his "first interview." However, unlike some who have recently arrived, he has been around Europe. He has worked in Italy for two years, in France for one year and in Germany for six months until they expelled him because his fingerprints were taken in Italy. He says "work is bad" in Italy and doesn't want to return and now has his heart set on Sweden. I want to ask him about the large scar which trails from one side of his head to the other and about the large slash marks/scars across his arms, but he says he needs to "work." With that he starts to mop up the liquid after the two Afghan men leave with their faces and hair still wet having washed.

The business of misery in Iraq: Hussein

A volunteer called Hussein then comes over and demands to see my ID. He stands tall over me as if I have entered a forbidden area, and all I can do is look up at him, but when I explain what I'm doing and show my ID, he relaxes and starts talking in his broken English. Because his English is limited he sort of acts out his journey passing through Turkey, Greece, Macedonia and on the border of

Hungary, he recalls how the police threatened to kill him. When it turned night, they crept into Serbia he says as he goes on tiptoes so they hired a man to drive them to Belgium. They heard that Germany was full so he went to Belgium. He shakes his head in disdain as he reflects on his home town. "Baghdad dangerous" and he talks about the murderous militia who kill Muslim Sunnis. "Police dangerous they kick us out of Iraq," he says. He gets me a tea as I wait for his friend who will help us translate the full interview. Hussein left Baghdad in Iraq because it was "dangerous, they killing Sunni, Militia tried to kill me because I am Sunni, they hit me and broke my teeth. They told me if you don't leave we will kill you". He says that because Baghdad is divided by both Shia and Sunni, there is constant conflict:

HUSSEIN: They will say give me your ID and they know you are Sunni because of your name. He will always try to make trouble with you, demand money from you or they will beat you. I have seen people been killed.

ASIM: They killed my uncle who worked in ex-Saddam government. They try to provoke you by calling you ISIS, they believe it.

HUSSEIN: They took my uncle as well and demanded $12,000 for him. They kidnapped him. We negotiated and he was freed after he was paid. He has family as well, a big family. I have a two year old I left in Iraq [he shows me a picture and as he smiles his missing teeth show].

While there is no law or order or even a replacement, there is a business attached to the disorder. And to leave requires parting with more money. Hussein left Iraq and had to pay to cross the border. "There was no real security, the police drink a lot and you pay them," he says before he laughs, "I bought the police a drink and drugged the police and then was able to pass." He passed to Turkey into Istanbul before heading down to Izmir. The dinghy he took with another 40 people cost $1,000 or, as he was told, "$1,200 if you choose the island you land on."

ASIM: I stayed in Izmir for two days to find someone but there is lots of cheating. We left at 2am at night, scary and we were with life jackets it takes three hours.

DAN: Did you know which country you want?

ASIM: Any country.

HUSSEIN: Me too, any one though my dream is to go to British. I would be prepared to go under train.

DAN: Why didn't you stay in Turkey?

ASIM: There is no job in Turkey, no good job, you work all month for almost no money. The Iraqi doesn't earn money from Turkey and government give nothing.

HUSSEIN: The police in Macedonia and Serbia were difficult, violent and we try to avoid them. Any border crossing is dangerous. They hit us, all of us, small children as well.

ASIM: But on the journeys it is not just Syrians and Iraq, Albanians, Afghan, people from all over Africa I don't know where. A lot of Afghan and Syria though.

HUSSEIN: In Hungary, we are in jail. They hate us there, they took us finger-print, we had no food, nothing, for days we were there. They hit us if we do anything else than sit there. If I take fingerprint in Hungary, I arrive here in Belgium and they decide I have to go back to Hungary.

Hussein then says there was a new way through Croatia, "we are refugees, we always find a new solution, along the way people charge money to take you. I pay $400 to go to Croatian border on a tractor." All the while, Hussein has his money and passport sewn into a hidden pocket into his trousers. While he wasn't robbed, he was threatened and had fights. His friends he says were robbed at gunpoint so he considers himself lucky. While "sleeping in the borders, in the forest, you can never sleep properly in case someone cuts out your passport from your clothes. It didn't happen to me, but my friend. We have to carry knives to protect us." Belgium, it seems, is the alternative to an overcrowded Germany:

HUSSEIN: I choose Belgium because they like refugees. In Germany there are too many thousands. I want to bring my family here and my son to be a doctor or lawyer.

The irony is that Hussein says that Belgium likes refugees yet, at the time of our meeting, he had already been waiting six months on an asylum decision after arriving in August 2015. While there are no bombs and guns in Brussels, there is still a long uncertain process which, in the meantime, he says,

> there are people sleeping in the street here, what of country does that? I was 20 days in the street. But 200 people sleeping in the train station? The police see us and do nothing, no one does anything. We come to the Centre but we are homeless. There is some space in the Red Cross but not everyone fit there.

While he waits for his asylum application, he is given €6 a week as recompense.

Food fight and lunch interlude

Suddenly, there is some commotion in the background as a couple of refugees start to fight over the food which is being handed out. Hussein then says, "come eat my friend," and grabs my arm. I am then practically pulled down and ordered into the dinner queue which is low in numbers. Younis, another young Iraqi man, also joins us. As we queue, one woman shovels out a spoonful of rice into a plastic container, while another sprinkles some curry substance on top before the toughest-looking volunteer/security guard jabs a plastic spoon into it and sends it effortlessly across the tabletop to the next person with a flick of his finger. When I receive mine, I am taken back by the wonderful spicy smell. It is certainly an improvement on the "something-filled baguette" they made yesterday. Asim leans over and says to me,

> In Red Cross, we were given some food the other day and I say to chef who is from Congo 'what is this?' and he say me 'eat, it healthy for you'. I look at it and pull a face and ask him again what it is and he say me 'I don't know what it is called, but it is potato and milk, and it is healthy, eat'.

We take the food and pass through the numerous others who eat away at the curry dish, the tables piled with empty containers and rice on the seats. On the sofas opposite, Afghanis fall asleep and behind me on the stage they line up to charge their mobiles. We sit down next to each other as if we are in a 1930s boarding school and tuck into the food. I struggle to separate the meat from the bone with my plastic spoon and, in seeing me struggle, Asim shows me a kind of chipping technique which seems to be effective in scraping away some meat. I try it and end up holding the meat and trying to separate the meat I can find before realising that my "meat" is basically a massive bone with no meat.

ISIS and the business of misery: Younis

Younis is only 21 and has made some journey from Mosul, Iraq, over the past 16 months. His home town, a city in the northern part of the province of Ninewa, was an area of which 50% was devastated by the 2008 drought and struggled to recover (Hall, 2019) because it was again hit by another severe drought in 2018 (Al-Quraishi and Negm, 2019). Each time he starts a new chapter from his life, I get more and more taken back. We begin by talking about why he left Iraq, and he tells me that last year ISIS "who are not traditional Muslims and come from all countries of the world like Canada, France, UK, America" took over his city with next to no resistance from the police or government forces. A strict Sharia law was imposed and people were "not allowed to smoke or do hairstyles." He says, "if people did not submit to ISIS, they were killed. All people who had contact or were in contact with police were killed." Alarmed by the new way of life, the decision to leave came when ISIS summoned the city folk by force to witness a public execution at which were his young sisters who "cried and screamed as a man had his head cut off" and as well when both his uncles were killed and his brother was put in prison by ISIS. He shows me a picture of his brother fearing that he is already dead because "if ISIS keep you in prison for more than ten days it mean you die."

ASIM: ISIS put sharia law, if they catch you smoking they will cut your fingers. If people do something wrong, there is an execution. In front of people. For example, if they hear you are with the army or you give information about Isis they will kill you. This is so you fear them.

YOUNIS: I saw ISIS kill people. Cutting their throats, line them up and cut them. They put cotton in their mouth and tie the mouth and cut them in front of children. This is why I couldn't stay and had to leave, when I saw this and all the children did. I worked in a shop in the centre and they normally kill people in the centre, they killed a man and his younger sister outside my shop. I have younger sisters, the youngest aged 6, and they saw this. When they saw this, they were crying and screaming. In the centre, there are many people. In august, ISIS came to my house, they arrested my brother, they took him to prison, they took him in front of his mother. He escaped.

ASIM: There is war between government and ISIS but you have to be with ISIS or they will kill you. They will give you a gun and you have to fight against the government army. When they first came to Mosul, they were only 1,000 but when they came the army just left. This is strange, it is like a plan between ISIS and the army.

YOUNIS: To leave it is difficult as ISIS put many mines in Iraq so you have to know the way, there are traps everywhere. I also had to bribe security people. They asked me where I am going and all these questions so I have to pay them not to have problems.

When his brother was arrested and put in prison for not joining the ISIS cause, he escaped by taxi with $1,000 in his pocket to get to Europe. When he was stopped at the edge of the city, he told ISIS, who were patrolling the roads, that he had a job in a nearby city and he would come back in two weeks, bribing the patrol guards in the process each with $24 each. He then got a flight the next day to north Iraq and crossed the border into Turkey. After getting a bus to Istanbul, he managed to get work in a café but says "many times the boss he don't pay me," and after living there for a year he decided to risk the boats to Greece. Only able to fund the journey because his mother sold all her gold and sent the money via Western Union, he paid a mafia $1,200 to travel to the Greek islands. However, he was caught five times by the Turkish Coastguard even when "the Coastguard called the mafias to check which boat it was, to see if it was a boat of their friends and if it wasn't they sent us back." When he finally was able to make the journey, the seas were rough and between Izmir and Lesbos the boat sank near the Greek coastline:

YOUNIS: Journey was dangerous, boat was very full of people and water. When you talk to the mafia people, they say 25 people in the boat but when you arrive there are 50. You cannot argue with these people because they have guns. They pick a refugee and say "drive" and this person normally goes free because you are not meant to survive. If the coastguard catch you and you are driver, you go to prison. Sometimes they take your bags and money before you get on the boat so you are also robbed. When they catch you, they ask you which mafia you use and if you are with one then it is ok. The boat is all the time sinking, family, children all the time screaming and crying. Some people are praying to Allah. On one journey, the coastguard caught us and hit everyone trying to find out who is the driver. On another journey, two girls died, they drowned, the sea too rough and take them away. You cannot be in the water too long, most people die because they are afraid and in the water, they panic. It was 2 or 3am, screaming crying the boat has sank, they try to call the mafia but this is why people die. This time the coastguard rescued me but we were waiting three hours floating around.

When the coastguards picked him up, they dumped him on the shores of Lesbos to walk 70 kilometres to register for travel to Athens. He went on a "big big ship, Blue Star lines" to Athens where he spent five days trying to negotiate a good price for a taxi to Macedonian border. In Macedonia, I asked him if he took a taxi to Sebia, and he laughed and patted his own legs saying, "this is the taxi." He then walked for four days, afraid to sleep because of the potential for robbery. After crossing the border of Serbia, he walked into a petrol station where he negotiated a taxi to the Hungarian border. When he reached Hungary, he found himself walking once again and passed four dead Syrians by the road with stab wounds to their bodies, someone telling him that "if people stop you and demand money, you give it to them." Once again, he barely slept afraid of robbery or injury. When he got to Budapest, he stayed in a grand hotel for €15 a night including food with hundreds of other refugees, and every 10 minutes mafias or illegal drivers would come in and offer €600–800 to Austria or Germany. He managed to take a taxi and on arriving in Austria was told that Germany "had too many people" so he bypassed the country and went straight to Belgium.

In the four months he has been here, he still awaits his "first interview" and even then there awaits a lengthy decision process. "They keep delaying me, telling me to wait": at that time he is given €7 a week to survive and spends the nights in the Red Cross and the days in the Centre. "I have been told a lie, there is nothing here for me, the people are nice but I get no support," he says. After that, it will also be difficult forif he is successful with the application, he will receive €800 a month but with that he will need to pay for rent, food and bills. And Brussels is not cheap.

> I am shocked here, they do nothing for refugees, people sleeping on the streets, in the station. I have been here for four months and not even had the first interview. I have registered but I still need to have two interviews, and I don't even have one yet! We have been cheated.

On an already forgotten street corner, an already forgotten man

We amble out of the Welcome Centre and walk down as a three. For their assistance, I offer to buy something for Asim and Younis. Younis is especially excited that it just happens to be a packet of cigarettes, but he will save them as he has a sore throat. It threatens to rain as we walk down. We cross the main road and not knowing which are the best, I just buy them two packs of Camel. We walk outside and cross the small road to the corner of the street next to a Metro stop. As we realise we have no lighter to light up the cigarettes, we ask a nearby man who they know. He stands tall as he reaches in his pocket to offer it to us and in return Asim offers him a cigarette.

The tall man retreats into a shop window to shelter from the cold wind. Asim then tells me he is a refugee as well who "takes the machine machines for money." Suspecting this is not exactly how he explains it, I go over the man and introduce myself. He stands leaning against the window smoking and looks out in the road. He is from the Ivory Coast, has been in Belgium for one year and France for three years and worked in both Italy and Spain for a combined eight years. He left the Ivory Coast because there was no work for him in his village and the political situation was "bad." In none of these countries, he says he "got papers."

> Now I wait for papers, I wait for one year but they no give me papers. It's a big problem this country, France as well, the work there is shit. I work in black [market] and see what happens for me.

As Asim does, this man receives €7 a week and describes it as "fucking shit". He adds "Belgium is shit, it is shit for refugee. It is big problem, big problem for Europe. More people come and Belgium don't care." He then stamps on his cigarette and comes away from the window and points down into the Metro station "it is so bad, people have to sleep in the Metro. I am lucky I stay at Red Cross Centre but even there it is not great." His work composes of waiting on the road with three others similar in orientation to receive calls or requests to take away heavy appliances like washing machines, fridges and freezers. He may be lucky to earn €10 a day but could get lucky and get several jobs resulting in €20.

6

THE BUSINESS OF MISERY

War commerce and its human debris

The tall man from the Ivory Coast – who remains nameless in this book and whom I met by chance in Chapter 5 – must have left his home country around 2003/2004 in the midst of the internal Civil War that raged from 2003 to 2007. One of the main drivers of the Civil War were increased conflicts over land and resources in the cultivation of the country's primary export – cocoa – the main ingredient for our chocolate. The Ivory Coast is part of a block of African countries from Sierra Leone to Cameroon that forms the West African Cocoa Belt, and over the past 20 years the area has diminished in cocoa production because of increased droughts which hinder the cultivation of the crop (Barima et al., 2016). However, it is more costly to replant ageing farms or use expensive fertilizer hence the migration to new virgin forest territory; the latter of which also yields greater return even if this is necessarily reflected in high wages. Farm workers are typically paid around $2 a day in a business which is estimated to generate $100 billion each year. This is aside from the child labour exploitation associated with the production of cocoa in the Ivory Coast, which is then used by global chocolate brands like Mars, Nestle and Hershey (UNICEF, 2018), which – though make ethical pledges to tackle exploitation and improve workers conditions via the "Fairtrade" nature of chocolate production – at best can only make limp "commitments" to reducing it.

Aside from the increased flood risks caused to coastal communities by sea-level rises around the Ivory Coast (IPCC, 2019), deforestation has seen the country's forest stock reduced to 16 million hectares in 1960 to 2.5 million hectares in 1990 to just 1.7 million hectares in 2016 (Despretz, 2019). This trend not only accelerates the process of climate change (because of the cull of forest stock) but also threatens the entire industry of production and this was evident in the build-up of the Civil War. The country's first president, Felix Houphouët-Boigny, made the ambitious expansion of the cocoa industry a central aspect of his politics so he opened the borders to neighbouring Mali and Burkina Faso to enable migrant Muslim workers to assist by increasing production: while underpopulated, the Ivory Coast was in need of labour. However, when the forest stock started to run low and following Houphouët-Boigny's death in 1993, the country was thrown into political turmoil.

The rest was history. Ethnic tensions increased and violent conflicts ensued as competition increased over fertile land and the what-was-left forest stock. The host farmers who were mostly Christian resented the Muslim workforce and saw them as a threat to their livelihoods. Thereafter a full-scale ethno-religious Civil War – that recruited child soldiers – that divided the country raged so climate change, cocoa production, migration and competition over natural resources were all driving factors in the conflict. Hundreds of people were killed, women and children were raped and tortured and thousands were displaced internally. Others like the nameless tall man in Chapter 5 simply fled. However, perhaps less documented is the arms supply to realise this coup. A report by Amnesty International (2013) states that spending on military arms made up of 10% of the national budget in 2004/2005. The same document highlights that munitions were acquired from China, armoured vehicles from Angola, attack helicopters from both Belarus and Bulgaria and drones from Israel. So inequality, corruption and war commerce are forms of *geopolitical entrepreneurialism* in the *business of misery* and play a part in *climate changed*, and this chapter shows the case for Syria.

Noor in Norway

On the train, I watch the landscape outside at the snow everywhere while man makes himself comfortable and takes his shoes off to read. Outside is white. Fresh 40-centimetre snowfall blankets the ground and makes for a heavy weight for the trees whose branches droop with snow. On train, we pass rivers and lakes half-frozen on which swans paddle and over which small clouds rise, giving the effect as if the water is on fire. As we pass the lake, the pockets of cloud start to join lower cloud which overhangs as if you could touch it from the ground. The snowdrifts like white dunes against forests and small groups of houses. As we pull up in Hamar in Norway, the platform is icy and inside the train station waiting in a blue jumper is Dag: he greets me and says yesterday it was −27°C and this morning it is slightly colder (−37 °C).

Dag is the Mayor of Hedmark – an area the size of Albania which covers 28,000 square kilometres. We drive around Hamar stopping off at a few places following a cautious pathway in and out of the icy streets of the town. The icicles seem permanent from the streetlights and even from the cars, many having snow stuck all over them. We drive to the outskirts past the frozen part of the lake and into what looks like a series of social work buildings. Not quite knowing where we are, we ask a man who drops off a couple of Arab women to a building and he sends us back down a snowy road.

We pull up and walking towards us smiling is the manager of the refugee centre whose name is Erling. He shakes our hand and welcomes us in. The centre accommodates around 80–90 refugees, all of which are young people between the ages of 15 and 18, mostly from Afghanistan, Syria, Sudan, Eritrea and Iraq. We walk into a room at the back where coffee and biscuits are made by the refugees. six young boys are then led in by Erling: from left to right Hussein, Mohamed, Noor, Ahmed, Hossan and Adjmal. Noor, aged 16, is one of the first to speak:

NOOR: My family were wheat and vegetable farmers, we found it difficult to survive in the countryside so moved to the nearest city. The crops stopped growing and there was no money in the business. My father then worked as a taxi driver in the Aleppo. [Field notes Hamar, Norway]

Syria: a context for *Climate Changed*

In Aleppo, Noor – then just turned a teenager – found work in a mattresses shop among other small jobs he could pick up. When I interviewed him in 2016, he was critical of the causes of what he saw led to his family "starting again" in Aleppo:

NOOR: It is not a revolution, it is a war. It was inevitable because of the tensions, the Kurds and Arabs hate each other. Some people are rich and more and more in Syria people are poor. This has got worse I mean more and more people are poor, especially us when we were working in the fields as farmers.

Noor's anger is not only at the consequences of moving from a rural area to the city of Aleppo but also at the social, ethnic and religious division in his country as well as an apparent wealth–poverty gap. His observations about climate change are correct if you recall when I outlined how this was one factor in the uprising in Syria and subsequent war (see Chapter 1; Kelley et al., 2015; but additionally Smiatek et al., 2013; Karak, 2019; Abel et al., 2019). *Water* (or lack of it) played a direct role in deterioration of Syria's domestic economy, and this essentially heightened existing tensions which were already historically bound to ethnic and religious division (Gleick, 2014). Persisting droughts and the decrease in precipitation which was the largest observed in the Gulf region at the time affected more than 1.3 million people prior to the uprising (Terink et al., 2013). Furthermore, during the worst stints of drought in 2006 and 2007, 85% of livestock died and 160 villages were abandoned so rural workers migrated to Syria's cities (Shank and Wirzba, 2013).

But as Noor hints, there were other processes we have to analyse in the outbreak of the Syrian conflict. Selby et al. (2017), for example, cast doubt over the role of man-made climate change as a feature of the Syrian conflict preferring to consider liberalisation of the economy and poor management of domestic policies relating to poor agriculture. In particular, they cite Assad's scrapping of agricultural fuel subsidies as one major factor as this inevitably pushed rural workers into debt.

This is a point picked up on by Martinez and Eng (2016) who suggest that these kinds of poor agricultural policies were additional components which lead to war in 2011. So, in essence, infrastructure which would be normally used to support the domestic economy declined. As subsidies reduced, food prices increased and caused discontent – thereafter with the onset of war, food stock was targeted as a way of starving rebel areas where the free army held. While there was little government interest in improving/rescuing agricultural infrastructure, there was also no formal means by which people could make this felt such as through a democratic election since Assad's rule was autocratic, and this was partly why rural workers and farmers joined the rebel groups as propaganda was circulated against the Assad regime. This, coupled with a rampant population increase, complex religious and socio-political factors, economic changes related to neoliberalism and a wave of political reform which swept the Arab states known as the Arab Spring (Gleick, 2014), produced what Noor and millions of other Syrians like Ismail and Takisha and their family experienced.

Syrian free-for-all

We follow the busy Istanbul streets as they get narrower, in and out of the puddles, and into the road to avoid confrontation with people on the pavement (there is only room for one person on the pavement). It starts to rain again, and the water quickly fills the cracks in the roads. Everything gets more intimate as it feels like the buildings and streets are shrinking, either that or it got really busy all of a sudden. After about ten minutes, we are met by smartly dressed man with a fresh haircut, who shakes my hand and leads us down through the mazy roads. We take a right and enter a quieter street. As we pass two women, they joke that we are Ismail's relatives. We enter a small door and climb two flights of steps. Outside the door, as it is custom, we remove our shoes and are welcomed into his home – a small and half dilapidated flat where he lives with his wife, two sons and daughter.

While Takisha, his wife, busily bustles off to make tea, he waves me into the living room and we sit down. On the wall hangs a cheap TV which is somehow wired to a box that allows them to receive various different Arab channels in countries as far as Egypt and as near as Jordan. Above the wall where Ismail sits is a copy of an old painting of Istanbul as if it were a reluctant symbolism of where they now live. We make conversation between watching some Russian news channel which favours Assad. "Some media says revolution is good and other says it is not a revolution but war is just for robbing the country of its riches," says Ismail before elaborating on how Homs, his hometown, was under siege for some months:

ISMAIL: The life was normal before the revolution, nothing bad, we earned money, we had a salary.

DAN: So you were happy with the regime.

ISMAIL: Everyone who didn't talk about politics were normal but people who did were in danger.

DAN: So do you think the revolution was a good or bad thing for Syria?

TAKISHA: In the beginning we were happy because we believed in the revolution, and we could get a free life, a good life like what happened in Egypt and we thought after a month it would finish but after longer we thought it is not good for us, we left everything we had, we had money and property. My children have cheap salaries, so I am spending my savings to survive. We sold the car and we sold the home.

DAN: My god.

ISMAIL: Government forces did a lot of robbery of the homes in the chaos… After the revolution, we left Homs and moved to Damascus for two years and seven months. When we were in Homs the army were all attacking us, the capital [Damascas] you can live normally, but there was no electricity, no gas, no water, it was dangerous.

When they reached Damascus, they didn't work because they were waiting for the war to finish in Homs – thinking they would only be away for a month, thinking it would pass and the security forces wouldn't threaten them for so long. All their family remain in Homs, some are teachers, still working and earning money there. They live in some safer areas of the city he says so there is no bombing because "it is under government controlled area so people are not protected but from bombs yes." The family have been in Istanbul since April 2015 and have two sons working in cafés full time to sustain the whole family while the daughter is hoping to start a Mathematics university course. His sons, now 25 and 26 years old, respectively, were most keen to leave Syria as they didn't want to do their military service, less so when it went to war. The rent is $400 without including bills:

TAKISHA: We are lucky, we have a flat, we have some money to support us, but there are millions in the border camps, they are the unlucky ones. They have no money, no passport, can't enter countries. They left immediately, they left with nothing. We left with our decision but some people were completely forced.

Throughout everything they say, no matter how hard it may seem, they remain calm about what has happened to them. We are offered more coffee and politely accept. As Takisha bustles off to the kitchen again, Mukhles proceeds to try and sort out a problem with their daughter's ID so she can register for university while Ismail talks me through some pictures he has taken of Syria. He flicks through a sequence of photos he took, all of which depict their home city as a complete wreckage – a ghost town with nothing other than broken, empty buildings and rubble covering all the roads. One can even make out the bullet hole on the walls. As more coffee comes in, on the Syrian TV, there is a propaganderous celebration of Syria's victory over Israel and they start waving their hands in criticism. The singing accompanies images of missiles and army and military movements as symbolisms of glory and victory. The "actors" sing of Syria's glory and Ismail recounts how in the lead-up to that war, Assad's bombs were blessed.

When Assad came to power in 2000, he aligned himself with powerful private enterprises and investors in the neoliberalisation of the economy. As foreign investment poured in, the public sector was drained of resources and funding, thus ensuring that production and profit stayed within the family even if it was state-run or private (Lund, 2018). One of the first investments the Assad family made was to modernise the Syrian army. Before the 2011 war, arms purchases were made from Belarus, China, North Korea and Russia, the latter of which was responsible for 71% of sales (Holtom et al., 2013). As the war began, the Syrian government made unflinching, widespread and heavy attacks using its new firepower which included chemical weapons, mines, airstrikes and bombings. Since there was a business in supplying the government the weapons, lo and behold there was another supplying arms to the oppositional forces. For example, the United States supplied the free army that opposed Assad with arms and weaponry which totalled $1 billion (Dick, 2019).

War commerce: the case for Syria

But weapons are not the only form of war commerce. As we have seen in this chapter, people like Noor were part of a growing population of mostly rural workers and fringe city dwellers were increasingly locked out of opportunity, turning in the main to odd jobs and illicit means to survive. This inequality fed opportunities for corruption at all levels within the Syrian social system and an increase in illicit markets (Samaha, 2016). Indeed, the increase of black markets began soon after April 2011 when, at the time, US President Barack Obama imposed, via executive order, the first of four sets of economic sanctions on Syria aimed at punishing President Bashar al-Assad's human rights abuses. The intention was to strangle and suffocate the Syrian economy by quelling its access to essential goods like medications and fuel, and blocking bank transfers (Cornish, 2019). This had immediate impact as oil exports diminished from $4.7 billion in 2011 to $0.14 billion in 2015 (World Bank, 2016) and plunged the country into even more desperation as queues formed at gas stations, fuel prices increased and Syria's currency depreciated significantly (Samaha, 2016). Syria's economy shrank and the diminished law enforcement ability only laid the platform for illicit business opportunities to exploit the misery via an *exploitative entrepreneurialism*.

Day-to-day life was intense and insecure. Perhaps quite obviously as a result of war, looting and robbery became commonplace and illicit markets quickly evolved around commodities like food, medicine, petrol, water and drugs like fenethylline – used to enhance the performance of fighters (Holley, 2015). Luxury brand goods, cigars, chocolate and even antiquities were among other thriving illicit markets which expanded (Steenkamp, 2017; Brodie and Sabrine, 2018). Syrians who stayed in the country, however, were also extremely vulnerable to kidnapping, hostage taking and trafficking (see Chapter 5) as a Syrian journalist called Quasim verified to me:

DAN: What is it like living under ISIS?

QUASIM: If you keep their law you will live, if not you die. While they have good things, like security, because no one steals anything or treats women badly, they are also very strict.

DAN: Is it a written law?

QUASIM: Based on religion. On a daily basis they are very aggressive with people, this is how they keep order.

DAN: What sort of things have you seen ISIS do?

QUASIM: I have seen them cut peoples' heads off, rape women, all in public. Some people say it is too much to punish people like this because these people did wrong things but they are small things and so some people don't agree with it. Is this a law if you say "if you touch this, you will have your hand cut off?" which also happened.

DAN: How does ISIS compare to Assad governance?

QUASIM: Assad killed more people than ISIS but ISIS show people what they do, Assad hides what he does like people disappearing or his centres where people go and don't come back. ISIS do public law. ISIS caught my friend and they know of his work as he was writing like me and I was scared that I would be next. I don't know what happened to him but probably he was killed. He disappeared. He also worked in human rights as well, he was documenting what ISIS was doing to people and how the free army was killing people, Assad regime.

DAN: How did you know your friend had been taken?

QUASIM: His family called me and told me that he had been taken. After one week, I then left, and I went by myself. They shouldn't harm my family but now I am wanted for sure by ISIS.

Disappearances and kidnapping are big businesses in Syria for evidence suggests that in 2014 ISIS earned $45 million alone just from ransoms (Lederer, 2014). Research also shows that soon after 2011 it became common for Syrian children to be forced into early marriages and potential forced labour and sexual exploitation (Steenkamp, 2017). ISIS, particularly known for their strict interpretation of Sharia law, have also released guidelines on how to kidnap women and use them as sex slaves, thereafter potentially forcing them into abusive marriages with the fighters. After having forced them to take "virgin tests," ISIS were also found to trade girls in "sex markets," sold off into unknown hands to become domestic and sexual slaves (USDS, 2018). Children, particularly boys, disappeared and either died or were smuggled into join the ISIS fighting cause. For example,

Before its liberation in October 2017, ISIS operated at least three child train-ing camps in Raqqa, where it forced children to attend indoctrination sem-inars and promised children salaries, mobile phones, weapons, a martyr's place in paradise, and the "gift" of a wife upon joining the terrorist group.

(USDS, 2018)

For many children it was either this or face death. The unofficial exchange of commodities means that control over territory can mean power and revenue. Given the oil-rich nature of the country, at the height of its power, ISIS con-trolled 80% of the oilfields and were earning $2 million a day from illegal trading (Lister, 2015). Bribes and large fees at under-sieged towns or cities and border crossings generate money for the government, free army or ISIS and poorly paid soldiers were easily corrupted. For example, the Syrian army have made mil-lions of dollars from the drug trade by simply taxing trafficking groups (Herbert, 2014). Even if Syrians can afford to flee to nearby countries, there was no guar-antee for safety. Research shows that young boys and girls were vulnerable to sex attacks by Lebanese pimps while in Turkey and Jordan, refugee children were forced into organised begging networks, illicit prostitution networks or exploited as a workforce in low-paid work (USDS, 2018), thus contributing to the continuing misery of war and its human debris:

These activities vary in profitability, but they generate sufficient funds to allow insurgents and the government to buy weapons, pay combatants, provide social services and establish institutions in the areas under their control. These factors are crucial in reproducing the armed groups and maintaining the conflict.

(Steenkamp, 2017: 1)

It is through these illicit dealings that politics is influenced internally (Herbert, 2014). Externally, there are other interested parties. As war continued, however, Assad's oppositional forces, such as the free army and ISIS, made arms purchases through foreign governments such as Croatia, Israel, Jordan, the UAE and the United States with much of the products going to Quatar, Saudi Arabia and Libya and being sold through illicit markets (Dick, 2019). Such illicit networks served to capitalise on the war chaos, making it more difficult to trace the origin of sales (Angelovski et al., 2016). For example, research by the Balkan Investi-gative Reporting Network (BIRN) and the Organized Crime and Corruption Reporting Project (OCCRP) found that Eastern European countries (Croatia, Bulgaria and Slovakia) made discreet sales to Syria – often via a third-party country such as Saudi Arabia – in the form of assault rifles, mortar shells, rocket launchers, anti-tank weapons and machine guns. This is notwithstanding the other interest in arms purchases in the general Gulf region. For example, it was estimated that €806 million was generated in weapons sales from Eastern Europe to Saudi Arabia from 2012 to 2016. The same period saw Jordan, the UAE and

Turkey make purchases taking total spent on weapons and arms to just under €1.2 billion (Angelovski et al., 2016). Other analyses indicate continuing interest in arming as much the Syrian government regime as the insurgent forces such as the free army and ISIS (Kedem, 2018).

These days, the trend continues: the United States continues to be the main exporter and the Middle East the main importer. The latest statistics show that the global the arms trade grew 5.5% from 2015 to 2019 in comparison with 2005 to 2009 and that the United States accounted for 36% of all arms exports, while 35% of exports were received in the Middle East (Wezeman et al., 2019). As I write this book and type this word in 2020, the war has raged for the last nine years and, with little hope of peace, the international sanctions remain in place, the foreign creditors await and with little hope that there will be political and social stability, investment remains absent. Instead, inflation, insecurity and unemployment continue to be the daily experience for people – those that remain there (McLoughlin, 2020).

"A friend with death": Latif, Athens.

We exit Dimitrius's office and stride towards the Syrian area of the camp. Dimitrius leads us to around the right, past the large pylons under construction in this forgotten industrial area of Athens. We turn right into a narrower pathway which runs between two different communities. We are introduced to an old and fragile woman who is the local translator. She moves her coffee from the spare seats and urges us to sit down. I sit on a broken plastic seat which surely will buckle under my weight as the translator balances her coffee on the wooden plank next to it. The sun continues to shine as a cold breeze takes the edge off the potential for winter warmth.

As refugees pass us, they greet this old and fragile woman. It doesn't take long for her to say to me how difficult it is for her as a translator. She leans across to me and looks below her glasses, saying "stories, the stories" as she raises her eyebrows and sips her strong Arabic coffee. This woman, who speaks four languages, seems to reveal all in just a few words: "all the stories, I have to translate, the children's, the womens', everyone. All their stories, everything which is happened to them," and she pulls a pained face.

Before I have any time to delve further into what this might mean, Latif is wheeled up towards me by his nephew. Latif sits crumpled in his wheelchair and comes across as a serene man. He invites me to Syrian coffee before politely asking his able family member to prepare it. As his nephew scampers off, I talk to this educated man about his life. "You have to be a friend with death" is his first reflection of his journey from Syria before adding "when we crossed the Turkish border, someone was shot dead in front of me – the Turkish guard are ordered to kill people who try to return and there was an Iraqi man to tried to run back to Syria but they just shot him dead."

Having studied languages and becoming an electrical engineer, Latif fled several times internally in Syria to escape the wrath of both ISIS and the government forces. It took him some months to get out of Syria because of this since there was no easy route and it involved bribing many officials and contacts in the warring factions to allow him to pass without killing him. Eventually, he left his family in one city before staying with more relatives in another city, slowly biding his time as he is disabled.

He recalls how he was arrested numerous times on the Turkish border. On one occasion, he had paid a smuggler to take him across but was told to wait by himself by a muddy river for a few hours to be collected. Aside from losing thousands of dollars, the only people who came were the Turkish gendemarie who beat him up, arrested him and left his wheelchair in the mud. Such was the degrading nature of this for Latif that he then had to be carried around by his nephew for ten days. He says, "they told me after they kicked me and put me in the car for arrest me" then said to him "why do you need your wheelchair, you get another one in Greece besides we don't want to get our car dirty and it has mud all over it." He tells me in a kind of empty tone which seems to be beyond humiliation or indignation and can only look down towards the floor into his own kind of space; a place where you can see him almost reliving the experience.

After a while, he lifts up his own numb leg and crosses it over the other and continues his stories. He continued to lose thousands of dollars, losing $2,000 on one occasion, and eventually did and made his way to Izmir in Turkey where only on the third time of trying did he manage to cross to Greece (twice before he was arrested by the Turkish coastguard). He was carried around again for nearly two weeks in Chios (a Greek island) by his nephew as there was no room for his replacement wheelchair in the inflatable boat: the smugglers considered it to be extra space after all and demanded an extra €1,500 as it was what someone else would pay.

Latif has not seen his family for nearly two years. He tries to make the best of what he can and is doing a TEFL course which would qualify him as an English teacher. He gets €90 a month from the Greek state, €50 of which he sends home to his family – not that this goes far for prices are so high for things in Syria because of the shortage of resources. This leaves him with a little over a Euro a day. He repeats it to me in a tone devoid of all indignation and disgust but one of utter disappointment and resignation at the reality of his current circumstances. "How can you live on one Euro a day?" he says and spits at the same time in anger. "The war of higher powers will go on," he adds as he tells me that the interview for his asylum application is 22nd July 2018. He says he is about to see a lawyer about moving the date forward. Remember that this is only the interview and thereafter he will have to wait for a decision which will likely take months. He adds "I just want a normal life for my family, I want to wake up with my family, play with my children, a normal life."

Human debris

As Latif's account clearly demonstrates, the human consequences of all this have been devastating for everyday people. By the end of my fieldwork in 2018, it was estimated that over half a million Syrians had died, 6.6 million had been displaced internally and 5.6 million had fled the country (Human Rights Watch, 2019). Even in the wake of bouts of intense fighting (UNHCR, 2016b), and international "intervention" in the form of airstrikes and bombing, investigations into civilian casualties are not transparent and there is often no compensation for victims (Human Rights Watch, 2019). "Siege warfare" or the strategy of "encircling" cities and towns, thus cutting off access to food, water, electricity and medicine, were other tactics used to slowly strangle thousands of people into poverty, desperation and death (UNHCR, 2018b). Other evidence points to 90,000 people "forcibly disappeared," detained in official or makeshift detention centres, and many of this number are believed to have been beaten to death or died as a result of their injuries (UNHCR, 2016b). One such survivor, however, was Wissam.

Torture and extreme violence: Wissam, Vienna

We walk towards Mohammed's flat and buy a few chocolate biscuits in the process for the long interviews we have lined up. Once again, we go to his studio flat and we start to make a few calls to see who is interested. I nose around his flat and at the books he has to study since his arrival in France. We finally get some success from a man called Wissam who comes from Damascus and who has managed to get asylum status in the city; they had met each other on the journey up through the Southern European countries and have since kept in contact. However, Wissam is uncomfortable about meeting in person so we continue to talk by phone. It transpires that Wissam has been in Vienna nearly two years, having waited over 18 months for his application to be accepted. During this time, he says he was "nervous every day" as he was afraid he would be sent back. While he says he didn't consider moving on to another country because of the delay, he seems somewhat frustrated by his current predicament.

Wissam has yet to start German lessons and he has been in Austria for over two years. The cultural courses, he says, leave a lot to be desired and there is very little formal assistance for translation. He relies on some of his friends who have been there longer and who have been able to pick up the language. However, he, like others, didn't know what conditions he was agreeing to when he signed his asylum papers. He says he knows about 50 Syrian refugees, half of whom speak some basic German but only a handful have very basic manual labour jobs. This seems to be his problem as well for his English is generally good having watched "films and read books." "I want to live in a country where they speak English, no one here does and I don't understand German," he says.

The lack of the language stifles his prospects for jobs as he also competes with other unemployed Austrians in the job centre though he is constantly told to come back when his level has improved. He struggles with leaving his flat some days because of the "depressing I have" he says. At first, he attributes this to the treatment he and some of his friends have received when they have been out together from "far right racists" (see Chapter 8):

DAN: You give me the impression there is something negative about Vienna.

WISSAM: Yeah, I mean, I got some racism. They don't like the foreign people. When I go to spend my time in public, they watch me like I am scum or I am dirty. If they could kill me, they would. It gets stressful and I am afraid, I don't want to go out of the flat. I always try to stay in. People ask me to come out but I say no I want to stay here.

However, as our conversation continues, it turns out that there are other features of his past which also cause psychological instability. There is a pause in the interview as he regains himself and tries to reduce his heavy breathing. "Who tortured you Wissan? What happened?" I ask. He starts to explain the scenario which relates to the persecution of people like him who are Sunni Muslims. Three years ago, as he was coming out of a café, he and his friend were surrounded by two police cars. They got out and asked for his ID and detained him in a cell. At first, they asked him to confess to his real motives and disbelieved any protest he made of his innocence. At first, they hung him by his hands for days. When he still protested innocence, they started to break certain bones in his body, starting randomly with some fingers. Without knowing what he was supposed to be confessing to, the torturers went a step further and stripped him naked and burned the skin of his back through to the spinal bones. Where they saw a bone, they applied a red-hot prod. As he tells me, his voice quivers:

WISSAM: No I don't want to go back to Syria, please. Even if it finished [the war], I wouldn't go. I had a special situation, they arrested me, put me in prison, they tortured me for four months and until now I have problems in my body and my psychological self. I cannot sleep and eat well. I have so many problems, so when I think of Syria I get stressed and be afraid again.

DAN: What did they do to you?

WISSAM: Er.. The government hate Sunni people and we are Sunni and everywhere when they catch me and see I am Sunni, they have to arrest me or kill me. They put me in prison, they broke my bones, strangled me [crying], electrocuted me, heated up a metal rod and put it on my spine when I was naked, hung me up from...[he breaks down in tears]

DAN: Are you getting help for this?

WISSAM: Yes, when I was in the camp I went 7–8 times and speak with the doctor and he gives me some pills.

[PAUSE: The climax of these descriptions is then met with an emotional outpour as he says]:

WISSAM: I came to this country to feel safe and hope they will like or love me, I want to feel like I am human and I am living, this is what I want. I don't want money, I don't want to be a millionaire, I just want to live a good life.

There is a silence as words fail both Mohammed and I. This – among other things which he doesn't go into – took place over four months.

In circumstances of war when the everyday fabric of social life is ruptured and replaced with chaos and desperation, the uncertainty and insecurity can unleash extreme situations of social suffering such as this. Similarly, and as we saw in Chapter 5 with Masri and Ahmed in Iraq, kidnapping was and is still commonplace in Syria.

Kidnap: Ziad and family, Istanbul

Mukhles and I board the metro and take a long ride to the poorer area of Istanbul, where the buildings are high-rise and the roads broken and potholed and evident perhaps by the boys aged about eight smoking in the streets and the others barefoot playing in the roads. We get slightly lost and then make phone call to Ziad only to see him waving at us from his balcony. We return to the entrance of the block and he shouts down instructions to help us open the door by fusing two of the four loose wires together. We finally get the wire combination right and the door buzzes and we enter. We walk up two flights of stairs and, again as it is customary, leave our shoes outside as he greets us with his five children who bounce around him. For Ziad this is no real trouble as with no effort he picks each of them up with one hand and gently wrestles them out of the way. His wife remains in the kitchen and he disappears to help her prepare coffee and distract the children. In the living room, there are covers over the sofa and a broken bookcase. The old TV flickers intermittently showing some sort of cartoon before Ziad comes over and switches it off. Even then, throughout interview three of his boys chase around us trying to turn the TV on again while his wife comes back and forth to restore order.

Ziad and his family left their hometown of Homs in October 2014. They, like thousands of others, left because of war: "there was no danger of bombs where I was living but there was a high risk of arrest, kidknapping, rape and assault. Many of my friends have been arrested kidknapped, some of them disappeared probably killed." During the time he was there during the war, Homs was a contested city and control fluctuated between Assad's security forces and the free army. He then goes on to distinguish the safe places from those which are dangerous:

ZIAD: In the "safe places," there is risk of arrest or kidknapping but in other places which is outside of Assad regime control then the risk is bombs, rockets everything.
DAN: If it is government controlled, then why is risk of arrest and kidnapping?
ZIAD: Well it is not official, like a mafia, they operate in the name of regime but sometimes they are not the regime. This never happened before the revolution.

Life before the revolution was "silent," and if anyone said anything against the powerful, they would go to prison but not "get killed." Now, the prisons are like "slaughterhouses" he says. He laments on how one of many protests took place in 2011 following the disappearance and likely murder of some teenagers which he says was one of many things which contributed to violent retribution from Assad:

ZIAD: When young people are killed, we do not bury them silently and we wanted to bury them together and their families would be in the big mosque in Homs, near the market at a big clock. It was not a place for funerals and not usual but people decided to do it there because it is in the city centre, there were seven at that mosque and another Babsiba (old city), there was 100,000 people there. People went together to bury them. After their burial and went to the new clock and it was the first time in Syria that such a high number gathered there before there were public demonstrations in public spaces. They sat down and they security forces started arresting and shooting them and it was the first big sit down in the revolution. At that time we didn't want revolution or change to regime but to change the mayor of Homs. Why do we do a demonstration, we started for two reasons because children was tortured by security forces, young people of 12–14 years old and all they did was write on the walls "freedom" and the head of the security forces, took them to prison, their fingernails were ripped off, they were burnt, they were tortured and then disappeared. The security forces even then insulted their parents. So the people started to demonstrate. It was because of this abuse of the children, and this continued. The other reason was because we had a mayor that didn't satisfy the people of the city, he wanted to change the markets and destroy the city centre and make malls without approval of people.

Ziad says these boys were "killed for fun" and after this event, Ziad moved to Damascus. At the time his sons were two and three, respectively, he had a baby and his wife was pregnant with twins. In Damascus, however, he had to move three times because of bomb damage to the block of flats where they rented. He and his family decided to leave when he heard that 1,000 people were killed in one night in and around the city. Even now he says it is still risky:

ZIAD: They tell me the same is happening, the danger is still there and we are talking about places of real danger. I have relatives who lives five minutes from a section of the city who can't get in, can't get out, can't get gas for their house, one tank of petrol is about 20 times its real price, bread is difficult to find. They close it because the free army is there and the civilians there are supporting them. At some funerals, they have guns to protect the demonstrators which is basic part of the free army.

He says the "free army" are made up of young men who refused to do mandatory military service as well as rejected rank in Assad's army when the 2011 uprising occurred. Generally, he sees them as a weaker force as they are not as well equipped; nevertheless, "the Americans don't want war to stop as they earn money from us, from the free army and Assad regime, they earn money from us," he adds. Ziad sees no real end a conflict which was instigated to "divide Sunni and Shia Muslims so they fought each other so they lose their power against the Assad government." Ziad is lucky as he has a job working as an English teacher, but for the majority of the four million Syrians in Turkey, there are few opportunities as he explains:

ZIAD: I had to work as soon as I got here, started teaching but less than 10% of us don't have work because there is not many Syrian schools and they can't teach at Turkish language. So many Syrian teachers cannot work in Turkey and it's the same with engineers, they have no chance here so they end up in knitting or making clothes which is just over €230 for them per month which just about covers some of the rent.

Shortly after, we finish our coffee and amble back to the nearby metro of Menderes. As we board, Mukhles recalls more stories of how for nearly nine months he was unable to sleep because of the fear of dying from bombing. But war also heightens injustices against women. As you will read now, Arsala is one of thousands of women as well as girls who are subject to rape, sexual violence and sexual humiliation (WILPF, 2016; UNHRC, 2018a). Many are detained against their will, subject to potential sexual slavery, sexual torture, mutilation and many reside vulnerable in camps with no social order and security (UPR Working Group, 2016). I met Arsala in a poor French social-housing area.

Rape: Arsala, Strasbourg

Mohammed makes another call as he pours me more strong black coffee and says, "now we go and meet my other friend from Syria." We gather our things and make our way to the tram before boarding and chug slowly south of the city past new plush city commercial investments; the change in urban landscape is quite noticeable as we leave the river which seems to distinguish the city and its outskirts. We get off near a supermarket which supplies the city with food products from places like Syria and Afghanistan and cross the road to meet Arsala. She has just come from the gym and is with her smiling friend Habiba from Morocco. We walk with them, passing Arsala's bike which is chained to a lamp post outside, to her nearby apartment in dodgy social housing block. We walk in and are led into a ground floor flat which, by comparison to Mohammed's, seems far larger. The space is made up of a living room, a bedroom and a large kitchen. The walls are blank white and there is an empty feeling to the place only countered by the bric-a-brac which Arsala seems to have accumulated combined with other bags, clothes and similar assortments.

Arsala barely uses the flat as for the first few months she has been here, she was unable to pay the high electricity bill as the government support money had not come through in time. She is now scared to use anything and instead spends minimal time there. In addition, for the first month there was a gas problem which was potentially life threatening as it leaked while she was sleeping. Despite this, Arsala fishes around in the half-empty fruit bowl, wipes clean an old plate with her jumper, fetches a nearby knife and puts it in front of me as typical welcoming custom. As Habiba sits and plugs in her mobile and starts playing a game, Arsala reaches into her rucksack and pulls out a bag of sugared ginger which she adds to our growing feast. She offers me her hand and says "please" indicating that I eat and offers me water.

When she has finished playing host, we start the interview while the loud children play outside in the patchy long-grassed playground which sits in the middle of the housing block. It's difficult to believe this woman is still able to smile for even when I ask her briefly about Syria, painful memories are quickly stirred. She left in 2011 when a bomb wiped out her family and her partner:

ARSALA: I lost my mother, there was a bomb in the flat. Everyone ran out, all my family died, my partner died. I left with nothing, in the same clothes that I was wearing that day. I asked people in the area to be able to pass the border to bribe the guards. I had nowhere to go.

Unable to find them in the rubble, and with nothing to her name, no money, no papers, only the clothes she wore, she borrowed money to cross the border into Lebanon. She fights back the tears at first seemingly pretending that there is something in her eye as she then goes on to say how she had to find her way homeless. She first found an abandoned house and lived with other seemingly orphaned children; however, when the police found them, they evicted them from the property.

ARSALA: I slept in the street for seven months, found a building to live in it with some Syrian boys and girls but the police raided it and we were put into a refugee camp. I registered with the UN.

She then stayed in a refugee camp where she was constantly attacked:

ARSALA: In the camp, I waited and one night some drunk people came and raped me and cut my stomach open. The camp is dangerous, people are robbed, they say they are police and they come in and rob. This happened to me twice.

As she says this, she really starts to break down and tears form quickly in her eyes before dropping even quicker down her face. She quickly wipes her face and smiles bravely. But it transpires that these were normal occurrences because she had to wait four years before her application for asylum with the UN was accepted and she was moved to France. Four years. In 2016, she arrived in France and was given a place in the flat, in this poor area of Strasbourg. She doesn't understand the asylum papers she has signed, doesn't speak French or wants to live in France. Since her arrival in France in late October 2016, she has struggled to integrate. She speaks minimal French as the language courses have only recently started. Government funding was delayed and she confesses to not understanding most of the things she has signed since being here – not that anyone has explained anything to her. She struggles with the concept of potential discrimination because she cannot understand the language and seemingly interprets things as directly against her. Still, she tries to keep a brave face and with that starts to offer Mohammed and I the rest of the very few things in the fridge for our nourishment.

All of the above + people trafficking: Assam and Naram and family, Paris

In a youth-hostel-cum-refugee centre in the poor banlieues of Paris, I meet a lively man called Assam who, before we sit down for the interview, shows me his most recent artwork depicting the "border stories" (see Figure 10).

At first glance, this painting may appear as something etched out by an eight-year-old, perhaps messing around with colours or the like. However, the artist is a 40-year-old Syrian man who has been in Paris for 55 days waiting to find out which French city he and his four children will make their new home. He and his family sold everything to raise the $10,000 to travel to somewhere in Europe (including $1,200 per person for the journey from Turkey to Greece and that doesn't leave much). They sold jewellery, clothes, car, laptop, land, everything.

FIGURE 10 Assam's artwork "border stories."

The painting tells the story of his journey with all his family, from Turkey by boat (the black oval) over the sea with many others traversing borders. The red dots in the blue are people in the sea he saw floating with lifejackets. The piano-keyboard-like stripe represents Macedonia where they walked for days without food and where his six-year-old daughter was beaten by the police. The stripe is Hungary where, again, the treatment from the police was harsh and violent, and they walked through dense forests not knowing the way and in fear of kidnapping from human traffickers. Thereafter entering into Vienna in Austria and Munich in Germany is the yellow in the far top left corner. "It is the light," he tells me. The numerous dots are the thousands he travelled with "…people in need and in pain" he says. He painted it in just ten minutes yet this is what he "dreams each night."

ASSAM: The government or someone took my friend, I never saw him again, I don't know what he did. He was kidnapped. We raised the money in three months but when we met with the kidnappers, they said he was already dead. Because he did, I had to take care of his son who travelled with us across Turkey, Greece and all those countries.

DAN: What have you told the son about his father?

ASSAM: We didn't know what to say to him for three months, as we just took care of him. We had to. His family is dead as well, home destroyed. The boy has no one. Daniel, can you imagine how many other children are in the same situation? Daniel, how many people have lost limbs, legs or arms or hands? [he starts to cry].

His wife Naram, who is 36 years old, comes with four children – two children aged 13 and 11, and twins who are 6 years old. But also, in the end, another child travels with them. Naram then and sits quietly in the chair. From time to time her children come in and linger around before finding things to do which involve running around a lot and shouting. However, her youngest daughter Maya who is just six years old yet looks much younger will not leave her mother's arms throughout the time we speak. From time to time she opens her eyes and smiles at me before nestling her head back into her mother's arms. Maya's hair is falling out and she has only started to recover from the weight loss and trauma of the journey Naram says. Every day she goes to a kind go school but cries each time she has to leave her mother perhaps thinking it may be the last time she will see her. As the interview progresses, it transpires that Maya was beaten by the Macedonian police as they, along with thousands of others, tried to cross the border. In the chaos of the lashings and beatings, Naram was thrust to the floor and also beaten, all the while protecting her daughter in her arms who was crying and screaming. For one week her daughter did not leave Naram's arms. As she explains this to me, Maya raises her head once again from her mother's arms and looks at me and smiles. They reflect on life in Damascus, where they too had to move several times from areas at high risk of bombing, before moving to another town with "no electricity or food":

NARAM: There was no electricity, no food, there is no safety. When my children go to school, I don't know if I will see them again and it is very difficult feeling when you have children and you can't feed them. I didn't want to wake up in the mornings because I had to look my children in the face and I had no food for them. We were surrounded by government forces in the end and we had to leave. Before life was comfortable, I felt safe and there is brotherhood, love between people.

DAN: Do you disagree with the revolution?

NARAM: I wish it didn't happen, I didn't want it to happen how it did.

DAN: How did other women feel about the revolution?

NARAM: Majority of women have same feeling because it was safe but now it is a chaos so we don't feel it should have happened.

DAN: Did you talk about politics and the regime?

NARAM: No, never. No one did.

DAN: What did you do as a mother when she needed to find food for her children in Syria?

NARAM: I can't do anything like all the women around me, there are 300,000 people living in this city and they can't do anything. However, we are all in the same situation so we share what we have between us, small agreements we make. Even young men give to the families with babies or children, everyone was working only for the families. All the citizens.

At times, the town under siege was allowed to let food supplies pass, but the price was high for basic products like bread which went from "25 lira before war to 1000 lira." Naram sent the children to school as she wanted them to study, but they didn't go on "dangerous days" when there was bombing or when they moved the place was surrounding:

NARAM: If it is not bombing, they kidnap the children. Women, young people, and children. It is to negotiate a sum of money from them. Both sides did it, the free army and also the government forces. The military tend to kill people they kidnap from the free army and vice versa but the civilians are used to make exchanges or make money.

The decision to leave came when her brother was killed:

NARAM: I saw houses destroyed, I have seen other terrible things. My brother lived opposite me and I could see his balcony from my house but when I was out on my balcony one day I saw a bomb hit his house and he was inside. I had to leave then. When there are bombings, people sleep outside as they think its safer. Obviously it isn't but still they think the buildings will collapse so they go to the streets. They do this if they have no bunkers. Really there is no safe place, nowhere to hide.

DAN: How did you prepare for your family to leave Syria?

NARAM: First we took nothing from the first place, just clothes. We thought we will come back but we didn't and the building was destroyed. We sold everything and came with $10,000 – we have no land, no bank account, no house, no clothes only that we have now. When we decided to leave, we had everything in a week. We didn't want to leave, we really didn't, we coped as much as we could but in the end we had to go. When we left, I had no time to think. I had no feelings, there was no time. We had to leave from the danger, we focus on leaving with the children. We must go, we have nothing and we leave and that's it.

They then left on a bus back to Damascus before taking one for 24 hours to Beirut, waiting an additional 22 hours at the Lebanese border, before taking a boat to Turkey which took 16 hours. Leaving on 28th August 2015, they then arrived in Turkey in early September with little idea what to do:

NARAM: We had no plan, no country, we didn't know. Only we knew we needed to leave to safety. We look for three days in Istanbul for three days to take us to Greece by boat. We found it difficult to find people who we could trust so my husband decided to call a friend in Izmir and we went there. It took 12 hours. For us it was $1,200 and the children went free, well the young ones.

DAN: How did you feel in that moment?

NARAM: I wish I hadn't come. I realised how real it was, I was afraid only for my children, not myself. I tried not to think about it, I mean think about what it was to do this. To Izmir we then went...

7

THE BUSINESS OF MISERY

Refugee border stories

We leave in the taxi which the boy has called and drive back down the hills into the centre of Izmir, Turkey. Pulling up ten minutes later, we get out at the train station area called Basemane – the hub for refugee smugglers. As I step on the pavement, I immediately see three men sitting on stools, in front of them selling on an upturned box, an array of extremely large power block chargers for mobile phones. Next to him, another sells waterproof covers for mobiles; next to him, I count three pairs of men who sit and smoke and have before them spread on the floor – as if they are home-made works of art for sale – various sizes of life jackets (see Figure 11). We pass Syrians with backpacks and black bags, filled with all these accessories which they have just bought, as Bulent tells me that the refugees congregate here to receive the "final call" which I suppose to mean when they will be picked up by smugglers. And this is just the corner of one road. Down to my right the stalls continue as they do behind me. Bulent points to the hotels all around us and says, "they are all fully booked," and then points in the restaurants saying, "they are all Syrians, all waiting for the final call": in Izmir I am told that the restaurants make more money from selling life jackets than food.

We cross the road to the main square where more stalls spread out – life jackets on floors, against walls, on boxes, already in plastic bags, hanging from the backs of chairs. The light is dim in the hubbub of the café talking and shisha smoking. We are approached by someone who asks us if we are interested in travelling somewhere, and we sound vague and answer in English which seems to create suspicion and he starts making a phone call. We walk off slowly and cross the road again to the mosque area. On the corner of the street is where the refugee queue starts and it goes for a few hundred metres. "Imagine how it was during summer and during the day now there are double the number waiting for the final call," whispers Bulent as we walk slowly from the light into the dark. The mobile phone lights aluminate the faces of young, old, families, some sit, some

FIGURE 11 Life jackets for sale, Izmir, Turkey.

stand, all wait. All their belongings and life are in those bags. As I continue to trip on the broken pavement, I see a young boy of two years old playing curiously with his life jacket as if it were a toy with which he didn't know how to play: when he looks at me, all I can see is my daughter's face. He is not the only one because these young children are everywhere, some restless, some asleep (see United Nations, 2020).

In Izmir at the time of this study and the peak of the refugee exodus in 2015, Basmane square was the operating hub for the smugglers. The *business of misery* is not only representative therefore of geopolitical arms sales, illicit commodity markets and in the chaos, bribes and miscellaneous payments needed for movement but also the way new illicit and exploitative business opportunities evolve around the misery caused by the refugee crisis. When I visited Basemane, an adult life jacket cost €10, one for a child €8 and one for a baby €5; the quality was very questionable as many people I spoke to complained that they burst or came loose on the boat journey from Turkey to Greece.

Of course, international condemnation for the continued arrival of people across the Mediterranean never gets beyond a low simmering perhaps broken only with a few spikes of indignation when media agencies close in on a rudderless ship in the Med. There is then some policy attention. An intervention or two. Some Twitter shares. But in general things return to how they are. This chapter looks at how these market opportunities arise as refugees continue to risk life and limb to clamber to some other country where additional uncertainty awaits them. This is told through "refugee border stories" with an emphasis on refugee narratives and testimonies in the depiction of their continued exploitation by others immersed in what I call *hardship entrepreneurialism* as part of the *business of misery*. For now, some attention is paid to migration routes and statistics even though they have to be taken with caution since many attempt these journeys and die without trace (Cummings et al., 2015; European Commission, 2016).

The business of misery continued...

In the six months prior to the commencement of this study in August 2015, 137,000 refugees had crossed at various points in the Mediterranean in falling-apart boats and rubber dinghies (UNHCR, 2015): this was an 83% increase in comparison with the same period in 2014 (Cummings et al., 2015). Many died including in one incident 800 refugees of mixed nationalities attempting to get from Libya to Italy (Bonomolo and Kirchgaessner, 2015). According to the UN-HCR (2019b), at its peak, the route from Libya to Italy saw 105,400 refugees attempting crossings from January to September 2017. When the Libyan coast-guard picked up its operations, many of this number significantly reduced in the same period in 2018 to 21,000. Increases were then seen in the other routes over the same period from 17,100 to 43,200 in the Morocco–Spain route and 20,000 to 37,300 in the Turkey–Greece route. However, this intervention came at a cost because 85% of those "rescued" or "intercepted" by the newly established Libyan Search and Rescue Region (SRR) went back to Libya and were detained in abysmal conditions (including limited access to food and outbreaks of disease at some facilities; some consequently dying).

Yet for refugees, sea crossings such as those depicted in the field notes are supposedly a final part of a journey which has already encompassed risks such as travelling by various means through conflict zones and risking the possibility of robbery, abuse (in various forms), kidnapping, torture, or death as well as the continuous threat from smugglers (Chapter 5 and 6). It is perhaps unsurprising that refugees experience high levels of psychological and in some cases physical traumas from exposure to war and conflict in their home countries (WHO, 2018). These experiences can be exacerbated – such as being forced by gunpoint by a smuggler to board an overcrowded improvised boat that will hopefully float towards its destination – as they journey. It has been suggested that when refugees are in transit, they are more vulnerable to disease and poor healthcare, debt, increased risk of post-traumatic stress disorder, depression among other mental health illness as well as physical complications, in particular those who have been victims of abuse, torture and trauma (UN, 2017).

This makes them a very vulnerable population and this vulnerability can mean that their trajectories are often difficult to predict as journey experiences shape decision-making and ambitions; for example, emergencies policies initiated to control/deter refugees, oppressive security measures at border crossings or indeed the closure of a border can alter migration routes (Monterescu and Rajaram, 2016). Border crossings can be cut short: despite having ambitions to go further, regulations, family circumstances or the like may mean they have to adapt themselves to a new reality as we saw with Ismail's family in Chapter 5 when the sons had to support the whole family by working in exploitative conditions in Turkish garment factories (see Kampanyasi, 2019). So because refugees make these travels outside formal systems, it means they take on additional layers of vulnerability: they are neither protected by the state nor able to purchase their own security.

While the "professionalisation" of smuggling services (Cummings et al., 2015) is partly related to this, it is also the function of the internet and social media which facilitate migration. Contacts are made as refugees arrive in new places, WhatsApp messages are exchanged, and advice and management of travel is organised through the internet. Moreover, it is the banality of harm in the everyday (Tombs, 2018) which is recognised by people travelling from country to country like this; the normality of risk combined with the almost inevitability that something will go wrong as Osama told me when I met him in Budapest, Hungary.

A fate worse than trying again: The "big industry"

> OSAMA: Now it is a big industry. The people who are running the boats are making so much money from them. My friend lost $15,000 from the first attempt and didn't even get to Greece! He tried to get from Turkey to Bulgaria but the land crossing was closed, it was him and three others, and one died and in the mountains the guide left them and stole their money. They walked for three days and had some food but one died. Then they reached a road and the police arrested them and took them back to Turkey. This is what I mean by the industry. He was an educated man, he was studying a masters and he had to start again. He tried again through Greece but again they sent him back to Turkey. In the end and he found another man who could get him to UK, to Angola and from a military airport they could go without papers. But my friend was so desperate. He wanted to work but there is nothing for him in Turkey. So he went there, he got arrested and was beaten there lost his money again, it is a very sad story and I talked to him via WhatsApp and he was sent back to Turkey. So he can't re-enter the countries he tries to travel to, he is like banned there so every time he is reducing his chances. At least he arrived eventually with another guide but so many didn't.

During the period of this research, there was a major increase in refugees taking what is known as the "eastern Mediterranean route" from Turkey to Greece – more than 85% arriving in Greece from countries experiencing war and conflict such as Syria, Afghanistan, Iraq and Somalia (UNHCR, 2018b). Refugees pay between $1,000 and $2,000 depending on the time of year, boat size and weather conditions – it often being cheaper when there are storms and even "extreme storms surges" because of climate change (Krestenitis et al., 2016).

The smugglers, however, also have precarious backgrounds and are looking to work themselves out of their own deprivation as one study found in Turkey that three-quarters (75%) were found to be unemployed (Günşen et al., 2015). They therefore work by a form of "*hardship entrepreneurialism*" as part of the *business of misery*: victims but also perpetrators of a system which equally makes their life circumstances complex and challenging. Typically, the smugglers are "loosely connected, informal and not strictly hierarchical. Different individuals and groups form flexible chains, where members can be easily replaced with little or no disruption to the network's activities" and can make around $100,000 in less than a year (UNODC, 2018: 111). No wage would come close to paying them that otherwise and the future is uncertain, so for them, refugees are a good business.

No choice: "Fast class" in driving boats

MOHAMMED: The economic situation is not good in Syria before revolution, a lot of people don't have money to buy food. A lot more people in the cities. It was getting worse since I arrived in 2005, there was more and more people out of work and then small group of people with lots of money so people feel there is something wrong and they start to protest for their rights.

The country experiencing more and more violence, Mohammed and his friend had no choice but to leave. He took several buses over several days into Turkey towards Istanbul taking "$3,000 in cash" before he looked on Facebook for a "friend who shares the knowledge about the boats." He paid someone $1,200 to cross, but it is "what we do". After three nights in a cheap hotel in Istanbul, he was taken on a bus:

MOHAMMED: There is many people on the bus, Iraqi, Syrian and Afghanis about 80 on the bus, for 8 hours I am standing. We all go to the same place a village. We gave the money to a person, then we do the boat trip, and then he gives it to whoever when we are safe and we arrive. We don't know but it is a company, there is many of them, a week before one was arrested for this. Stayed for 2 nights in the mountains waiting to travel all 80 of us. About 50 of us are young men, but there are many babies and children. One child didn't have one [lifejacket] so I gave him a rubber ring.

DAN: Who is driving the boat?
MOHAMMED: They choose someone and teach them a very fast class, say 15 minutes and how to direct and steer. They don't have a choice.
DAN: What were you thinking?
MOHAMMED: I was praying: 55 Afghani in one boat 6m long and 35 people in another, like Syrian and Iraq. I sit my legs on someone and they are on me. Water was getting inside so we were bailing the water out between as there

FIGURE 12 Stormy night across the Aegean Sea between Izmir and Lesbos.

are high waves. We feel we are all dead and we will sink. It took one hour. Some people take 6 hours, other sank, police take them. We were lucky.

When he arrived in Lesbos in Greece, he was 56 kilometres from the ferry to Athens. He said, "some people take us like a taxi 20 Euro and take us to a village but it is not the town, so then we take another one 50 Euro and we are still 12 km away. Everyone wants to make money from refugees."

Gunpoint: Even "faster class" in driving boats

KASIM: In Izmir, there is a lot of people selling lifejackets and they are all there to make money from us. We are a group of 50 people waiting and we are with eight-month pregnant woman, families, old people, and like 13 children. We are waiting and together we paid more $46,000 dollars. $46,000 for a journey which we take, which someone with no experience does because they choose the driver of the boat and if they don't do it they put a gun to their heads. The mafia organise it. It was cheaper I think as the children and babies go half price they said so only $600 for each of them. We wait in the night, children crying, women praying. The waves were 3 m high (see Figure 12). The coastguard rescue us because our boat is sinking, it is full of water and some people are out of the boat. Everyone is cold but no one died we are lucky.

DAN: How did you feel in that moment?

KASIM: I see the children and I thinking about them, not me, forget myself and I feel I want to help them and some of us helped them in the water.

Somewhere floating in the Mediterranean: Bushra

A woman in her late 20s then sits in the chair opposite me in the Parisian cáfe in the refugee hostel, and we start to talk through our translator Mohamed. Bushra left Syria earlier this year for Saudi Arabia with her three children and husband. There he was able to get a basic job to cover their living needs. However, the increasing tensions between Saudis and Syrians, as well as competition for work with other lower paid Pakistanis and Afghanis in the exploitative construction industry did not permit them to fully settle, and they decided that she would travel to Europe. She flew from Jeddah to Istanbul where she paid smugglers $1,700 to travel by boat from Turkey to Greece. On the boat she said that the Turkish coastguards circled them and tried to capsize it by boarding it ut she and others fought them off. She quickly ran out of money in Serbia and relied on the kindness of other Syrians. She walked for days without eating she recalls and spent three days in a Hungarian prison. In there she met a woman who had "gone mad" having been separated from her husband and children a month ago. As the interview draws to a close, she starts to cry when she thinks about her children. Her hands remain in her face for several minutes before she then sits forward; wiping away her tears, she shows me the only memorable moment of the journey. In the clip, she allowed me to have, the whole boat unites to celebrate after fending off the Turkish authorities (See Figure 13).

Meanwhile on Lesbos beach in Greece: Eva, a British tourist

EVA: We were on the beach and a boat came in and capsized and people did nothing around us. We were eating in the restaurant and we heard screaming and shouting, so we left our food and with the people eating with us, some Dutch, we started to go into the water. They were shouting that a woman who couldn't swim was in the water and they couldn't save her. One of them went in to save her and we helped get the boat in, we gave them clothes, tried to calm them down. We took them back to the restaurant and bought them food. I was like "why is no one doing anything"? They were just lying there in the sun, putting on lotion, enjoying their holiday. There was another day when like five boats arrived and people just watched as if they were zombies.

(Eva, UK)

FIGURE 13 A snapshot from Bushra's video celebrating victory against the Turkish coastguard.

Hungry but not Hungary

During 2015 and 2016, it was common for refugees to find routes from Athens into Central Europe. Countries like Hungary were a risk for the refugees because of the high chances of arrest and imprisonment:

MOHAMMED: 50 Euro to go to Macedonian border, at night crossed and waited an hour for papers to be processes and 20 Euro bus to Serbian border – arrive middle of night, tried to cross but get lost so just walk towards the light, some villagers give us clothes as we walk – found policeman who told how to get to Germany, walk 2 hours and bus to Belgrade then all the time no sleep because we want to arrive. We heard Hungary were building a wall so we have to get to Germany quick. Get a private taxi 1,500 for each person to take across Hungary as the border is closing. I call my family and they send

FIGURE 14 Bushra in prison in Hungary.

me the money. This was my big mistake but we are afraid we don't want to be caught in Hungary as everyone is going to jail as well. We get to the border and he tells us to get out and drives off.

Such was the vast number of refugees passing through the country during those years that Hungary erected large barbed-wire fences and employed 3,000 border police to deter refugees seeking asylum or even daring to pass through the country (see Figure 14). In 2017, the Hungarian Prime Minister, Viktor Oban, passed some of the bill for this which was estimated to be around to €400 million to the European Union: good business from the proceeds of misery.

Meanwhile in a cold town in the UK

Sahil has in total moved across 15 different European countries. He was born in a rural town on the east side of Syria near the Iraqi border. His family business was affected by 2007–2010 drought, hence them leaving to Aleppo, the closet city (Chapter 6). He spent half his money on bribing officials to leave Syria and the other half on the boat from Turkey to Greece. Managing to borrow money from other refugees, when he arrived to France, he was jailed four times when he was living in the Calais Jungle and the camp was subject to high levels of police control. He describes this as "horrible but character building." "In the Jungle there are people who have been kicked out of everywhere," he says, mixed with "a lot of smugglers who give people false hope of travelling." Hoping to board a boat or a lorry, each night for seven months he went to the port. When he finally made it to the UK, he travelled north to Edinburgh in Scotland. Feeling partly relieved, he reflects:

> The main problem is finding work. Most people don't come to look for work, they look for safety look for new safe life. I was hunted by ISIS and the Assad regime at the same time. We had a dictatorship controlling our lives, making it miserable when the revolution happened it got worse, Everyone wants control, crime increases, everyone wants to seize the land resources for political interests so it creates a vacuum and more conflict. Now I have a new challenge which is my new life.

He estimates to know about 20 refugees, 12 of whom have low-paid jobs, but the rest can't work or are on benefits. He is not alone. Refugee employment rates across Europe lag behind those of economic migrants and even though refugees tend to be overqualified for the menial work they can find (Desiderio, 2017). Traumas from the past make transition to work complicated as Sahil he knows one refugee friend with a war injury and another has a sniper bullet in his neck: even then he says both would rather work than depend on benefits:

> Refugees can't have the same jobs as everyone, they have almost been cho-sen to work in crappy jobs. I had my first job in an Amazon warehouse, but I don't call it work, I call it slavery. I couldn't handle it and I quit. I work now in a cash and carry even though I am a graphic designer, artist, elec-tric welder and joiner. Now I carry boxes and displaying items but there is nothing for my field here. I have lots of ideas but I am restricted and lots of us are in the same position.

The business of misery transcends suffering in home countries and repressive border experiences and well into the "new life" (Chapter 8); Witness the labour exploitation to which Sahil is now subject. Yet there is little choice in the face of poverty and debt.

New life, old memories and new worries: Nasir and Zafira, Athens

We are then led across the dusty path and between a few more metal cabins into another narrow pathway where sit more cabins. We pass and smile at the families who have their children playing among the dust and chasing each other and are introduced to Zafira – a Kurdish Syrian woman in her early 30s who has three children. She stands in the doorway and smiles warmly; she has her hair tightly platted at the back, thin painted eyebrows and is adorned with lots of make-up which covers some skin condition.

We are invited in and take our shoes off and skip over the soaking wet porch to enter their humble home. The cabin is essentially the bedroom, living room, dining room, kitchen and whatever else you can think of. It is probably no more than a few square metres. As we sit hunched under the bunk beds, Nasir comes in and starts to translate. He sits on the sponge thing which is one of the children's beds as we try to make ourselves comfortable on the bunk beds.

Zafira has three children, the eldest of whom didn't speak for one year after the journey from Syria because of the atrocities which he saw. He is seven years old and attends a Greek school, and he has a brother (Rashid, three years old) and a sister (Rihanna, six years old). Nasir lights up a cigarette as Rashid comes in and jumps all over us. At first he is shy and says, "I don't know you," but soon after he is running around and jumps over to give me a kiss on the cheek. As Zafira places down freshly cut apple and puts on the stove to make some Syrian coffee, he gulps down my water and rams the apple down his mouth; he smiles as his nose runs slightly. It's a miracle he is smiling. Zafira, however, is not so keen to talk – even if Nasir half insists. It seems they shared the sleeping area in Chios which is how they got to know each other and Nasir became friends with Zafira's husband – who is currently in hospital for some unknown illness. He has been there for three days now.

It seems the family owned a factory, but after it was bombed they sold everything to leave the country and fled to Turkey. They didn't nor now seem to have a plan in mind about where they want to go but want safety – not that there seems to be much hope for them here as their asylum application has been rejected for the second time (the last application took only a month to process). They don't know what will happen to them or where they will go as they have no home in Syria now and no money. As she says this, her eldest daughter comes in and robs chewing gum from her mum and gives us a piece each; she sits and plays with me in the corner and makes faces at me.

In the end the family managed to muster up €400 from members of the Syrian community for some legal representation and now have to see if they can over-turn the decision. These informal favours seem to pay off in some small way in the absence of a secure and dignified home, or even a more certain future. There is even one man who has wired up illegal satellites to half of the houses so the community can watch Arabic TV.

Nasir continues to answer questions I direct at Zafira, probably because he knows the answer but also because he seems to foresee the pain which may be caused if I asked her directly. After another few questions, I ask him to address a question at Zafira. It is about their journey here. She briskly does something of insignificance in the kitchen as she smiles and says how "when we crossed the

Turkish border, they [the gendarmerie – or the armed security force who patrol the borders] were shooting at us. They have orders to kill. Five people in our group who ran with us in the night in the forests, were shot dead." Maybe this is the reason that her son stopped speaking for a whole year having witnessed this.

Thereafter she seems to play off sensitive questions by laughing and smiling. It's clear she has a lot of trauma so I ask her about the counselling and social services, and if she has seen them about this but it seems not. This only seems to confirm the disparity between the work the professionals in the camp do for the refugees and the real suffering which has gone on undetected since their arrival. Zafira then places the hot Syrian coffee on a small stool, and we sip intermittently and talk more to Nasir as he is mauled by Rashid. "He is my best friend, he stays with me," he says as Rashid starts to reach for his Batman outfit. He puts it against him as if he were the strongest man in the world; for what I can see he certainly is the toughest three-year-old in the world.

There is then a sort of silence in which Zafira sits with her phone and nervously plays with it. She checks her Facebook several times before closing the phone. When I ask why, it seems that it has been ten days that she has heard anything from her family. Not one message, not one word, not one phone call. She fears the ethnic tensions in the area have resulted in their death but clings to the hope that they will say something on Facebook which will mean they are alive.

We finish the coffees and are dragged out by the hand by Rashid and Rihanna. They want us to buy some more chewing gum with them so Zafira reaches into her purse and pulls out 20 cents. She gives it to them and they run off outside before weaving in and out of the metal cabins to another cabin. They knock on the door and pass in the money without the door even opening further than ajar. There then pass some seconds and the same hand delivers their chewing gum as if it was some illicit transaction. We are given yet another piece of gum as they lead us up to the broken playground which sits under a tarpaulin. They take it in turns to slide down the makeshift slide and laugh before we must say our goodbyes.

When we return to Dimitrius to thank him for everything, he reminds me how, as he puts it, "we give them hope," but it's difficult to see what "hope" that is since most seem pretty resigned to either being ejected from the country or having no future in Greece.

New life, old memories and new worries: Ramiz and family, Hamar

We conclude the interview, I walk outside and Dag disappears to do a few errands. Snow starts to fall as an Eritrean family come out of reception; against the sun it looks like glitter is falling from heaven. I report to Ralf who is packing his things away for the day and says I need to look for Tariq whose English is very good and he is the man who can help me with the next interviews. When I knock for Tariq though, it seems it is time for prayer and I need to hang around

FIGURE 15 Passing the kids buggy.

for 45 minutes or so. As I wait for Tariq, I start walking around the square onto which the cabins overlook, each time passing a kids buggy which gathers snow (Figure 15). Abdul then emerges with his daughters and they trudge off towards their Norwegian classes while I return to my walking. I manage to circle square 31 times before I retire to the cabins because I don't feel my face any more from the cold. Dag then returns and soon after Tariq comes down, and Dag and I are invited to meet Ramiz and his family. Inside, we remove our shoes in the welcome warmth as his wife prepares Syrian coffee. His youngest son of two plays in one of the bedrooms, while the other two daughters have left for Norwegian classes.

He sits calmly with his hands clasped and sips his coffee slowly. We begin the conversation and he says how he was working as a driver between Syria and Dubai (about 3,000 kilometres) when the conflict broke out, and while they hoped it would calm down in Aleppo, they lost their patience as his wife approached her third pregnancy and they left – literally walking over the border. The most fearful part he said about living in the city was the bombing. Now he says that ISIS threaten to intervene in the city though the major conflict is between the free army and the government security forces. They stayed in the Kurdish area of Turkey, but Ramiz was unimpressed with the education which his daughters were getting as he continued to drive between Turkey and Dubai. When he left for Istanbul with the intention of coming to Europe, he had no idea which country to go to. To be able to afford the journey from Izmir to Samos, and whatever it may cost thereafter, he sold the car taking the total amount to $13,000. Of the $13,000, $4,000 was paid to some smugglers to get them on boats to Greece; he closes his eyes as he shows me how he held all three of his children in his arms during the five-hour journey made complicated by the high waves and storms. "If they die, I die with them – I could not live without them," he says.

Thereafter things were relatively problem free until they reached Hungary where they were imprisoned for a week because he refused to have his fingerprint taken. In prison, only the children were given food and they stayed in overcrowded cells where most people had to rest standing up. In the end, he gave in and made the fingerprint. Such were the problems at the border that he ended up paying €2,000 for someone to take him to Austria. On arriving in Germany, there were hundreds of thousands of refugees, and he was advised to go to Norway and after more trains across Germany, into Denmark and Sweden, he arrived in Oslo with less than €200 to his family's name. He says Norway has a "democracy" and prays for a successful asylum application though it can take months since his fingerprints were taken in Hungary and Germany and permission needs to be granted from those countries so that he can stay in Norway. He may be waiting some months.

Families may reason the best thing to do is to get as much money together, pack up as much as possible and send the strongest or at least most likely candidate to another area or, in this case, another country so at least they may be safe. This was the case for Shizar, a young man with multiple sclerosis (MS) whom I met in an old Second World War hospital-converted-refugee centre.

New life, old memories and new worries: Shizar, Oslo

We descend to the dirty-snowy roads and drive for about ten minutes past a hospital complex and double back Refstad Transittmottak which is where refugees are housed as they make their application. From the outside it looks like an old school, but it turns out it is a former Second World War hospital used by the Germans who occupied the country. The surrounding area is sparsely residential in this sort of forgotten suburb of Oslo – a city which has seen "hate crimes with racist motives" triple from 2013 to 2016 (Taylor, 2017). We buzz and the front gate opens slowly and to the reception we walk. We speak to the receptionist whose insincerity seems to brush off on everyone in the room.

We stand around, sit, look out of the window and, for nearly an hour, spend our time basically looking at each other and at our phones. Perhaps we will get rejected I fear and won't get into talk to the refugees. Each worker I note wears a fluorescent jacket with "Hero" written on and look like they have just come in from doing roadworks. Turns out Hero is named after the two Norwegian businessmen who founded the private company which operates asylum services to the government.

The receptionist gets some company, and between them they seem to keep endlessly busy with cups of coffees and phone calls to their friends as Dag and I wait endlessly as if time had almost stood still. In my boredom, I read a few leaflets and work out that the Utlendings Direktoratet of Immigration (UDI) is the government department that checks the refugee applications. "Hero", on the other hand, is the private company that delivers the housing and social support. When I start to investigate further on my phone, I find other interesting facts.

It turns out Hero – a supposed "non-for-profit" philanthropic enterprise that charges the government in exchange for the care of refugees – generated $63 million and a profit of 3.5% for its two owners in 2015. What "heroes" the owners are. This was not as much, however, as the $99 million which was generated from "ORS Services" who offer the same sort of assistance in Austria, Germany and Switzerland (Donahue, 2016) and have been regularly criticized for their treatment of employees (Loewenstein, 2015). Again, that's good business from misery.

I peak my head around the corner at the refugee children play fighting in the corridor where three youngers take in an older one who protects a girl: their shrieks and screams echo bring alive the lonely, drab corridors of the former German Second World War hospital. I can wait no longer and make a glance behind me to make sure the receptionist is not looking and tell Dag I'm going to the toilet. We have been waiting an hour and I decide I'm not going to waste my time. Of course, I go to the toilet but deviate on my return and get talking to a group of Syrians, one of whom has a good level of English. One talks to me on behalf of his four friends, two of their wives and three of their children including a girl of two with an enchanting smile who keeps taking off her shoes and throwing them at me only for me to give them back to her only for her to take them off and throw them at me again. The adults are all in their mid-20s and say the food is horrible and claim that the only reason they cleaned the centre today because there is an official UDI visit; otherwise, the place is normally a shambles. The young girl it seems has been ill and not received adequate treatment they add. The rooms are overcrowded and of the capacity of 300, easily reaching 400 though it seems numbers have decreased since Sweden started to intermittently close its borders (as many of those arriving in Norway come through Denmark, Sweden and into the country). I'm later told by some workers that they will probably be sent home as their application is not from a country which is considered to be war-torn or to be subject to levels of life-threatening political violence.

We say our goodbyes and I start to walk around. I get lost as all the corridors are carbon copies of each other and there is this odd clinical feel about the place. I am then accompanied by one young refugee who decides to give me a tour. I explain about my study and he seems interested. We pass old toilets being gutted and I am shown communal areas where refugees watch programmes on their mobiles and message family and friends. Upstairs I am shown the nursery – the best and cleanest room – I pass a table tennis set, which, despite its temporary repair with brown tape, sits broken as a consequence of people "jumping and dancing on it." There is a decrepit feel about the place as I suppose that Hero, the private company charged with its upkeep, doesn't want to invest too much as it could jeopardise profit levels and the government contracts are short-term (which has repercussions for how the staff do their jobs) so all the support could be withdrawn within a month.

The young refugee man tells me to wait in a room with an open door and runs off: "I get someone for you, wait". I go in and sit down and shortly after at the door is a young man with a crutch in his hand. He asks if he can enter and I say of course, saying as he sits "I am a mess." Shizar's English is flawless perhaps because his mum teaches the language as a civil servant; his father also works for the Syrian government.

SHIZAR: I left because of war mainly but first I graduated in Syria and studied engineering then I tried to get a job or work but because of the bad situation there were no jobs so I had to travel. I could not get work. But my town was controlled by the regime, while other places around it controlled by the free army or other troops. About 15–20 rockets fell in our area every day. You had to obey everything under Assad. It was not a fair society but it was safe. We had to live like that.

DAN: What did you think when you saw the revolution?

SHIZAR: I said to myself this man Assad is supposed to be educated, he studied in London. Maybe he will leave the country but I was wrong, he did the opposite. He stayed and war was next. At first I agreed with the revolution but then after I saw the revolution changed into armies and war and killing people and ISIS I said no.

Most of Shizar's family still remain in this village in the government-controlled outskirts of Damascus. They are reluctant to leave because of their job security as well as the care requirements for Shizar's brother who is blind. "He had a tumour in his head and had surgery when he was 8 years old and he went blind in one eye and weakness in the other eye so all his life he studies with a severe impairment," says Shizar.

Leaving Syria because of the conflict, he moved to south Russia because of family ties; his sister had married and lived there as well as his grandfather who was from that area. There he rented an apartment, taught himself Russian and attempted to get by. Even though he has a degree in civil engineering from Syria, he was refused permanent residence twice, putting it down to the onset of MS. Though he was given some medicines, he had to keep working, taking on jobs making ceilings and in shisha cáfes. However, the long hours and physical demand of the work massively took its toll on its body. His condition worsened and he lost the ability to walk, having to be carried to hospital one day. When he was released again, he was just about able to walk with the crutch but then decided to try to leave Russia as his temporary residence was terminating. He first tried to go through Estonia to Germany but was rejected at the border so took an alternative:

SHIZAR: I took two flights from Miramut to Moscow then to Murmansk. I took a taxi to the border then I took a bike. There were four of us, three friends of mine and that day we were the only ones but when we came across the border there were many Syrian people inside the border, we didn't see them on the road but when we came into the border we saw them.

Because of an agreement between Russia and Norway, it is illegal to cross the border by foot so he, like thousands of other Syrians and Iraqis, bought second/third/fourth-hand bikes which had faulty brakes and cycled 50 metres into Norway.

SHIZAR: I got to Oslo in September 2015 and we were given new clothes then we have to wait while we are processed. We stayed in the corridor all night and we stayed in a hotel until they move us to a residence. They sent me back here since they find out I have MS. It is still being processed, I have had two interviews, one with the police and the UDI. First they send people to Russia without informing them. My friend he is right now in a camp in Turkey close to the Norwegian border until he is transferred back to Russia. He was rejected. He is Syrian like me. Now I am really afraid because the Norway is sending people back to Russia because it is considered to be a "safe country." I am afraid of this.

We finish our conversation and we leave. He shows me his small room where he stays with his cousin; one bed lies empty as his cousin escaped to Iceland fearful he would be sent back to Russia where he seeks asylum there. We walk up the corridors as small refugee children chase around his limping figure. We walk into the communal areas which smell of human bodies and the children are arguing over the computer games and small groups of refugee men play cards. Two women appear as they encourage their one-year-old to walk to them; one does so like a zombie with a big grin as if she has just mastered the most complex of life riddles.

Shizar is only 25 years old and shows such willing to work, but the stress and problems in Russia coupled with the border crossing and delays of access to medication have advanced the MS. As we walk towards the reception area, he tells me he struggles to "concentrate" and "feels dizzy" when he walks as the disease has increased its grip on his body.

8

A FORMULA FOR FAILURE

Welcome to Europe and the realities of the "new life"

One month later, in January 2016, I receive some WhatsApp messages:

SHIZAR: Hi Daniel, today I had the chance to buy Norwegian sim card ... so I
  bought one.
DAN: Shizar? I just arrived back in Madrid. Do send me updates on what happens
  there. I'm interested in what you do and the conditions you have to live in.
SHIZAR: Ok I will keep you updated with everything
DAN: And take care. If you think something may infringe your rights let me
  know and I can see what I can find out.
SHIZAR: Ok thank you so much ☺

In the following months, Shizar grew more and more anxious about the political
situation in Norway when government started to send back refugees who had
come via Russia – the rationale being that technically they had not fled from a
"country in conflict." Our messaging desisted at the end of January 2016, but
suddenly two months later, in March, I received some messages from the same
number with some news:

SHIZAR: Hi Daniel how are you? I left Norway.
DAN: What??? You ok?
SHIZAR: I came to Germany. I lived in the hospital for five months full of nerves
  and tension because of the Norwegian government decisions about refugees who came from Russia and have valid residence in there. Eventually I
  couldn't wait any longer I decided to go to Germany.
DAN: How?

SHIZAR: The Norwegian government is confused about me because I have valid residence in Russia until October and I have this sickness so they thought a lot about my case whether they reject or accept me.

DAN: I suppose it was a risk to wait.

SHIZAR: I came by bus and train.

DAN: And passport control?

SHIZAR: No one noticed.

DAN: When did you leave?

SHIZAR: Three days ago.

DAN: Who are you staying with?

SHIZAR: I applied for asylum here then they brought me to the camp. I'm living with two other Syrian refugees in the same room.

DAN: I'm glad you are safe.

As we saw in Chapter 7, refugee trajectories can be uncertain and even arriving in a potential host country can immediately present problems. This is what we see here with Shizar. Delays and uncertainty on his application, social pressures in his accommodation and hearsay going around about people leaving plus government action on returning failed asylum applicants and diminishing health were all part of his decision to try Germany. And why not? What is the worst that can happen? It would only be a *fate worse than trying again*. So rather than being "individual free will decisions" taken by refugees, it is more about how they make decisions and take actions based on various elements of governance around them combined with social pressures and their personal circumstances.

The other problem was that Shizar was entering Germany – a country where hundreds of thousands of refugees had previously been accepted for asylum and a similar number rejected, even if left-liberal Europhilic sections of the media hail the country as the "beacon of European integration." However, the rhetoric of "welcome refugees" seems a distant reality in real life. The rapid influx of refugees in 2015 ignited already fragile feelings particularly among working-class Germans evident in the protests across the country and rises in hate crime with "anti-foreigner" sentiment (Entorf and Lange, 2018) – some of the most recent examples being the continued arson attacks on refugee hostels; the murder of Walter Lübcke, a pro-migrant politician by a man with far-right links; and the more prominent murder of nine "foreign-looking people" by a supporter of the extreme far right (BBC, 2020b).

These events took place in poorer regions and cities where unemployment is high, housing is crowded and substandard, and where there are fewer foreign-born residents' and instead a legacy of anti-foreigner feeling is present - hence the increased likelihood of violent attacks (Klikauer, 2018). In these areas refugees are seen as a "threat to German culture" (Funk, 2016), particularly those in East Germany in cities like Dresden where Shizar was eventually housed. Settlement is further impeded with the presence of the PEGIDA or the People against the Islamisation of the West who, during the course of this study and specifically in the election year of 2017, were vocal against the refugees. In the periphery of Dresden at the time of Shizar's arrival in 2016, an organised group of eight people were under trial for undertaking knife attacks on refugee shelters (Haase and Somaskanda, 2017). Only a year earlier, in 2015, an Eritrean refugee had been murdered in what was thought to have been a racially motivated attack (Connolly, 2015).

We will find out more about Shizar later on as I look to challenge questions around – having travelled to Europe – what kind of "settlement" and "integration" is achieved. In doing so I will consider the management of the refugee crisis and the binary between the "help" European institutions supposedly offers which is countered by the rejectionist political stance they have to their welfare. When this ideology combines through politics and the media, it forms a kind of generic negation of the origin of the refugee issue as well as collective branding of the same group as "invaders" to the European project.

Welcome to Europe, a fine continent: twinned with its own demise

It's no wonder refugees seek Europe: 85% come from climate change-affected and war-ravaged countries in the Global South, around half of which have a GDP of less than $5,000 (Hansen and Randeira, 2016). In 2015 alone, around 333,000 refugees were granted asylum and thereafter awarded protection status by the 28 of the EU member states. Over the two years of 2015 and 2016, the number exceeded one million per year (Kancs and Lecca, 2018). The sheer numbers arriving caused significant tension among EU states, attacks against refugees from the far right, thus threatening the identity of Europe and challenging the legitimacy and credibility of democratic institutions (Winlow et al., 2015). One of the main issues was the lack of consensus between member states about how to deal effectively with the issue which jeopardised refugees' human rights (Barbelescu, 2017; Heldt, 2018). Stevens (2017: 188) suggests this to mean that the EU is "clearly content to maintain an asylum system that grants certain rights to the very few." This is because as Crawley et al. (2017: 60) summarise,

> The EU has focused almost exclusively on policies designed to contain refugees and migrants prior to their arrival on European shores, at the expense of addressing the reception and protection needs of those arriving from situations of conflict, persecution and human rights abuse. There has also been a failure at the national and EU levels to address the longer-term integration needs of refugees and migrants arriving in Europe.

Yet it is perhaps even more basic than this for there has been widespread criticism of European institutions for their confusion and then failure to properly examine the reasons for the refugees arrival and related issues to their settlement (Wolf and Ossewaarde, 2018; Peace and Meer, 2019) – hence the rationale for this book.

In addition, according to Bauböck (2017), there was no "harmonisation" of normative standards related to (a) a refugee relocation scheme and (b) contradictions in the Dublin convention principle of assigning responsibility for refugees according to their "country of entry." Increased right-wing populist political presence among EU states also almost certainly assisted in the disagreements about establishing permanent refugee quotas which would have eased pressure about the allocation of numbers of people (Zaun, 2017). Allsopp and Chase (2017) note how EU policy frameworks instead promoted a "state-centric" view of migration and a "static conception of belonging" which taken together disfavoured anything other than a political preference that they return to their country of origin.

When such state mechanisms failed to support refugees, charities, volunteers and civil society picked up the pieces free of charge (Vandevoordt and Verschraegen, 2019). One such case was over the summers of 2015, 2016 and 2017, respectively, which saw refugee camps spring up in one of the central parks in Brussels. In a climate of rejection towards the refugees and, when nothing was done by the government, it was some citizens and volunteers who provided support. Here, Thierry, the manager of the Welcome Centre, recalled it thus:

THIERRY: It was the first time in Belgium we have seen these kind of things so open, so in front of us. It was so surprising when they came to the park and how it was possible that the government did nothing and they were in tents in terrible conditions. This was September 2015. Minimum police, no political interest, they did NOTHING. It was the citizens, a group of people who stepped forward to help. They were shocked that the government didn't welcome them and left them in bad conditions. They had to register and wait in the rain and with no shelter. The people stepped forward and started to donate tents, clothes, food. Now the government have not done much more. They were like forced to open this pre-welcome space where the Red Cross work and there are 300 beds, we forced them to open more, then they opened 200 more, then they opened to 1,000 places but it is still not enough. They forced us to do their job. They realised this, they didn't want to do it. It is for refugees, we don't like them here in Belgium.

DAN: Is that reflected in what Belgians really think of refugees?

THIERRY: Yes, Belgians are not really interested. The camp we set up was good but it was a small number of volunteers. Generally Belgians don't like these people. There was a poll late in 2015 "do you accept refugees in Belgium" and more than 60% said no from the Dutch-speaking region and more than 70% from the French-speaking region said no.

DAN: Why are Belgians not interested?

THIERRY: Because they are different, the feeling that they come for money, but they [the people] don't know the stories of the refugees.

DAN: How do the media project their stories?

THIERRY: The media didn't talk about it a lot...They did it when there was something special, when people were sleeping in the park, but then it disappeared from the media. In Belgium, it is liberal right, more nationalist. I find it a problem and they are populists and take their decisions according to the opinion of people and this is dangerous even if it is a bad decision. They just want to be re-elected.

Other barometers of failure were evident in the continuous breaches of human rights, lack of protection for the refugees and the number of deaths that occurred during the exodus (Niemann and Zaun, 2018). The lack of agreement was perpetuated by the rigid system of the Common European Asylum System (CEAS) which was supposed to uniformly assess asylum applications and how, coupled with sparse instructions, this could best settle refugees and asylum seekers (Schweitzer et al. 2018; Peace and Meer, 2019). But there were further cracks in the system. Niemann and Zaun (2018: 1) note that,

> While a CEAS with common protection standards and a clear distribution mechanism had been introduced on paper in 2012 through several EU directives and the Dublin Regulation, the absence of such rules in practice was becoming strikingly obvious since late summer 2015. At that time, the Dublin system – according to which border countries are responsible for any asylum-seeker entering the Schengen area through their territory – had already broken down and border countries waived asylum-seekers through towards traditional host countries in Northern Europe. In late August 2015 severe human rights violations were becoming obvious in Hungary, a country with only a recent history of receiving refugees. Germany, later followed by Austria and Sweden, thus unilaterally suspended the Dublin Regulation for (Syrian) asylum-seekers in Hungary.

Much attention was given to the "refugee crisis" to alleviate the fact that Europe had also failed to offer security to ordinary working people and society's most vulnerable, many of whom were becoming increasingly restless and discontent (Winlow et al., 2017). As some European economies continue to struggle to shake off the hangover of the 2008 financial crisis – and will almost certainly need to shake off the fallout which will follow the 2020 coronavirus outbreak – many people continue to be left behind. Increasingly social ills are blamed on people like economic migrants, refugees and asylum seekers, all of whom are often projected as a social and economic threat to nation states livelihood and collective well-being (Garcés, 2015). Instead of, for example, the collective media and political attention being focused on how refugees have come to seek a better life, they are blamed for having left what they had – even if it had been destroyed in front of them (Briggs, 2017). In the words of Fekete (2018: 105), they are "criminalised twice over: first, as illegal immigrants and secondly, as an army of preying destitutes, scrounging off the welfare state". This is why it is common to find present in European discourses a reference to a "crisis of values" which, according to Onghena (2015: 7), is that,

> While on one hand border closure initiatives and restrictive migration policies come about, on the other, messages of unity, resistance and moral panics come about.

The growth in nationalistic rhetoric therefore pertains to this supposed crisis of European values – even though the same Europe is responsible for leaving its own citizens behind in the wake of the financial crisis having imposed austerity measures on the working population in exchange for allowing inequality to continue to expand at a rate never before witnessed in history (Žižek, 2016). As Zimmerman (2016: 1) aptly summarises,

> The refugee crisis soon became a political crisis that gave rise to populist parties. The topic was more and more mixed up with other migration issues, economic or educational migration, welfare migration and even internal EU labour mobility. Brexit, the surprising vote of the British to move out of the European Union was another unforeseen act fuelled by miscommunicated migration concerns. The migration topic suddenly is determining elections in member-states and causing large disagreements about possible European approaches to solve the crisis. Hence, the migration issue acts like a catalyst in an endgame of the European Union, although it is only misused in the face of weak political structures. The current crisis can be seen as a crisis of Europe and its institutions, and not one of European migration. Refugees and internal labour mobility have not been the cause of the crisis, although for some it is a most welcome by-product.

This provokes, suggests Slavoj Žižek (2016), a kind of "ideological blackmail" in the way in which Europe is welcoming refugees in with "open arms" while at the same time "pulling up the drawbridge." For example, hundreds of thousands of people have been given asylum in countries such as Germany – given the potential for their contribution to the economy at a time when an increasingly ageing population needs them – yet at the same time, countries such as the UK, Norway and Denmark have deployed a political rhetoric of rejection coupled with revanchist social policies against "foreigners." The latter in particular was internationally criticised in 2016 when it introduced a new law which made family repatriations more complex and confiscated refugees valuables, arguing that they would need the revenue to pay for their support (AFP, 2016). Nations have instead tightened controls on irregular access to Europe, but these restrictions have instead made refugee border crossings more precarious and risky (Zimmerman, 2016). This is reflected in the asylum statistics. The EU received 1.2 million applications for asylum in 2015, but by 2018, this had dropped to 580,845 (DW, 2019b). More and more people were rejected. In 2018, for example, the number of accepted asylum cases dropped by 40% to 333,400 people compared to 2017 (DW, 2019b).

Plug the hole that drains refugees into Europe

The EU then controversially paid Turkey €6 billion to reduce the number of refugees entering into Europe and to assist with funding, for example, the cost of over half a million Syrian children (Haferlach and Kurban, 2017). Research from the United Nations International Children's Emergency Fund' (UNICEF) in 2017 found, however, that 40% of "school-going aged" (380,000) children were missing out on education. Many were instead often working in exploitative conditions or were homeless. Having seen Istanbul, Izmir and Ankara littered with homeless children over two visits in 2015 and 2016, it was difficult for me to see indications that this money actually reached the most vulnerable children in this study.

This was evident one day when I met Emre – a young Turkish man who works for an NGO which helps Syrian children in Ankara. His agency was founded in 2011 just after the Syrian war started and was meant to help the children since at the time there was none. "There is still none from the government," he tells me as we walk around the city. "This year alone, I have been involved in helping 400 children directly and that is just me," he says as we collect donations of food and clothes from his office before driving to various neighbourhoods around the city depositing them. "Here it is bad but the camps at the borders are the worst, there are thousands of children there, none with ID or money or basics. The government give poor people some money in this country but not Syrians," he adds. He then recalls how he found a family in a bus station in the city. He says "family," but it transpired that it was just five children since their father had died in Syria and their mother had been sectioned in hospital for mental health reasons. The five children were sleeping in a bus station and the eldest who was just 15 years old sold tissues to stationary traffic, while her brothers and sisters begged and cleaned shoes.

From terror to terrorism

In any case, despite this funding, it didn't mean that refugees still didn't get through on the Turkey–Greece route. As this study concluded (in August 2018), already 102,700 refugees had made the same crossing (UNHCR, 2019b). They come into a politically and socially fragile Europe, perhaps even more so because of the increased terrorist attacks across the continent (Dimitrov and Angelov, 2017) which have carefully been exploited by political factions to increase social alarm about the pseudo enemy of ISIS and the "Islamic terrorist" (Žižek, 2016). Refugees journey from one threat (terror) to be on the brunt of another (terrorism). Curiously, the concern has continued to be exercised about the "refugee" even though in numerous cases the attackers/perpetrators of these very same attacks have almost all been European-born citizens (Briggs, 2017; Žižek, 2016):

FIGURE 16   Refugees follow the news about the Paris terrorist attacks in November 2015.

Three days after leaving Paris in November 2015, I receive a message from Mohamed attached with a photo (see Figure 16). In the picture, refugees watch in horror at the atrocities unfolding from the suicide bombers in the suburbs. The message reads, "We are fearful too. We did not expect to flee violence and death to then see it happen where we want to be safe." Throughout 2017 and 2018, there were sustained protests to speed up asylum and integration programmes in Paris. Nevertheless, hundreds of refugees are still sleeping rough in France's capital (see Wilkins, 2018).

Hence, a sort of self-punishing rhetoric has evolved in which Europe blames its own free movement approach for the installation of radicalisation and related problems to the seemingly never-ending influx of people from outside its borders. This has translated into a kind of warped social fact which has since evolved into increased nationalistic policies, increase in far-right popularity and hardened social attitudes towards refugees, migrants and asylum seekers – perhaps most evident in the increase in hate crimes across Europe, particularly against those who follow Islamic faith (EUAFR, 2016).

And what happens on the ground, in the streets, in the camps, in the centres? How do refugees experience their "new life" as they come to terms with having left their country and now face the stark reality of starting from scratch under these political and social conditions. Remember that many arrive with traumas and mental health illnesses related to the experiences in their countries and the border crossings (Bogic et al., 2012; Strang and Quinn, 2019). Reception centres are overcrowded, the conditions are inadequate (Chapter 1; Peace and Meer, 2019) and, in the face of homelessness, refugees have to be creative with the alternatives (see Figure 17). Social housing is often unavailable in large cities (Kearns

FIGURE 17 Overcrowded reception centres means some refugees wash in polluted wastewater from Melilla, Spain.

and Whitley, 2015; Doomernik and Ardon, 2018; Glorius, and Doomernik, (2020) even then housing is often inadequate and substandard (Zimmerman, 2016), and this perpetuates problems with refugees' mental health because of a lack of stable housing (Porter and Haslam, 2005). Learning languages are complex, education systems are different, and adjusting to the mode of life including the meritocratic expectancy there now is for them to work themselves into security (Briggs and Cordero, 2018).

This is despite the fact that managing labour integration hinges on the receiving country's "complementarity/sustainability" and whether there is a demand for the kind of skill set refugees or other migrants bring (Peace and Meer, 2019). In Germany – the country which has received most asylum applications – it is estimated that the country needs 260,000 new migrant workers per year until 2060 to meet labour shortages because of an ageing population (DW, 2019a). Similarly, labour demand is required in the UK. The Brexit vote of 2016 in the UK divided the country and perpetuated anti-migrant sentiment. Foreign workers, both skilled and unskilled, started to leave the country because of the high levels of xenophobia. In 2017, it was estimated that there was a 20% labour shortfall in the fruit- and vegetable-picking industries (Carrington, 2017) and in 2019, thousands of European workers in the National Health Service left their jobs (Savage, 2019). Yet many of the new arrivals to Europe during this period of this study of 2015–2018 were either low-skilled and already economically vulnerable or overqualified for many menial jobs. Both cohorts faced more difficulty due to technological change, thus complicating their medium- to long-term integration (Barslund et al., 2018) – even if there is a demand for labour.

Contractual integration

The graphic engineering course Shizar had started in Syria some years back suddenly looks quite redundant and out of date when he arrived in Germany and subsequently reapplied for asylum. Tired from the journey, and already weak from a lack of medication, meant he spent the early part of his time in hospital in Dresden. There the doctors made change after change to his medication for his Multiple Schlorosis (MS) which left him tired and docile. Even after eight months, he was still hospital-bed bound, and on receiving a successful application for asylum, he was required to sign a contract stipulating his commitment to language and integration courses to eventually be productive in the labour market. His slow recuperation from changes to his medication, however, jeopardised the commitment he could make to the language courses, and this slowed his progress: he had only 18 months to complete the language course and embark on a training programme. He also felt edgy when he went out in public feeling an air of social tension from "people who look at me, staring at me."

The refugee exodus evident in these refugee testimonies clearly tested the foundations of European social and asylum policy as well as the structural limitations of domestic asylum systems and processes. Such was the system stretched by the demand on it that a general trend was for refugees, having been granted asylum and protection for a limited period, to have to sign contracts binding them pass integration or language tests/exams. The mandatory courses which followed presented more challenges, of which many were adversely affected by if they failed to pass tests/exams (Carrera and Vankova, 2019). This was reinforced by the fact that integration measures were often not well designed for the specific needs of refugees, which increases the risk of discrimination. Additional conditions such as income thresholds, long waiting periods and pressure on housing and reduced financial benefits further restrict family reunion and settlement by making procedures more burdensome and ineffective. In the following field notes, all of the above become evident. I travelled south to Córdoba in Spain to reunite myself with Abdul, whom I met through my first contact Abbas in Melilla, Spain. We were reunited at Easter in 2017, 20 months after having met in August 2015.

Tapas but no success

On a humid and overcast day, I arrive in Córdoba at the height of the Easter festivities and floods of Chinese tourists. Parking on the outskirts, I walk in past the closed bars, of which some start to slowly get out the tables looking heavy-headed in the process. There are a few markets out at this early hour for a Sunday and among them are coin-collector stands, jewellery and bric-a-brac table which has old children's comics on sale next to second-hand porno magazines.

As the old centre of the city starts to warm up, and the bars and cáfes get busy again, I get a call from Abdul. After I left him in August, he has spent a few more months in the camp, even less time in Spain, and then tried to seek work in Germany. Like three of the five friends I meet who also did the same, there was a belief that – regardless of the Dublin convention which requires you to stay in the country in which you seek asylum – Germany would still take them in. That offer expired, however, at the end of August 2016 when the German govern-ment started rejecting more cases – as I found only a few weeks previously when I found myself talking to numerous Iraqi refugees from Dusseldorf in Germany who had had their applications rejected.

I wait around at the entrance to the Roman Bridge in Córdoba and soon after a shaven-headed, cleanly trimmed beard Abdul embraces me. "¿Qué tal amigo mio?" he says as he smiles broadly; he looks well and healthy. He shows me over to a pack of eight other refugees who wait and look over the brown river which runs through the ancient arches. I shake all their hands and speaking in English and Spanish just hope I can hold the interview. Last time, Abdul and I had Abbas as a translator, but this time I rely on his new friend Masood who has a good level of English. We walk up past the Mezquita and into the depths of the old city, passing droves of tourists and drunken locals who make polite fun of us in the festivities as they drink and enjoy tapas – we stand out like a sore thumb. It's clear that Abdul and his friends don't really come into the city centre much.

Eventually we arrive at a square and sit down and order some refreshments. Jesus on my immediate left, who smokes continuously, barely speaks Spanish but manages to convey to me that in a few months he hopes his whole "family will come from Syria." Masood sits opposite me – who is from a small town in Syria which was geographically set between the war factions of Assad and ISIS – his hometown more than anything being the place where most of the bombs and missiles failed to hit their intended targets. Diagonally to my right are two brothers – Muhamad and Ahmed – whose Spanish is non-existent and have a his-tory of working in ceramic industry in Syria; Ahmed seems constantly nervous and has numerous burns and scars up his arm. Denra, a young man in a cap with a beard, arrives shortly after – a man who tried for ten months to cross the border from Morocco to Spain, trying on average he says "ten times a day."

As we start to talk, the main problems come to the service immediately: the language support and training is at best extremely poor. It relies on vol-unteers, since there is no direct funding for refugee language courses, so it

FIGURE 18 Discussing "integration" in Córdoba with Abdul (bottom left corner) and his friends.

means as Denra says, "some weeks there is a class, other weeks there isn't." "It is just not serious, you cannot call this serious, I can learn Spanish from my friends but if I want to learn it so that I can take a course to then be able to take a job, then it is just not enough," says Wasel. Research shows that in Spain, despite the high demand for programmes and classes relating to language, culture and training, there are limited spaces and, in the long delay of having to wait, this "interrupts" their integration (CEAR, 2016). Refugees have no choice but to leave the country or find irregular, poorly paid and exploitative work.

They have been on mainland Spain for nearly eight to nine months now, a few having been sent back from Germany having tried to go there. Even then, they say, that even if they were to be able to improve in the language, there are no real courses which they can take to be able to get work. They compete with tens of thousands of other Spanish people in the region who are unemployed. The Andalucian domestic economy is still depressed having failed to recover from the exodus of its rural workers during the 1980s and 1990s and major deindustralisation from the turn of the 21st century, which was exacerbated by the crisis of 2008. Time is also running out for the contract they signed to learn the language which had bound with it the €300 per month which expires in ten months in February 2018. In this time, they are expected to learn a language, get secure housing and get work. After that, integration is supposedly "complete": they lose the benefit, and they lose the accommodation and will be on the street. They say they know 50 other Syrians in the city, 10 who speak reasonable Spanish but none of whom have a job.

Housing, education, employment and health

We sit there and the conversation comes to a natural standstill. I sigh and turn off the recorder. There isn't much you can say. "You know we escaped death to come here," says Wasel before Jesus starts to mumble in Arabic, and Wasel translates, "he says that in his town, he saw ISIS kill people." "In my town, if you didn't join the army, they killed you – if you didn't show you would die for Assad, you died yourself, I saw this, I saw people lose their heads for it," says Abdul pausing from time to time. They then say that there was some offer of work in a strawberry factory which someone told them when that they "needed 100 workers," but "if you are not first in the queue, then forget it," says Denra. "This has happened a few times, we have found out about this low-paid cash in hand work, but it never comes off. They say they will call you but you end up waiting and no call comes. In the end, they only need a few people rather than 10 of us," says Wasel. Note how, in the absence of full capacity in the language, the only opportunities are in the black market or informal economy where refugee labour is open to potential exploitation. No surprise that, after starting again in Spain, at the beginning of 2018, Abdul fled to Germany to "start again" – once again.

All aboard the fast train to neoliberal meritocracy: destination "integration"

In this study, asylum and subsequent protection from the host state were riddled with varying conditions which bind refugees to housing, courses, programmes, training and exams, among other things. While I haven't compared distinct ways in which how EU states have done this, the main message seems to be "we will protect you for a while as long as you learn the language and get a job in that time – if not, well you're on your own." The degree to which this "alignment" process is achieved felt easier for younger refugees, perhaps reflected in this brief exchange with these two Syrian young men while on the train in Essen, Germany.

At the next stop in Essen a young German woman with heavy make-up and thick eyebrows boards. Another young man sits next to her and next to me sits a large German woman who sits and breaths heavily as she plays Sudoku on her phone. The young woman who can't stop using her phone gulps down a can of fizzy drink and leaves it on the small table by the side which has other rubbish dumped on it, while the young man next to her bobs his head slowly to his music. A beggar then comes up and down the train aisle with his hand open, and as he passes, a stale smell follows him. He speaks openly, from what I can gather from my broken German, about needing some money for food and gets either cold looks from the passengers or no look at all.

There we sit for 15 minutes or so until all three get off at the next stop. Soon after, two young men who speak Arabic to each other get on: one sits next to me and his friend sits opposite. Seconds later, an old German man squeezes between us to insist on taking the spare seat opposite me. For a while I look out of the window, but as the one diagonally opposite me starts to sift through his plastic folder of documents, I get interested. He takes out first a certificate where I can see it has his birthplace as Syria so I interrupt him.

"Excuse me, is this a language certificate," I say, and the old German man opposite me stares at me and the two young men look at each other before the one next to me who is unshaven tries to speak English "Ja, I mean yes," he says and laughs to himself. I ask if I can take a closer look and reach across at the papers and take a closer look. The young man who sits diagonal to me as I try to understand this achievement. The certificate says that Fayiz, who is 23 years old by the looks of his date of birth and from Syria, has attained C1 in German. I congratulate him and ask him how long it took for him to achieve it and he says, "18 months." He eagerly digs around in the folder and hands me another one. This one is for "business German" it seems as he adds, "I studied business in Syria before I came here, soon I will start an internship so I can try to get a job." I smile and flick through the other certificates for cultural courses and other exam results, all of which look high. Meanwhile his friend, who sits next to me, looks slightly envious of the achievements. Still, he also smiles and says, "it is very hard but we have to study every day or we don't get an opportunity for a job." With that, they suddenly shuffle the papers together as we approach the next stop.

While I am not able to conclude how many people were "integrated" over the course of my study, it was clear that it very much seemed to be an ongoing process which people hoped to obtain over the period in which they had been given asylum protection. While there is debate around what "successful integration" is (Dubus, 2018), and a lack of directive guidance on behalf of the EU, most empirical research tends to analyse "case studies" or "programme evaluations" which produce "best practice policy advice," particularly at a regional level (Niemann and Zaun, 2018; Scardigno, 2019). In this study, I have favoured covering what Ager and Strang (2008) call the four markers of integration: housing, education, employment and health. While these markers appear as separate variables in their work as it does in that of other researchers (Zimmerman, 2016; Oduntan and Ruthven, 2017), in mine, I found that they very much overlapped and intertwined with each other. By this, I mean that it's to say that secure and adequate housing correlated with better educational performance and health outcomes or a combination. For a minority of the people I met such as Modar, this was their experience.

I board the train once again and travel some 20 minutes to Den Haag or The Hague in the Netherlands. Down the stairs, and across the familiar organisation of Dutch train stations (which resemble those in Belgium and Germany), I walk around to the end of the hall. There, turning left into a small passageway, waits Modar, a young 24-year-old man from Syria who has been here in the country for about 18 months. I greet him and look for a suitable café to talk. As we walk, he moans about how his second bike has just been stolen (the first he bought for €200 and after that was stolen, he paid €50 for the second – it is common for bikes to be stolen in the country). After wandering around the train station aimlessly, we find one and settle for a table inside. Perhaps less nervous now he has been granted asylum, this young man only smokes between 20 and 25 cigarettes a day: while awaiting the asylum application he was going through between 40 and 50 a day.

We start our conversation in the plush and clean surroundings of a café. He left Syria in 2015, shortly after I began my study in Melilla, North Africa. In fact, as it transpires, we both were in Izmir in Turkey at roughly the same time – though he was boarding the rubber dinghies and I was simply passing among people who were waiting for them.

Like all young men in Syria, he was approaching an age at which military service was expected of him. And like most of them, he "didn't want to kill anyone" as he says. Though his family is still in Damascus, he left with about €3,000 to make the journey into Europe. Though he was not alone, he had agreed to leave with five friends of similar age – all of them studying university degrees. The military service would normally be delayed, but he explains that such was the demand for young men to enter into the army to fight for Assad that he would have had to cut short his studies to serve.

None of his friends wanted to kill either which is while, even though they left at different times, after crossing into Lebanon, they met in Turkey to board dinghies. This was only after he slept in the streets for two days as he tried to cross the border. When he met his five friends in September 2015, they tried three times to board boats to Greece; the first two were cancelled because of the presence of the Turkish coastguard on the nearby waters. On the third, they were lucky for two reasons: (1) that among them there was a fisherman from their city in Syria who was able to drive the boat and (2) that the weather was calm. In Chios, he stayed for several days before taking a large ferry to Athens, all the time with his friends and all the time heading for his desired destination Germany.

He took a bus to the border of Hungary, which left him several hours walk to the border. As he crossed, international journalists said it was safe and that their fingerprints would not be taken as the border police were taking a break. They walked and then took another bus to the border of Austria, got off, walked again over the border and boarded another bus. "After I arrive in Vienna, I start to relax as I know that the tough part of the journey is over," he says.

In Vienna, however, things were complicated as his friends in Germany said it was difficult to get in and that he should try another country which was when they suggested the Netherlands. After being separated from two friends in Germany, he continued on with the other three to the Netherlands where they presented themselves to the services. Within 26 days he had crossed from his home country to arrive in Den Haag and had only six months to wait for a decision on his case. "Every day I was worried, worried they were going to send me back," he says reflecting on that uncertain period.

However, he was granted stay for five years and is expected to, within that time, achieve a B2 in Dutch and make himself useful in society. Of course, this was tricky for the first six months as he was moved from refugee centre to refugee centre, and after being granted stay, settled in Utrecht. There he has stayed sharing a flat with another young man of a similar age from the city of Homs. In that time, he made some good progress with the language. His English too has improved. However, it's difficult to see how he will be able to continue his law studies in a country in which legal system functions very differently to his. Moreover, he worries that he will never get to the standard where he can learn the relevant legal terms.

Welcome to hotel neoliberalism: reservations only, and even if there were vacancies, no special discount for refugees

While it may be the case that Modar won't be able to use his university studies in the Netherlands, he still has a good shot at integration and a future in the Netherlands. His housing is secure, and he is learning the language and making good progress and has started to make friends with other refugees and Dutch people. I found, however, that the reverse of this equation seemed also the case – that is, poor or unstable housing encroached on educational possibility and/or performance as well as had negative impact on health thus making it almost impossible to get work. Evidence shows that during the time of this study there was a lack of information about the skills and competences of refugees newly arrived in Europe (Bordignon and Moriconi, 2017). This means that previous experience almost counts for nothing and this was the general experience for most of the people I met.

In Amien, France, I met Galal in an overcrowded run-down hostel for refugees. He is from Damascus where he studied for two years a Mathematics and Economics degree but was not able to finish his studies because of the onset of the war. He had wanted to go to Germany, but at the time, French NGOs had started to try and ease the burden of refugee reception and he was among 50 who were taken into France. While "Amiens is a beautiful city," he says, "there is no work here not only for us but also for French people. We make protests about it." He lives in an overcrowded hostel where this is a lot of "tense" as he describes it between people. He is deeply critical of the support:

GALAL: We spend our days looking for work, going to the library to learn French as we don't have too many French friends. I speak a basic French. I understand it but when I talk it is very difficult. The programme is very bad, the classes. It is a waste of time. We had to wait three months before we went on to a class and then we attend and we have already missed the basic part so this is why we go to the library. One day it is culture, another day history, there is an exam on the same day and we don't understand the questions and there is no one to translate so we take the answers from answers. They are not serious courses as sometimes the teacher even tells us the answers. We can't get jobs as we don't have the basic language.

The structure of support does not go far enough and local charities have to support him as well as others:

GALAL: Because I am under 25 I don't receive money from the government, I get a charity donation of 180 Euro a month and I don't pay rent as I am housed with young people. People over 25 get 400 Euro. I know all the Syrians here, about 40 of them: three of them have work and about 15 speak French quite well.

DAN: So even the ones who speak French well don't find work?

GALAL: Like the French, there is not work for them either. We are afraid, always worry especially Marie Le Pen when she talks about sending us away.

This causes him much stress as he feels he doesn't have a future in France, on top of the fact he has not seen his fiancée in two years and their arrival relies on his settlement: learning the language and getting work to support them all. "I would go back now if only the war finish," he concludes. This is what European states want, isn't it? Note how the political climate impinges directly on Galal's emotional state, adding more anxiety and worry to his settlement experience (Chapter 2). Naturally, Galal's story is not representative of every refugee, but the way this research has been done specifically highlights the shortfalls of intervention and integration efforts because the fieldwork has been in precisely the places outside official government premises and formal processes. This study is not an evaluation of a particular integration programme nor has made an assessment over one particular mode of refugee integration. Galal like many almost every one I met experience major difficulties concerning the language, culture and education and work opportunities and find it complicated to simply culturally adjust to what is expected of them. This seemed mainly to do with an unfamiliarity with the meritocratic cultural expectation to work for oneself – a concept which was almost alien to most since they had come from countries where social capital seemed to be more prevalent rather than human capital (see Bourdieu, 1984; Briggs and Cordero, 2018). For me, the mismatch between cultural and professional expectations of refugees in Europe is out of sync with their cultural heritage, life histories, experiences and circumstances as was confirmed to me when I went to revisit Abbas in Germany 18 months after having met him in Spain.

After an emotional reunion at the train station, Abbas introduces me to Ahmad and I am invited to see where he is housed along with 40 other refugees. He locks up his bike and says, "come this way, but we need to come back as I need to borrow a bike for you." "Why?" I ask. "Because the refugee friends are a few miles away and we need to go by bike," he answers as we cycle down the intimate streets of this sleepy, rural German town. We come to a junction, cross over the road and turn right and between nice houses; there is in the middle of this square next to the fire station, one of numerous refugee housing centres.

I can only describe it as a building nobody wanted even when it was in use for something useful; it is a kind of hut-annex thing which is yellow and dire need of modernisation.

We walk inside into the dirty floors and the whiff of fried onion hits us as someone cooks a basic dish combined with pasta. I follow the smell to the kitchen which is a large room with sealed windows, three small cookers decorated with impregnable stains and a few pots and pans; the only window available to open is forced as far ajar as possible so the odour can escape, but it ends up circulating into everyone's bedrooms. Refugees come in and out and look at me oddly as they fiddle with the stoves on which they have their food cooking. To my left as I come out are the toilets and showers, and stepping over the dirty puddles, I take a look and say how they could probably do with being replaced. Opposite them are where the rooms begin, each one sleeping about four to five refugees from mostly Syria and Iraq: as Germany shuts its borders and tightens control over admission in the country, Iraqi refugees seem to be the ones having their cases rejected.

Abbas shows me inside his room which composes of four bunk beds to the right, a single bed on which his friend Ahmad sits cross legged, a small fridge, a table and a very makeshift mirror brown taped to the wall. I see a drawing one of the German children did for Abbas and take a closer look before sitting down on the bed opposite Ahmad as he moves the cigarettes from the side and offers me a coffee. I duck my neck under the bunk bed and sit on the unmade bed putting my coffee on the stool in front of us. Ahmad starts to share his story. He left in 2012 having only been able to save enough money to get to Turkey. There he did poorly paid packing jobs and worked for another year to be able to afford the high costs for the boat crossing. Having left his fiancée back in Syria, and having not seen her for nearly five years, he was finally able to afford the boat crossing – even after the low wages mostly went on his high rents for refugees in Istanbul. Remember there is always a business attached to misery.

When he finally did cross in the middle of the night, he remembers the training given to one of the volunteer drivers lasted about ten minutes and consisted of advice such as "head for the lights, that's Greece." Thereafter the 70 people who were crammed in a boat with a capacity of 40 set off on the rough waves, and on the way, they passed two overturned boats and numerous bags and rucksacks floating aimlessly in the sea. He used the rest of his money to get to Germany, but his dream of getting to the UK was cut short as he ran out of money; he was told that smuggling costs to get to the British Isles exceeded €2,000 and they were not guaranteed. So he presented himself in Germany. It took one year to decide his case after which time he was only given one year of protection in Germany meaning, after that time, he would have to leave: unless he formalised a legal challenge which is what he is doing.

When I ask about learning German, he says he struggles and can't access the courses yet because it is related to his legal status. While he concedes to being safe which is the main thing, he is worried for his fiancée and family who are still trying to survive in Syria. He bites his nails as Abbas sits next to him on the bed with a cigarette. The danger is that Ahmad will complete that year and become a nomad in Europe.

Stateless citizens

Thus far, I have talked about a small number of refugees who seemed to have made some slow progress towards some form of "integration" and a wider group who, while having received asylum status, struggle on courses, with languages and work and, consequently experience high levels of stress and anxiety and like depression. There are another pool of refugees who await a response and feel stuck in a stagnant system. Many abandon their application having lost hope or, having received rejection, drift around Europe (UNHCR, 2018c). Eurostat estimates that since 2014 there have been 3.6 million asylum applications in EU countries, of which only 1.8 million have resulted in legal protection (DW, 2019b). So where did the other 1.8 million people go?

Other data confirms this trend as the rejection rate for European asylum applications almost doubled in three years, from 37% in 2016 to 64% in 2019 (Tondo, 2019). Even Germany, the country which at the end of 2017 had "protected" 1,410,000 refugees, then rejected almost three-quarters of family reunification applications from Greece in 2019 (BAMF, 2019). Unsurprisingly, the experience in reception countries like Greece and Italy is one of frustration and permanent delay. With the explosion of the exodus in 2015, a relocation scheme was devised in reception countries such as Italy and Greece. However, by 2017, of the 106,000 asylum seekers who were part of relocation schemes in Italy and Greece, only 13,546 had been resettled in other European countries (Dimitrov and Angelov, 2017). With Turkey taking extremely slow steps towards integrating the millions of refugees coming through the country (İçduygu and Millet, 2016), the EU relocation programme in essence was a shambles and left reception countries disproportionately overloaded with refugees (Bordignon and Moriconi, 2017): the sheer volume of arrivals clogs up a Greek social system already overburdened with debt, reduced public services and relative little political interest in funding what are seen to be "problematic groups" (Moris and Kousoulis, 2018).

Permanent delays to "integration": Eleonas Camp, Athens

We meet outside Eleonas metro station near a mass industrial estate in suburbs of Athens. The traffic is heavy and constant as we cross the broken road past rubbish bins and take a right turn down a dusty road. All around us are buildings which are something between Half started, half-finished and half-forgotten. Heavy lorries whisk up the dust as we reach the end of the road, where there is a huge pile of rubbish; a stray dog fishes out some food and scampers off just before the rubbish is run over by another lorry.

This dusty road gets busier as we walk past a deserted factory and start to see a high wall beyond which the metal cabin roofs peak over. We have arrived at the Eleonas refugee camp, marked by a slow-moving metal door which opens and closes as if only god commanded it so. We walk in and are greeted by three reception staff who ask us to wait under a corrugated iron roof as they go off to find our contact, Dimitrius. As we wait, some workers feed a small puppy; it hungrily scoffs down a sausage pie even mistaking the paper bag for food and eating it.

Dimitrius then comes out and invites us to his office – a similar sort of metal cabin to the refugee homes. He invites us in and sits back in his chair and says how they [the workers] "give them hope." This is something which he keeps saying to me over the course of the day as if to reassure himself that his role is not completely impotent in the housing, social and emotional support and relocation of 2,000 refugees.

As I explain about the research, he leads us around the camp. He says up until 2015, 8,000 people were arriving each day to Athens but at the moment it is more like 5,000. "They still come by sea although the winter not so busy (although its cheaper)," he says. The camp as such holds 2,000 people but given the current renovations, made obvious by the scattered broken mattresses and bed springs which sit piled up awaiting attention, should only hold 1,500. The metal cabins were moved here only as recently as 2015 when the camp opened; interestingly they were recruited in from an area outside the city constructed to help the 50,000 people who were displaced after the 1999 earthquake.

We walk around this small community in this forgotten part of Athens and in and out of three different zones determined by nationality and culture. There is a safe zone where minors are kept under guard 24 hours a day and in the middle is a makeshift football pitch. In the main activity outside the metal cabins is minimal and most people seem to keep themselves to themselves.

We walk on and down to an area which houses the Afghani community. "We see more Afghanis," Dimitrius says to me: perhaps unsurprising given that the mess between the Taliban and the US army continue to wreak havoc on the country. Quite impressively, here in this narrow pathway where one can almost touch the cabins opposite, the quality of the buildings seems better and the pathway is adorned by plants and shrubs, other thrown-away bits and bobs and unwanted industrial bric-a-brac. This is because the refugees have searched the surrounding derelict industrial sites for rubbish and disused material to complement their small abodes. It is clear they have been here for some time. As we walk, above us hang an old tarpaulin between the narrow alleyway, outside the houses on the steps the children's shoes sit neatly in order by size, and even small plants sit on window sills which have been laid to create a sense of dignity. A cat runs between us as an Afghani man holds his baby daughter and gets her to wave at us as we pass. I say hello to another woman in the window who smiles and we walk to the end where there is another tarpaulin hanging from between a tree and a low electricity pylon. In the middle there is a rag which covers a series of stacked wooden pallets which is a table and around it panels a mixture of cushions and foams – it is the communal kitchen.

We are then shown into the camp's nursery, which is composed of one metal cabin. Inside 15 children or so, mostly under the age of five, potter around and find things to play with. One young boy comes up to me, smiles and shakes my hand. Though these are the youngest children, others who are older go to Greek schools, and a few already speak the language quite well. In the camp itself, English and Greek are available to learn, though most seem to see little point in Greek because of the dire circumstances of the economy and even "Greeks can't get jobs," says Dimitrius.

We walk back and turn left into the second zone where mostly Syrians are living. The dusty path widens and between the cabins sit old bikes, rubbish and some broken toys. In one such space there is a cracked mirror which perches on an old dresser cupboard and opposite is an old office chair which has been repaired with gaffer tape. On the floor around, and scattering the plywood panels which overlap each other, is swathes of hair – it is the local barbers (see Figure 19). On we walk, past an old woman who sits cross-legged and sets up a stove in the middle of this small community; she folds over the small stove and starts to prepare food over the fire she has just lit, before cutting up vegetables with her frail hands. She also smiles at us.

FIGURE 19 The local barber shop.

Dimitrus then dumps us at the door of the social work and psychology office. Inside it is warm as the team of five women sit in their coats and look timidly at us. We explain the nature of the research and the two young students do most of the translation. There are little more than quite official and short responses to our questions about the refugees' problems. The responses are also fairly surface like for they seem to think that the only stresses the refugees have, the men and women, respectively, relate to the fact that the men can't find work and the women were stressed because they have to look after their numerous children. Absent was much understanding or explanation of the likely traumas the refugees experienced, and it felt more like the professionals were guessing what the refugees were worried about and had little insight into the refugee experiences. This certainly seemed to be confirmed when we were led to meet one of the local translators and the Syrian families.

In 2018, Greece entered its eighth consecutive year of recession, Gross Domestic Product (GDP) had shrunk a quarter in ten years and unemployment was nearly one-fifth of the population (19%) (Voutsina, 2019). Note how the stagnancy of the Greek economy directly affects motivations to learn languages and work. The longer people wait, the more their hope and motivation wanes to "integrate." In Eleonas there was evidence of some families making more permanent their homes, while others, as we saw with Nasir in Chapter 7, start to see their mental health deteriorate.

In Hafeez's case, it was his physical health and difficult with the Italian language that impinged on hopes that he could find work and settle in Italy – a country which continues to grow in public debt and inequality (Romei, 2018). At the time of our meeting, he was 18 years old having arrived in Siracuse, Italy, more or less one year ago. He came alone and left family back in Syria. At the moment, he attends an educational day centre in Palermo, Sicily, and has been there for the last eight months undertaking different languages courses but has made slow progress as the standard seems basic. "It is not enough for you to get work," he says. He has grave health problems, in the main caused having contracting a disease while travelling from Syria to Libya and not been able to seek medical help. While he is getting better, he has "weak days," he says. The educational centre helped him complete his asylum application when he arrived as a minor one year ago. He says the most difficult things are the language and looking for a job. Though he has attended carpentry workshops and been making a bench for the refugee centre, he can't see how this will translate to potential paid work, adding:

> It was hard to arrive in Italy, with a different culture, habits, language, etc… But what is most hard is my health situation. I have a safe place to sleep but that is all. I wonder if I have a future here.

Médecins Sans Frontières (2016) indicated that between July 2015 and February 2016, 89% of people they attended in Italian reception centres had suffered traumatic experiences from border crossings and 60% had suffered the same in their home country. Like Hafeez, this had left them with either psychological or physical injuries. When either delays to asylum application or difficulty in attending/completing courses or finding work within already squeezed domestic economies combines with wider political processes to destabilise refugees, it damages motivation to integrate (Marbach et al., 2018). There is almost a reluctant acknowledgement that it may have all been in vain. Others having heard about the state of the economies in Spain, Italy and Greece, as we have seen, simply move north to the stronger states. There I found many who, having got tired in these reception countries or passing straight through them, simply were pinballed around central European countries such as France, Germany, Belgium, Austria, the Netherlands and Denmark.

Maybe this is where the other 1.8 million lurk: fallen between the nooks and crannies of "democratic societies," that promise equality and all its feel-good components but in reality are uninterested in really ensuring their safety. It is in these miscellaneous places, I found people who hadn't filed for asylum, perhaps feeling intimidated/fearful by the system, and/or having previously been rejected somewhere else. This pushes people into informal economies and illicit opportunities and heightens the risk to which they are exposed. It should be no surprise that ghetto camps like the Calais "Jungle" evolve to accommodate these surplus populations of stateless people, whose once burning desire to start again somewhere else at best now weakly flickers dimly.

The last corner in Europe: Calais "Jungle"

As we leave returning to the mud and rain, we take a right up the main pathway passing portable toilets which flap open revealing piss and shit everywhere. We pass suspiciously radioactive-coloured dykes and bushes from which dangle bits of rubbish and old clothing. We make our way towards the church – another wooden structure made in a similar fashion to most other buildings: a solid wooden frame which has nailed around it boards and insulation, covered with tarpaulins with a set of plastic roof panels; each Sunday it attracts up to 1,000 people. We walk in and are closely followed by the man who made it – Soloman, a tall Eritrean man who wears surprisingly few clothes and speaks excellent English. He stands tall and wide over us as he explains how he also wants to go to the UK and how his wife is already there. When he tells me he has lived in these conditions for one year, I shake my head in disbelief. He towers over me and puts his hand on my shoulder and says, "You think I joke with my life? I tell you that the French and British government joke with my life. Here is not Europe, here is place for animals. I will lose my wife because of this [and points around the camp]."

After we make a donation to the upkeep of the church, in the main to assist with the expensive heating costs, we continue in the mud passing mostly Afghan restaurants, cáfes, a liquor shop, makeshift hotels, hardware stores, supermarkets,

FIGURE 20 "3 Star hotel/restaurant" in the Calais Jungle.

everything which can service a small community and does so. There is then a gap in the road which leads out of the camp and about 100 metres away police vans line the street randomly stopping people as they enter. We continue for a few minutes longer before returning to eat exceptionally good food in one of the camp's restaurants (see Figure 20). Inside it feels like a hippy camp as people with unusually smiley faces and middle-class accents exchange their stories. They look to have come of their own volition from the UK to "help" in some way though from what we see they don't seem to do much other than pose for selfies and talk to some of the refugees.

We order two kebabs, rice lentils and a spinach thing and another yellow-coloured thing which Jeroen recommended. As we eat, we talk to a few volunteers from Oxford who have come a few times with donated goods. One of them says she "does the volunteering because I would hope someone would do it for me if I was in the same situation" before showing disdain for the BBC and its inaccurate reporting of the issue. She flicks her hair around before throwing it into a pony tail, while her husband muses on his mobile phone before saying in her middle-class accent how "[the refugee crisis] will be one of the defining moments of our generation." They then revert to their mobiles and Facebook profiles.

Jeroen and I then talk about the refugee situation in both France and Belgium and conclude that Belgian officials don't allow for camps to evolve but at the same time don't offer much in the form of accommodation and social support. It reminded me of the €7 of spare change which Asim showed me in Brussels two months ago, telling me it was his weekly allowance while he was waiting for a decision on his asylum application. As we continue down the straight road, Jeroen tells me a story of Syrian refugee who tried to swim across the 22-mile stretch of the English Channel, but instead his body was found half rotten on a Norwegian beach – he had drowned and his body had drifted up to Norway (BBC, 2015). "They traced the serial number of his wetsuit to a Decathlon in Calais," tells me Jeroen.

To this day there similar attempts, the most recent being in 2019 when an Iraqi man suffered the same fate having been swept up dead on a beach near Zeebrugge, Belgium: the report quoting Carl Decaluwé, the governor of West Flanders, by saying how he was found "covered in fish nets with plastic bottles, I think to make it more easy to swim for him." This is because there is never *a fate worse than trying again* as we found out in the Calais "Jungle" when we spoke to numerous refugees about their motivation to get to the UK by any means and at any length.

When we leave, we take a detour off the main road into some flooded areas of the camp where the mud level increases and head towards the dome – reported to be some discotheque by the Daily Mail. Today, however, it is rammed with anyone who can fit inside. As we wrestle ourselves inside somewhat, it seems there is a press conference to announce that the eviction of everybody in the camp has been postponed because a charity has found that more refugees were living in the camp than the French government suspected, and there were also unaccounted minors (the youngest being 10 years old) who have no parents here, which means more measures need to be put in place before people can be resettled elsewhere. There is cheering and celebration for some reason though the pressure of forcible eviction put in action by the French Government is sure to return.

We walk further into the heart of the camp away from the main street, and the paths become more hazardous and muddy. We come across a waste site which is connected to a nearby lake which if it rose any higher would easily flood around 20 tents. We pass several broken bikes with their wheels removed, and Jeroen says that in Dunkirk those parts are used so the refugees can peddle on them to charge their mobile phones. Here some tents lie in tatters, while others are left abandoned. As we approach the exit, three children walk up towards us with toys in their hands, while above us the helicopters continue to circle. Heading back to the car, a police horse van passes and we see blocks of ten police vans lined on one end of the street where we had parked our car. Even as we drive off, we pass a water cannon, and rows and rows of police vans. But there will be no eviction today. Celebration? I don't know. They are still stateless people living in appalling circumstances, and this is not the only camp in the region for when the last corner of Europe overcrowds, there is always the very last corner of Europe in Dunkirk.

The very last corner of Europe: Dunkirk

Within less than half an hour, we are pulling into Dunkirk, having past the uninhabited camp where the current camp will be moved with time between a highway and an industrial area – out of sight out of mind. We come in via the ring road turning right at the first roundabout into what looks like a standard

FIGURE 21 "Residential dreams, refugee realities."

residential town community, the houses sitting new and organised around finely cut lawns and public spaces (see Figure 21). However, within a few minutes, we see a few people standing around caked in mud on one street corner before a few others walk up the road. As we slow to take in what starts to appear, it can only be described as one of the most surreal things I have ever seen for behind a thin wall of trees sit hundreds of refugee tents sitting in a sea of mud a stone's throw away from these residential dreamworlds. Indeed, as we pass the entrance, one can see the project it was supposed to be before the camps developed. Not so much of a utopia now.

We drive on past droves of people who walk back and forth to the volunteer vans where clothes and shoes are distributed: the vans literally turn up and a sea of people crowd around to get what they can. The road bends around and we park up in a retail park which is next to this thin forest/refugee camp. We cross the car park and across to the pathway leading to the entrance, passing large stacks of untended rubbish as people pass with bags of new clothes, some even clutching new footwear. Every 10 or 15 metres, there are thrown away wellington boots and/or shoes which have been caked in mud. At the entrance, the police busily stop everyone entering and leaving the camp, looking in bags and coats – the objective being to deter major construction work taking place which could lead to the amplification of the camp. Jeroen tells me that the French government have tried to avert the camp expanding by preventing some types of donations but recently gave permission for any aid or material or donations to come in for one day. On that day came lorries and vans from the UK, Germany, Holland and Belgium. Though in practice the police presence at the entrance is a little tokenistic because one can easily smuggle things through the forest further down the road. We walk over and the policeman asks me to undo my jacket and open my bag before waving me into the mud camp.

FIGURE 22   The main road in the Dunkirk camp.

At the front is some information desk which looks to be mostly coordinating volunteers and the like, and inside there is a chaos about the place. Rubbish piles high in small mountains, tents look as if they have sunk in what I can only describe as a grey clay mud which varies in its density – in places it is watery and shallow, whereas in other places it is thick and deep (see Figure 22). There is a real lack in infrastructure and the organisation of Calais is far away. Here it is more like aid, urgent aid though one has to question why resources get used so quickly – half of the things which lie in the rubbish just need washing yet there is no service or intervention to do that. When things get wet or muddy or both, they are just thrown out. Valueless in a way because I suppose people know that there is a fairly endless supply of new goods; the concept of possessions seems to completely disappear. The closest thing to washing, just as in Calais, are the portable taps which are found from time to time where people shave and wash their hands and faces. Of course, there is no room for everyone and I see one young man crouching and balancing on one leg as he pours a bottle of water over his naked foot to wash it.

Walking up in the watery clay mud, white vans sit parked here and there and unload food, drink and clothes as people queue and argue with each other in the queues. To my left down this main channel, some children step on and off a wooden pallet which lies sunken in the mud before finding sticks to hit it. To my right, a boy sits having his hair cut in a t-shirt, tracksuit on a chair with what were white trainers now black. I stop from time to time to make an assessment of what it's like off this watery-clay pathway and look into a darker slop in which people wade through between their tents.

Here it is also estimated that 3,000 live and it is nothing short of dire. As we turn the corner to the free food kitchen, a child explores the toilet cubicles for

FIGURE 23 A typical pathway off the "main road."

one which has not been totally ruined; she opens several doors before pausing in the mud and returning to her family. Off the main pathway, there appears an open space which Jeroen says was a month or two ago a massive swamp mud pool (see Figure 23). Now it is just uninhabited. However, there is a rickety pathway of wooden pallets sitting over the mud leading to the food kitchen. We step between burnt tents and rubbish on to the pallets and follow the "grey-bricked road." Inside it is warm and there is a good feeling about the place. At the end, a team of volunteers man the kitchen dishing out food and drink to whoever needs it, while to the left, there are some seats and tables where people sit taking up half the room and smoke — mostly occupied by the volunteers leaving many of the refugees standing when they eat. On the other side, a few more tables have been armed with mobile phone chargers so people crouch round with their mobiles. There is little room other than to look around.

We leave as new boots and shoes are distributed to a queue of refugees on the walkway. Heading back towards the main path to the right, we follow a smaller path behind some tents and almost get stuck in the mud. We come out next to a dyke full of rubbish and the orchestration of a new wooden structure manned by volunteers who seem to be in the midst of discussing a logistical hitch related to what goes where and how. We manage to cross the improvised bridge without slipping and head towards the school which is next to a few other small camps. As we approach, we get talking to some Norwegian and Danish volunteers who live in the UK and have recently started to help. As they stand there with boxes of fruit which they distribute to people, they say that a refugee camp has been here for four years. At that time, there were 40 people they say and even then numbers diminished, estimating that there were only 20 people two years ago. However, in 2015, they say, the number just exploded. "The situation is not getting better," says the Norwegian man, and will only get worse as countries close their doors and as more come in. He points around the camp and says, "all want to go to UK." His wife or friend or wife's friend seems to drift off as she holds the box only to be brought back to reality by the acquaintance of another man who has travelled from Calais to see the school. He joins in on the conversation berating the governments for their treatment of the refugees criticising in the main the Belgian officials who he said had put permanent marker on some people and order people not to feed them because "others will come." "In Zeebrugge," he says, "they sleep in bus shelters."

There is a natural pause in the conversation before we say goodbye to each other only then having to go the same way together and spend five minutes doing so to navigate the thick, clay mud. It wasn't awkward whatsoever in the slightest. We continue to press on through the mud, passing a large green tent where provisions were kept when the government permitted aid to come in one day and wade through more mud and in between trees to an opening which Jeroen had help clear. It seems to be less damp and there is a natural pathway with trees bordering each side, each with the branches dismantled to allow for tents to be placed between them. However, Jeroen says that the NGO primarily involved in running the camp and managing the volunteers said it was not possible to put tents here because it was too close to the smuggling mafias: at this point, he points at some settlements beyond some smaller trees. We walk towards them weaving in and out of the thin trees and come out into another muddy track where sit at the end an overturned car and vandalised white van. We walk past these supposed settlements where the smugglers operate and hear only voices from the tents.

On our way back, we slow as the mud deepens and pass a huge pile of rubbish — well considered to be rubbish but really it seems to be goods which don't serve in a purpose, more muddy things which need a clean more than anything else. This is a public health hazard to say the least as Jeroen says that the size of the rats area alarming. We move on and I ask to see the family tents at the rear of the camp which look like small circus tents, certainly much larger and more durable than some of the things people use.

As we walk towards them, we walk past a family cooking and next to them is a man in black jeans, green jacket and scarf; he crouches on the floor in pain as he holds onto a baby buggy which has the wheels caked in mud. I ask how he is and he starts to hold his stomach, "something I ate from the food kitchen," he says, as his eyes roll around and he returns to his crouching position. Hiwa, meaning hope, is his name and he has been here for four months, leaving Iraq a year ago. Having received death threats he left with only his violin and camera, coming through Turkey on the inflatable boats and up through Europe. He says now he normally attempts to stow away about three times a week on lorries or ships bound for the UK and has his heart set on either Maidstone or Liverpool where he says he has family. He says that his journey has been possible after making an agreement of a payment of €5,000 to cover some travel costs and is only transferred when he reaches the UK – the price having been negotiated in Iraq.

As he shows us his small blue tent, a friend of his arrives with a tatty plastic bag and pulls out a bunch of pills and medication – all seemingly donated from the UK. He passes me the small damp boxes, most of which don't have instructions, and asks me which one he should take for a stomach pain. Though I don't know really, he continues to pass me the boxes and asks me to look. Fortunately, his friend intervenes and says "paracetamol" that I can find. I pass him some pills and he asks if he can take two every hour, but I advise that he should take two every 4 hours and if he still has the pain after 24 hours he should see a doctor though this is probably unlikely to happen. He is grateful and washes the pills down with some water and seems to make quite a quick recovery. So much so that when his friends offer us both a rice dish they have been cooking, he is able to eat it.

Last chance saloon (just don't go into the bar): Zeebrugge

States are uninterested in what happens to failed asylum seekers and are content to threaten them with expulsion after their rejection, and in many instances, this rejection is bolstered by local communities. Just like the man I met in the close of Chapter 6 and the beginning of Chapter 7 who had been stateless for years across Europe, there is a danger that the pinballing is never-ending which makes *a fate worse than trying again* a worthy option as I found out when I visited Zeebrugge in Belgium.

After a coffee stop off in a petrol station at which Jeroen has two double shots, we pull up in Zeebrugge – a small coastal port town in the north Belgian coast. Though there is some tourism, Zeebrugge seems really a place where Belgians retire and spend their time between the beach and the bar. As the wind blows sand from the wide beach, we pass through deserted streets where the only lights on are those in peoples' apartments and the few restaurants and bars. There is not a soul walking around on the streets and it's only 7:00 p.m. in the evening. For a few months, groups of refugees, mostly from Iran and Iraq, have been turning up in a group of about 20–30 each night to see if they can board the ships which go once an evening to Hull in the UK. Some it seems make it, while others have tried numerous times without success. Their general profile has attracted organised mafias operating specifically for the trafficking of these people from Iran.

We park up at the church which has an eerie feel in the dark and get out into the wind. As we walk around the church in the empty streets, the lights shine against it as we come out into a square where sits beneath what looks like to be a bus shelter a man talking on his phone. We walk towards him in the dark and in the corner past some abandoned refugee bags. We wait near him hoping he ill finish his phone conversation, as Jeroen picks up that he is from Iran. We ger for a while before deciding to get a drink and come back. We take an unlit ow pathway towards the beach promenade and see a few dog walkers pace up and down the deserted walkway; the roar of the waves echoes in the background as one can just about make out where the extensive beach stretches. On the long promenade, there are only three places open: two fancy restaurants with a handful of clients and one local bar where the youngest clients are around 55.

We walk in and there are immediate looks from the locals as we approach the bar to order a drink. As the waiter polishes cutlery and studies us below his glasses, the waitress busies herself to get us a couple of beers. We sit at a table near the door, still seemingly getting the glances from the locals. When the waitress comes over, we start up a conversation. It is not hard to draw out her views on the refugees because she quickly corrects us saying they are "illegals" – going seemingly beyond a technical reference to their illegality for not seeking asylum or at least registering their application. She says people are fearful and residents have complained about them even though their public crimes in the town are that they sometimes sleep rough in the square because they are homeless and at other times seek refuge in the church which occasionally opens to them. The other harm she accuses them of is to try and to board the ships bound for the UK in the nearby port, often cutting fences and truck tarpaulins to climb aboard and hide.

As she talks, she gesticulates in frustration and indignation as if their presence is a major infraction on the townspeople's way of life. But it seems the refugees are guilty of more criminal activity. She even goes as far to say that during the day, some lie down on the benches by the beach so the locals can't sit there and speculates that some may have started to squat in house further up the promenade. Really what she doesn't like is the fact that she can see them; their visibility troubles her because it breaks the safe compound of how she has constructed her existence according to what is written about refugees or "illegals" as she calls them. However, this feeling is not restricted to Zeebrugge as Jeroen recalls that in a nearby town where some refugee presence has started to grow, the refugees have been banned from the seafront because the residents and council fear they will blemish the image of the town. As she finishes her rant, we finish our drinks and peanut snack and walk outside to see if we can talk to some of the "illegals."

Winlow and Hall (2012) note that the refugees' social infractions amount to being the ugly face of the "other." They are not the surface "other" or those minorities that should be embraced as a symbol of diversity, or at least tolerated under liberal democracy for those people have the capital to buy into its expectations on how to behave. Neither are they the minorities whose differences must be celebrated through culture – music, art, theatre, etc. These are the ones that take the benches up so locals can't sit down, sleeping in the town square disrupting the parochial social order and despoiling their beautiful little town. The resentment here we can locate in how the far right have garnered significant support over the last decade, culminating in success in the 2019 and 2020 elections in Belgium. The new right parties cite a change in social feeling attached to the "increased terrorist attacks" and the "refugee crisis" and a feeling of a loss of "Belgian culture" – further evidence of the crisis of democratic institutions (Chapter 2).

The "illegals" and the fate worse than trying again

Just after leaving the bar we walk back to the church as it hits about 8:00 p.m. and sitting in the shelter are two men while another talks on his mobile seems to disappear as we approach. We say hello and smile and shake their hands as they emerge from the shadows and the dim streetlight lights their stubbly faces. They both stand there in several thick coats, hats and any kind of clothing which will stave off the cold wind. The man with the best English is just 24 years old and his name is Iman, while his friend in his early 30s with a few missing teeth is called Hossein. They both are from Iran and have already spent six months in the "Calais Jungle" having left it because they had had no success in finding a way to the UK: "no chance," repeatedly says Iman.

We produce our trusty cigarettes and offer them around to them as a way to try and warm them, and in the process, they immediately recognise the impro-vised foil which wraps the *Jungle cigarettes*. Interestingly, they say they spent only one day in Dunkirk because they said that the Kurdish mafia groups who control the camp area told them "if you don't pay, you don't stay." "Jungle not good," mumbles Hossein in his best effort to speak English before producing out of his pockets a piece of paper which Jeroen tips into the light. It is an order to leave Belgium. Iman then produces his: they have until the 26th February to leave the "territory" as it states so in five days they should not be here. They are fearful of deportation, but as there is no agreement between Belgium and Iran to deport the threat to ask them to leave the country carries little meaning.

For the past week, and between the time they had spent trying to board the ships, they have been sleeping in the shelter and in the church when it is open. Tonight – a Sunday night – however that opportunity is not available. Given they also have not eaten all day, we invite them to the only place which seems to be open in Zeebrugge – a kebab shop. At first, they politely decline, but when their friend comes, Ahmed, he sways them to accept out invitation. Finally, they accept another cigarette before we amble off to the corner.

We walk up the empty streets in this seaside town to one corner shop which is also a kebab restaurant. The Afghanistani owner looks sternly at us as we enter starts to rearrange his menus. At the back is a mini supermarket, to the right is the mean on the skewer and to our left a group of other Iranians occupy the tables drinking beers. We order them some small kebabs for €5 and a drink and sit down to talk as the TV blurts out some news. In the light and heat, they start to remove their layers of clothes. Back home Iman was a chef, Hossein was an electrician and carpet weave worker while Ahmed made and fixed shoes. They are all in relationships it seems, as Iman proudly shows me a picture he has of his girlfriend on his phone screensaver; she is waiting for him to arrive to the UK so she can travel from Iran. Hossein shows me picture of his nine-year-old daughter and five-year-old son who smile in a picture in his car; he takes the phone back with a large grin on his face, cleaning the cracked screen in the process.

Europe it seems for them is constructed as a "promised land" where there is not only safety but jobs, security and safety for their family. Yet this seems to be in conflict with what they have seen so far obviously aside from in the Calais Jungle but also in the main cities they have travelled through. Iman says, "I thought this was Europe so why are so many people begging in the train station in Brussels? I don't want to end up as beggar."

We ask them about how they will get to the UK and between them they can't remember how many times they've tried. One reason why they say they haven't tried this evening is because Iman's body is in pain all over. It transpires that a few nights ago he had managed to balance himself on a plank no wider than 25 centimetres and no longer than a metre and a half on the underside of a lorry in the night. He and his friend waited for 20 hours and the ferry went but the truck under which they hid remained stationary. The UK is their prime target as they say they have family there.

We then ask them why they left Iran and there is a pause: it is as if they don't really understand or pretend not to understand. They ask me to type the questions on Google Translate. They look between each other and relay that all three had converted to Christianity and started to have problems from the authorities. "Iran good country," says Iman, "but I seen as betrayer" (because he converted). Hossein then passes us his phone and shows us video of a Christian man being hung and I start to see what is going on. There is a silence before Iman starts to break down in tears as Ahmed pats him on the back. Hossein starts sweating below his hat and wipes away the tears from his eyes. It's not only a fear of what happened and what led to them leaving but also a fear of what will inevitably happen as they see it if they go back. "Everyone who goes back…who get the deported is killed" and as he stutters his speech, he says "they killed my friend this way." There is a silence as Iman has to leave to get fresh air. When he returns, we collect up the rubbish and walk outside into the windy darkness.

To our right as we walk out is another Iranian man smoking. He tells us that four police vans are circling the area so he had fled so to not make it look like he would be waiting around and considered someone who was trying to board the trucks/boats bound for the UK. We leave him and walk back towards the church. As we walk, a police van passes us slowly and the officers inside look directly into our eyes. For now it doesn't stop. We walk up to where they will be sleeping tonight and exchange contact details "Inshallah you will arrive to where you need to," I say clasping their hands. As we walk back, we wave at them before passing the church towards the car. Later that night, once we are safely back in Gent in Belgium, I am awoken in the night by a WhatsApp message from Iman "Tnx daniel for food and drink nice to meet you ok no perblem."

9

CLIMATE CHANGED

The future is already here

This is normally the part in the book where the author, which in this case is me, tries to link all the sections of the book together: the aims and methods with the literature, theory and key arguments drawn from findings. I am not an expert on climate change, but I have used refugee accounts and observations of refugee camps, dodgy housing projects and other derelict spaces from all over Europe to formulate the terms "climate changed" and the *business of misery*.

"Climate changed" firstly refers to how the climate has changed in that despite scientific and technological advances which could otherwise secure an alternative future for us, man-made climate change seems now irreversible and has left indelible evidence through higher temperatures, increased droughts, rising sea levels and extreme weather conditions. Secondly, the operations of neoliberal capitalism have assisted and powered this change which is exercised through the *business of misery*, and it is this that has seemingly already eaten away at our own future: the almost permanence of a gaping inequality; the inevitability of war, conflict and social tension as the world's natural resources become the world's next battlegrounds; and the unescapable consequences for poor populations as they are forced to face their own death or flee and trudge on to somewhere else. Whole countries rendered lawless, useless then lifeless in the race to secure the world's diminishing natural resources, which powers on this self-harming system as it limps towards own demise.

Lastly, and perhaps most worryingly, is how *we are complicit in this*; we literally watch on impotent as if it is happening to another planet or like it is some weird futuristic twisted and violent sci-fi film with no plot yet which has unusually accurate and obvious parallels with our current circumstances. Still we deny it. Social feeling is confused and distant on issues like refugees and people displacement because we are bound to consumer distractions so when economic instability arises because of the workings of neoliberalism, the ideological attention via politics and media is directed on to the refugees. The new arrivals blamed for everything which could possibly go wrong in society and all they were trying to do was seek safety. Yet in the boardroom of neoliberal capitalism, morals and principals are not on the meeting agenda, which is why, despite the misery and deaths, it is simply business as usual. The experiences of the people in this text should consistently be the headlines, but instead they rarely even make the news unless there is association with something negative. This is why time and space in this book has been put aside to explain their stories correctly, without bias, without gain, and this was why this particular study was done in this way.

Thinking (and researching) outside the box

This study started from nothing other than some simple observations of African migrant workers and evolved into a three-year longitudinal ethnography which interviewed 110 refugees in 14 different EU countries and made observations in border crossings, refugee camps, inner city spaces, social housing and other forgotten areas. All I did was ask myself "what are these people doing in this space, selling these holiday trinkets on the beach?" "How did they get here?" "Where do they live?" "What are their stories?" "What has happened that has meant that they are now here?" And this became the blueprint for my whole study, its objectives and thus my questioning.

Unlike many studies that make use of case-study evaluations of refugee programmes or consult refugee populations about their "needs," this project looked beyond these micro experiences and sought to document their lives, experiences and decisions over a period of time to see how politics, social policy, security and illicit networks figured in the decisions they made. Unlike many studies set in clinical conditions where refugees are protected in safe environments, this research asked the refugees careful yet challenging and sensitive questions and took risks by critically interrogating the "European project," straying into the ugly corners of the city, scowering the late-night streets and delving into the dark shadows of the camps. In contrast to studies that present their suffering in statistics or their poverty in pie charts or gloss over their frustration in graphs, it sought to *humanise* the moot point of the refugees' predicaments through their words and accounts. Rather than over-romanticising their resistance and "never-ending ambition" or mistaking them for fully integrated subjects when they appear smiling in glossy-photo reports, it attempted to challenge what "success" they had managed to glean from the experience of moving country and starting again from scratch even if that "scratch" often really means "starting again" once again. For these reasons, this project found little evidence of successful integration precisely because it looked *in this way*, deep into the widening cracks of society where millions of these people have now fallen.

It evolved from no funding call, so it couldn't have been a priority for any government policymakers. Three-year research studies of this kind are certainly almost non-existent in this field. It sought no money to support it so it therefore had no conditions or pointless bureaucratic processes attached to how it should have been undertaken or what reporting should occur throughout the project. This eased the burden on me and allowed me to maximise my time in the field with these people as I was able to listen to them and document what was taking place while at the same time read around the issue. This freedom allowed me to adapt my methodology or questioning or destination according to the refugee's circumstances. From what I have reviewed for this study, I could find no other project as diverse in its attempt to follow refugees through different countries over a period of time nor one which has united an ethnographic approach with digital research methods through WhatsApp and Facebook to continue contact and relations with the refugees.

Academics will either laud me or heavily criticise for undertaking this without ethical approval yet I would even question the value of obtaining it in the first place. Having researched the vulnerable for some years and undertaken numerous policy-related studies, I don't believe the current parameters around how research is funded and undertaken do enough justice for the people under study. We are increasingly cornered into doing research in a way which actually prohibits access to the severity and gravity of social harm so processes like ethics committees negatively constrain ethnographic research methods and unnecessarily harness this research approach to a particular set of moralised positivistic ideals which are drastically out of touch with 21st-century realities. There is only so much we can anticipate and stipulate about how we do a project before we actually start. If we state we will not put ourselves in potentially risky situations, how else do we feel the risk attached to the circumstances of the people under study? If we do not ask carefully testing questions about someone's past, how do we access the more genuine experience? If, to some degree, we do not feel the trauma of our participants, how else do we find the words to contextualise their feelings? If we do not see first-hand how they live, what they eat, where they wash and sleep, how else do we find the motivation to help counter the myths and stereotypes about them? Adherence to ethical procedures, while important, is more I think about being honest about how a researcher works in the field and how he or she diligently goes about their documentation and with a sense of empathetic purpose. It should be about being human and showing humility and understanding.

Yet in a context of the "businessisation of higher education" and "academic capitalism," we are drawn away from these realities. If we do not get out of our offices and encounter these experiences: break away from confines such as the ethics committee, then we will continue to produce bland reports and uncritical articles which do not come close to the experiences found in the pages of this book. We will continue to reproduce the same theoretical interpretations we did 20, 30 and 40 years ago when we first started our careers. So my pledge to you is in *the way I have done this research and what it can reveal.*

Of course, by no means is it perfect. The sampling strategy is unlikely to be recognised by any reviewer of a high-impact factor journal, and this will do detriment to my chances of publishing. Some of you will no doubt point out that I have not separated issues such as gender as a variable which heightens vulnerability, but this hasn't meant I have overlooked it though. These are realities which are happening now so we need to be ready to research them so, no doubt, the theoretical powerhouses will surely weigh in with a critique that the study lacks theory: but I think it's better to be free and nimble in the ring than plod around thinking the championship is already coming home again. Here, I have made no punches below the belt but simply offered a new way of competing.

Green criminologists may also be upset with me as I have ignored referencing most of their work. But why should what we do only be about citations or tweets because to me this is what most academics are interested in. If you fall into any of the above, then I would wager you (a) are pretty much subservient to "academic capitalism" (not necessarily your fault) and/or (b) miss the point of this study (necessarily your fault), and this was to present to the reader an intimate picture of this dark reality. As I stated in Chapter 1, my intention was more about exploring the moral absence behind refugee displacement and how this was embedded in geopolitical business relations and economic and commercial enterprise. So the words and photos which make up this book are about how this is *passed down* to the refugees and how it is *felt* by them. My message is then that we need to work with them in these ways to be able to work for them.

Climate changed

We are at point in time where capitalism has evolved to such a degree that to sustain further expansion, it must continue to sideline the ecological warnings and abandon collective commitment to reduce global warming and instead excavate deeper into the earth's natural resources in order to preserve its own lifeblood. It must seek, destroy, exhume and benefit, before making market evaluations on where next to seek, destroy, exhume and benefit. In charge of this aggressive archaeological project are various powerful government players whose own structural and societal architecture hinge on the demand and need for those resources. These players claim that when they stir up the need for their own business enterprises, destroying natural habitats, raping the land and thus uprooting millions of people and making redundant whole countries, they do so in the name of "free market business." They then sell it to the troubled domestic economies where those resources reside as a way out from their uncertainty only to douse them with the toxic consequences of it in return.

South American rainforests make way for our increased demand for burgers. The tropical rainforests of Africa and the Far East are cleared to harvest palm oil, just so we can wear make-up and eat Doritos. Old, decaying forests are abandoned for new virgin forests just so we can indulge in chocolate. We buy into "Fairtrade" products hoping to vicariously assuage some of the guilt harboured around our existing consumer rituals yet all the while, these practices contribute to the eventual plight of the refugees as their homelands are decimated by man-made climate change(d) and the plundering of natural resources. There is no real care or attention paid to pollution and the environmental damage as a consequence of this because that could offset potential profit even if those people working on the front line of these industries are paid only a few dollars a day. Poor social groups are therefore those on the front line of neoliberal policies and practices, but it is their spatial and structural disadvantage coupled with their unfortunate place in history that authenticates their vulnerability in the context of climate change. While the wealthy elite have better adaptive capacities largely because of their affluence, status and political influence, conversely the poor are set in negative and violent competition with each other as the altered environmental changes advance.

By doing this we not only slowly suffocate but strangle ourselves as the severing of our natural forestry reduces our oxygen and replaces it with CO_2. When the CO_2 can't escape, instead it heats up the planet, melting ice caps and glaciers, making sea levels rise which flush out whole communities and jeopardise the survival of millions of people. Changes in the environment produce irregular weather patterns: flash floods, extreme heat, hurricanes and droughts wreak havoc on the most vulnerable and precarious workers in these industries and the stark connections are overlooked. Of course, there is little political will to join these dots together, which is why they appear in the media as anomalies: standalone events that have mysterious cause without historical or ecological context. But extreme weather patterns like floods and droughts expose millions and put them into negative competition against each other as well as pushing them towards already over-crowded cities where already inequality and limited opportunity fester. As the rural areas become abandoned and the workers are left to fight it out between each other, violence, conflict and political abandon ensue. In the chaos to make a living, and in the absence of political investment and environmentally friendly and sustainable policies, whole provinces and states crack, fracture and collapse. When crops fail, livestock die, conflict arises and political and social anger goes from simmer to boiling point. And when governments continue to ignore their obligations insurgent and terrorist groups step in like the Taliban, al-Qaeda and ISIS to provide "security," and thus, a diffuse criminality arises.

Notwithstanding, the war, the speculation of war and then the investment in war, and subsequent misery caused by generally Western commercial enterprises and complicit governments in the obsessional chase for valuable minerals and natural resources. After all, they want to secure a future control and profit to sustain the same system which has started to teeter and wobble. As we saw with Afghanistan (Chapter 5), Iraq (Chapter 6) and Syria (Chapter 7), war is the fast-forward crippling of countries already in a downward social, economic and ecological spirals; it perpetuates their ability not only for political and social stability but to respond adequately to climate change in their respective countries. In fact, the lack of action accelerates their demise.

Media, politicians, powerful kingpin business people from the industries which hinge on the maintenance of this status quo and even "academics" draw doubt over climate change as it threatens to impede the flow of their lifeblood – capital. Large-scale, intergovernmental agreements such as Kyoto and Paris are drawn up in an effort to make countries accountable for their actions against the environment and to make commitments to ecological improvement, but projections continue to be ignored as milestone after milestone is missed in the race to slow the impact of these processes down. We are swiftly approaching the endgame for humanity, the point at which we pass a point of no return. Our economies and social systems are too reliant on neoliberalism, and even in spite of the evidence on climate change, our politicians are too resolutely subservient to commerce and profit to reverse the tide.

The business of misery: *geopolitical, exploitative* and *hardship entrepreneurialism*

Maybe this is because they are part of the web of incestuous weapons and arms dealings around the world. State governments love bragging about their strong Gross Domestic Product (GDP), robust economies and more so about the power they can wield on other nations that step out of line. The business attached to defence, security, and war runs into the trillions, and this fills the coffers of powerful arms companies which are tied to those very same political factions, content to profit from anything which arises from geopolitical squabbling to all-out war. The West's hunger and thirst for control over countries where the world's valuable natural resources are rich become the theatres where tension, conflict and war are acted out. Indeed, this industry is the main lifeblood for neoliberal capitalism: it is the most profitable industry in the world and is a form of *geopolitical entrepreneurialism.*

Whole countries like those discussed in depth in this book such as Afghanistan, Iraq and Syria are left breathless from continuous pounding of bombs and rocket fire, and their infrastructure left lifeless in the aftermath. But just like war, there is also more business in the consequences of war, which represents the Naomi Klein's disaster capitalism thesis. More troops, more missions, more interventions resulting in more death, more suffering and more misery. Not to worry, the righteous West can supply solutions to prolong the suffering and misery by providing miscellaneous weapons drops and illegal deals with rival factions in those very countries. In the fallout, martial law mixes with a widespread violent insecurity as support for terrorist affiliations increases. The economies fold and illicit markets prevail as basic commodities like bread and water become scarce while petrol and oilfields are seized so that more deals can fund illicit arms trading and quickly evolve means of *exploitative entrepreneurialism.* In the fallout, the insurgents seek spatial control over these markets and support from disenfranchised citizens – failure to submit resulting in violence and probable death. This is on top of mysterious disappearances, kidnappings, ransoms, rape and other miscellaneous violence which is exercised on the populace. The refugees see and experience all this.

The subsequent "new democracies," still wobbly from the increased insurgency and terrorist presence, can do little else than count on the West for further business, sorry I mean further intervention. This "intervention" is often just sustained presence in the country until a deal can be penned to secure them cut-price natural resources. Sustained control and political influence in these countries become the norm, and resentment against the West is fostered by this and bolstered by the terrorist ideologies and practices. Yet, the new terrorist factions are just what the West need to rationalise further militaristic action in the very same zones: all the time refugees become the victims of anyone in particular be it rebels, government security forces, "police" or other organised entities with weapons posing as police or authority, and Western soldiers. There is no one they can trust.

While many resign themselves to this fate, as a refugee, leaving all this means there is no choice but to choose and as Latif said to me in the Eleonas refugee camp in Athens, "you have to be a friend with death". To navigate a country where at any point you could be wounded, tortured or as much likely killed, bribes need to be paid. Inflated prices on safety means that large sums of money are requisite for even basic short journeys from area to area. Most of the people I had met in this study, aside from suffering first-hand these gruesome experiences of war and terrorist control, were injured or threatened on such journeys towards their new lives. Many even witnessed others in their party getting robbed, beaten or killed just like Nasir and Zafira who watched five people being shot dead as they ran through the night in the forest across from Syria to Turkey.

There is only some distant idea of an alternative life for these refugees, and it is often idealistically juxtaposed as some "promised land" to generate some hope from all the misery – to keep them going as they leave their homes in rubble, having sold everything for nothing to be able to afford a one-way ticket to somewhere in particular. Crossing out of their countries doesn't mean they are suddenly safe because they are only vulnerable to further exploitation. Aside from some NGOs and volunteers here and there, no state entity is really interested or meaningfully committed to their protection as they would rather let them swiftly pass through on their way to somewhere else to become someone else's problem. This said, many of the people do try and make a living in Turkey, perhaps recuperating money and saving to be able to afford the trip to Greece. However, with a population of four million refugees, the competition for basic work is high. Instead, many survive in illicit markets or just beg on the streets as children work long hours under oppressive conditions for abysmal wages.

Most reason that sooner or later, they will have to move on as Turkey is no permanent home and seek out transport across the stretch of sea between Izmir and Lesbos. Remember even in illicit contexts, neoliberal capitalism always looks for new markets to exploit and exhaust, and the array of smugglers and transporters are evidence of this. More often than not, these people are already locked out of opportunity by neoliberalist forces – they too are its victims. So the smugglers and transporters working the different routes which drain into Europe are also working out of their own precariousness on the front line of the *business of misery* because they are working tirelessly to recruit potential clients. They work these margins by a form of *hardship entrepreneurialism* – seeking meritocratic opportunity from their very own lack and deprivation. Just as they approached me in Basemane Square in Izmir, Turkey, they seek to recruit anyone who is so desperate to leave their country that they will buy overpriced faulty and poorly manufactured life jackets before paying thousands of dollars to be then forced at gunpoint on to an overcrowded, substandard inflatable dinghy which is driven by someone with no experience over a stretch of the Aegean Sea which, more than ever, experiences more "extreme storms surges" because of climate change.

In the sea, thousands die and on the shore, the duff life jackets are swept up on the beach. Just like Eva, a tourist from the UK said, everyone looks on at them confused; wondering how is it that the third world could come to the first in this symbolic manner. More money is needed to cross from Greece, through Macedonia, Hungary, Serbia or a combination; all the time, vulnerable to violence, arrest, detention, robbery and exploitation, and despite some nice gestures from host residents, who feel good about the solidarity they show, it is not enough. European governments know that with each refugee fiscal commitment is required on their behalf, which is why routes traversing the above countries are aggressively policed and refugees are exposed to violence – like Naram and her daughter (Chapter 6) – to send a clear message of unwelcome. New fences and walls are erected and the defence industry expands but it's just more business from misery.

The idealised picture of the new life is suddenly shattered as refugees engage with long, bureaucratic asylum procedures which are designed to filter and test their "commitment" just like the process to "register to register" their application before waiting for an "interview" in Belgium (Chapter 4). Welcome to neoliberal meritocracy. Delays cause stress and uncertainty as we saw with Asim in Chapter 5, and support for all the traumas the refugees have experienced is either overstretched or limited or both. Yet like Farhad (Chapter 2) many have their applications for asylum denied which keep them transient and stateless, while some end up abandoning the settlement country and seeking out another to start there like Shizar and others return to their home countries, sometimes with shattering consequences:

WhatsApp conversation with Wasif, 2018

DAN: Are you in contact with anyone from Melilla?

WASIF: Yes, a lot of friends.

DAN: I would like to talk to them again…

WASIF: Some have already returned to Spain while some are here in Germany now.

DAN: Really? They got sent back?

WASIF: Yes, Germany rejects asylum claims and some returned to Algeria and Syria.

DAN: Shit, how did they feel when they were rejected?

FIGURE 24 Celebrating freedom (momentarily).

WASIF: I knew someone, he returned to Syria and a month later he died there. My brother also got refused and they sent him to Spain but he came back to Germany to try. My friend who you met in Syria was killed by the Syrian army.

[He sends me a picture of him and his friend, the man with white hat, celebrating "freedom" on the beaches of Spain (see Figure 24)]

For those that drift around Europe stateless, there is no real end point and no real settlement, and the threat of upheaval is ever present and sadly real as we saw with Iman and Hossein in Chapter 8. As European governments reduce their support for refugees and instead invest in defence and security, there is only an existence between the charitable handouts and the streets as we saw with the tall man from the Ivory Coast in Chapter 5. For those that get asylum, more challenges await them. Social stigmatisation, racism and discrimination are present in various forms as declared the waitress in the bar in Zeebrugge against Imam and Hossein and reflected Nasir and Abbas all revealed in Chapter 8. They are often housed in the middle of nowhere or in city slum areas, the housing often leaving a lot to be desired. Neoliberal policies and systems require them to work their way into integration. They are firstly contracted into a meritocratic system which, in exchange for a finite number of years' protection, becomes the trade-off demand to show further commitment to their own cause by attending courses, getting exams and finishing qualifications. At the end of it all, the "successful new citizens" will either be slaving away in low-paid, low-grade jobs for exploitative companies like Amazon like Sahil in Chapter 7 or be locked out of work, receive meagre and demeaning benefits from a system that conceives them as "undeserving scroungers" and so likely have to find an illegal substitute, not with standing the continued social pressure and stigma many are exposed to on a daily basis.

By spring 2020, Wasif – having been in Germany for five years – was no closer to finding work. He now spends his days filling in forms for work, even this year he has submitted 70 applications for jobs. Notwithstanding, of the 60 refugees he knows in Saarbrücken in Germany, 6 have jobs in domestic cleaning or construction work. "All my friends in the city survive by illegal means," he adds. He finds life in Germany difficult, does not trust anyone and regularly receives random racist messages from Germans on Facebook. It seems worse for his sister who he says "daily when she goes with her children to school a person threatens her with death, every day. They signal cutting off neck or shooting her with finger." The trauma of losing his friend from Melilla, as well as other friends and family in Syria, the journey on which he took to Europe and the experience of racist abuse in Germany dents his ability to trust:

WASIF: I had a lot of problems with my close friends, and the problems started in Melilla. Since that day my relationships have become few. I don't even like to meet new friends. Perhaps because of the war, immigration, and the loss of many friends, it caused us psychological problems. I am by nature a very social person, I have many friends in Syria and Algeria. But in Europe, I no longer wanted a new friendship.

Although he is "protected" until 2022, the lack of work, friendship networks and missing his wife, son and mother in Syria make him depressed:

My only fault is that my mother gave birth to me in the Middle East. I find no respect from anyone. I didn't know where to go, there is no place but Germany welcomes me. But I do not have work experiences. Nothing. I am a hopeless person, I cannot help my family in Syria and I cannot help myself. 23 years of learning and studying and I did not benefit anything from it. I think a lot about suicide, but I fear because I am a Muslim and in Islam suicide is forbidden.

And thereafter? The geopolitical resource wars continue. Conflict rages over the strategic positioning of minerals. Governments and corporations collaborate to move in to exploit the next market opportunity which further harms the earth. For on the front line of it all are the people in this book. They are testament to this social failure. They are the unequivocal victims and this text has examined the particular layers of this victimage. The vested interest of capital trumps across all levels: the corporate elites and their webs of private enterprises, corrupt European institutions and nation states, and ineffective international helping entities down to the local functioning of the security industry and organised crime groups. In the end, the lack or bungled international protection/intervention can only ask them of their human capital from which they must initiate to forge their own future. With all the will in the world, very few come through it.

Climate change and refugee displacement are therefore an extension and by-product of neoliberal capitalism – the vehicle powering the engine of all this destruction being the *business of misery*. It is responsible for the differing levels of entrepreneurialism at play – geopolitical, exploitative and hardship – which inadvertently and directly impact the livelihoods of the refugees and produce the various layers of their victimisation. As I have declared, I'm not an expert on climate change or on the industry of war or EU asylum policy. All I have done is attempted to talk to as many people as possible who have suffered like this in a way that most other studies haven't. I don't want to offer much in a way of policy recommendations because having researched the consequences of these people's exodus and arrival in Europe, I can find nothing from the existing systemic structures which would repair the damage, return the dignity and remedy their lives. All the responsible entities are too incestuously intertwined with commerce and economic expansion.

It would need something far beyond social policy, government and international collaboration for us to be able to reconfigure the current status quo because the aforementioned have no real control over improving things for the most neglected and forgotten people on the planet. It would require a seismic and systemic jolt to neoliberal capitalism and all its complicit parties – from corporation to citizen, from board member to road mender, from politician to pastor, from adult to adolescent – to force us to think otherwise, to wake people from their ideological slumbers, to force them to revaluate their privilege while at the same time fully recognise the components of this social suffering and carve out an alternative.

10

THE BEGINNING OF THE END

While this study took place over three years, I have kept in contact with some of the refugees who are now friends of mine. Though two years on from the end of the fieldwork, to this day, they continue to struggle as the time variable seems to be no marker on the level of integration they have achieved or sense of feeling settled. As I said at the end of Chapter 9, it would take a seismic and systemic jolt to break us free from the status quo which produces all this misery. It would have to be something which brought all political, social and commercial institutions to their knees. It would have to be something which made the world stand still long enough for us to envisage an alternative future.

At a European summit on youth learning

At breakfast, I get talking to the man making my omelette in the hotel. I say how I am grateful to be able to have food and he agrees. He mixes the vegetables with my request for cheese and turns it over as I watch. "Some people don't have food in the world," says the tall, chubby chef, "and all we do is complain about stupid things," he adds. "I know," I say. "Trust me, they don't know what it is to suffer," he says as he loads a juicy pile of omelette on my plate.

Shortly after

At breakfast we have scheduled a meeting with the team about our presentation about migrant and refugee political participation. I tell them I will be talking about a harsh reality, one which is unforgiving and which will be difficult to grasp for the audience, some of them at least. My colleagues nod at me as they write pointless notes in their diaries.

A bit later

After a leisurely walk to the conference centre, inside it is busy and there is nowhere to sit down. The conference theme is about fair and equal society for young people and a body of predominantly German social workers and educators are among the 20,000 participants who will be circulating between the sessions today. The conference is so well facilitated that personal earphones are available for people who want English/German translations.

Later still

As the time draws closer to the sessions, I sit sipping sparking water. The room slowly fills with about 70 people, most of which are German. In the 20 minutes available, I have to try and fit the findings of my refugee study into a meaningful narrative and relate it to "political participation." Unfortunately for some, given the current far right climate, I say that this kind of participation sounds good, but we can't expect to see it soon and present the gravity of the refugee situation in Europe. I try to ask the audience to consider it less a "humanitarian crisis" – which is how it seems to be framed by the organisers – and one related to climate change, global capitalism and economic neo-colonialism, and how a strategic resource-motivated, geopolitical game is at fault for the global uprooting of millions of people.

Aside from the social policy and political distance from wanting to really organized meaningful intervention and integration into "European values," and the blockages which populism present in our current politics, one element which I reflect as a major barrier is the cultural organization of social life which, on the one hand, works horizontally in countries like Syria (social capital) and how this is in conflict with how societal expectation in Europe is vertical (human capital). Social workers and educators moan about the lack of motivation of refugees to complete language courses, but they are designed around a meritocratic philosophy which demands the subject to muster their own initiative and self-motivation and many people arriving from countries where social networks underpin the completion of goals (and less of individual merit) which is difficult to muster. Many of these people have been emotionally eroded to the core many have severe traumas having lost family or friends, been subject to violence or victimization and thereafter left having sold everything to place their faith in smugglers and other beneficiaries of misery for their own welfare. It's not easy to trust and just do what is required of them.

Sooner rather than later

After the feedback session, in which I literally ended up banging my book against my own head because most people didn't understand my message, we are released from duty. So this is why I do this research: to challenge people to think differently. The world of youth work is often very distant from the grave reality of the people it should be representing. Why do I do this? Not only to write and you read it but to speak at events like this where the real people that matter – the policymakers – are far away and the people who do matter ebb between the conflict of living in a closed world of their own success stories with young people and adhering to performance outcomes to keep the funding coffers full, and that which I just described to them. My lecture is both applauded for its refreshing approach but criticised because I didn't "counter my negativity with positivity."

Youth work seems to be a sort of keep-busy strategy for both the people who work in the field and those who end up receiving its intervention. All the help mechanisms are designed to empower young people who fall into misfortune, but very often they don't nor will ever counter the processes which put them there in the first place. This is what I tried to explain. I suppose we all want to feel what we do is important and that it helps in some way. What would happen if you realized one day that what you did was essentially pointless and changed very little? Well that is what I see every day and it's not because I only focus on negative aspects of society – things really are that bad because I talked to the refugees, I saw where they slept and met their families. All we can hope for, even if the hope is false and ideological, is that sooner rather than later, we can start to reverse these oppressive economic forces which have robbed us of a decent politics which can represent our most vulnerable and balance out how what we think is important in life: our children, other people and the collective future of the human race.

La revisite, Strasbourg, April 2017

I sit with Mohammed as he starts to call a few friends to whom he had introduced to me in Paris. Assan it seems is now in Narbonne with his family and Abu-Ahmed in north France near Rennes. Assan still looks for work and struggles with French; his children are, however, happy. Abu-Ahmed and his family of seven are still out of fortune with work. Though safe and happy with the cultural conditions of living on the outskirts of Renne, there are few opportunities, and Abu-Ahmed resents the idea that "we came here to take money from the State." He also says that he is very worried about the "terrorism in Europe as it will give us a bad name" and thinks it will damage the image of his people. We finish the call and sit and finish our coffee while looking at Abu-Ahmed's recent Facebook statuses which condemn the recent terrorism in London.

Burnt fingerprints, Amsterdam

After traipsing across Amsterdam to find a former-secure-children's-centre-turned-refugee centre, we join the near canal and follow it to the river Amstel. Up the Amstel, life is calm and people breakfast in the cáfes and on their private boats. It is an unusually sunny day. We deviate from the riverside as there are some roadworks and cross the busy bike paths and come to a smaller canal. On it is the Wereldhuis – or world house – a Church-funded initiative for people at the bottom of asylum chain, who assist mostly if not all rejected asylum cases. During the day, around 100 people queue to get accommodation from the Bed, Bath and Bread (BBB) government programme and attend the service. Because they are undocumented, they get no money from the Amsterdam authorities so the Wereldhuis relies on donations and support from other charities. They essentially provide food, training and language courses, and it is open from 9:30 a.m. to 6:00 p.m. and run by volunteers and refugees, who normally do their own cooking.

We are led in by a tall Eritrean man, past some refugees cleaning and drawing, and are shown into the manager's office. Layers of dust sit among the piles of paperwork and the coffee cup marks on the table where a tall blond woman types away on a dated laptop. She invites us in and we ask a few questions. Antoinette says they used to be open on Saturdays, but a recent incident in Utrecht involving refugee who had his asylum application rejected resulted in a stabbing between two refugees. "People are very tense and stressed when they have nothing," she says. "Normally, people who would get asylum protection for five years would receive temporary support and after that time they would have their case reviewed say if the country was considered 'safe' – which most aren't in reality – they would have to return or they might get citizenship," she adds.

However, it seems that many people can't simply go home: either they have no money or the papers or neither of them. "They need to have papers to be received again but many of these people have nothing," she adds. So what happens is that they just end up existing between these night shelters and the day centres like Wereldhuis – stateless people, citizenless persons. I am told the service sees mostly Eritrean, Somalian and other African countries with a sprinkling of Syrians, Iraqis and Afghanistanis. "This is the last stop for many people, the only thing they have," she says as she comments on how the coordination is improving between the church and other voluntary services so that the support does not overlap. She is deeply critical of the local government but says that "some people in Amsterdam want resolve for these people but say those who live in Vollendam, a far right area, there is little sympathy for refugees and they think they should go back to their countries." "We are lucky that enough for some left wing support has got into the local government here otherwise there would be absolutely nothing for them, and in this respect there is a massive tension between the church and politicians," she concedes.

The service is strictly for refugees, and many times they have to turn away homeless street people like drug and alcohol users. She then comments that they have helped overturn some asylum rejections, giving the example of many of the women who access the service who don't always reveal everything in the initial interview where they presented their asylum in Italy. She adds, "This is because they felt ashamed of what happened to them and in instances the Italian authorities rape them. Many were forced to give their fingerprints on the boats and are then detained before they then face the process in Italy. While they wait, many are abused and raped which is why many end up burning their fingerprints and leave the country. These people then end up in places like Holland and they have no papers and are practically untraceable unless they tell the government the whole story, which as you can imagine, is not easy."

Virtual face time vs real face time, Hamar

Dag passes me the phone number for Abdul and his family and they agree to take a face time call. When I met them in Hamar two years ago in 2016, I did the interview through Abdul's 20-year-old daughter. Leaving Syria in 2013, they tried to make a life in Turkey. Abdul got a job in a Syrian school as he had a teaching certificate, but it was not enough to cover the rent and to support three of his daughters. This mean the eldest (19) and the youngest (13) had to work 55 hours a week between them in a sewing factory to make up the required $250 a month – that is about a dollar an hour. Abdul recalls how "it was no future for her." They stayed in Turkey for two years, and then left. They didn't have enough money for everyone to travel so they decided that one member of the family should leave and then later the others would follow. He paid €10,000 to travel by land to Bulgaria with his sister-in-law, mostly walked through Serbia and was imprisoned in Hungary and sent back to Serbia only to re-enter the Hungary to pass through without detection to Austria. Each time he needed advice like a car or a driver, he called the smuggling contact he had made in Istanbul. Thereafter it was easier to come to Norway as he passed quickly through Germany, Denmark and Sweden. All this happened in July 2015. Three years later, he has been reunited with his whole family. They were unable to travel over land because they didn't have enough money; it had practically run out after the money generated from selling their house, land and car in Syria. It took over two years before they managed to get the money for the boat from Turkey to Greece, and thereafter made a quick 12-day journey to Norway because, by then, many NGOs had been established on the route to help. "We are family again, we are happy!" "Finally!" I say as her eyes well and she looks back at her dad from her mobile.

The third world still continues to come to the first, Brussels

By 2018, Francesca, a volunteer nurse I interviewed in Brussels, had finished her nursing qualification. When I met her, she had just started her course, and when thousands of refugees started arriving in Brussels over the summer of 2015, she volunteered herself:

FRANCESCA: There was so many tents in the main park so we need to more present but so many people came that the small bus we had meant we had to open a large tent but there was so many needs, so many children. We opened a consultation from 2pm to 10pm but people came during the night so there was a conflict and we realised we had to be open 24 hours so this is how it started it was pretty crazy, a little village, lots of solidarity which has never really been seen in Belgium.

DAN: In what way?

FRANCESCA: Because people realised there was a need. It was nice but also confusing because suddenly there is this poverty in the city and the migrant crisis has been going on for so long but it came to the city centre and it worked well for a time as there were other agencies doing things but it forced us to work together even if it was cold and there was no shower.

Indeed, during the summers of 2017 and 2018, the central park next to the World Trade Centre – where I met Amir and his Afghan friends (Chapter 5) – filled with refugees once again, many in dire need of physical, emotional and practical support.

DAN: Why don't they want to apply for asylum?

FRANCESCA: Some just feel abandoned by the system and so they themselves abandon the system. They have tried and stopped because they have been rejected here and there, we are talking about 20% of our population. The problems are more about how they do the interviews with the refugees, how they ask questions about their personal lives and the traumas and this is what the refugees find difficult. If they don't answer they can't be processed. They have had too many people waiting so they get an interview and have to wait months so they just give up and move on. I mean they have left everything, walking for months, they want to move on with their lives. The way they are welcomed, the way they are spoken to in that registration centre it made me feel ashamed about how we treat them.

But the first world still blames the third, Madrid

Late in 2018, the *Fourth National Climate Change Assessment* was presented to Donald Trump's administration. The report essentially made stark warnings about the impact climate change could have on the United States, even stating that effects of global warming were already having sizeable consequences for the US weather systems (NCA, 2018: 7):

> With continued growth in emissions at historic rates, annual losses in some economic sectors are projected to reach hundreds of billions of dollars by the end of the century – more than the current gross domestic product (GDP) of many US states. Without substantial and sustained global mitigation and regional adaptation efforts, climate change is expected to cause growing losses to American infrastructure and property and impede the rate of economic growth over this century.

When asked about the report, which was produced by his own administration, Trump was quoted as saying, "I don't believe it," after reading "some of it." He went on to say that

> Right now we're at the cleanest we've ever been and that's very important to me. But if we're clean, but every other place on Earth is dirty, that's not so good.

Since then, Trump has initiated a new panel to examine connections between climate change and national security, some of whom were experts in nuclear weapons and had links to the fossil fuel industry. This was only a year after Trump disbanded a whole federal climate change panel in 2017 and only a month after Trump had said that "climate scientists had a political agenda" when convincing a news station that humans were not responsible for earth's warming (BBC, 2018). Only last year, in 2019, Trump dropped "climate change" from the list of threats to national security and formally began the process of withdrawing the United States from the Paris Climate Change Agreement signed in 2015 which, if re-elected, will come into place after the 2020 elections (Holden, 2019). The United States, however, still leads the field in global arms and weapons exports (von Hein, 2020) in the competition to see how much more turmoil and misery the war and conflict industry can create.

One foot in integration, Oelde

When I met Abbas in Madrid six months after having met him in Melilla, he was planning to travel illegally to France and then to Germany. He paid hundreds of Euros to cross into France, but he was dumped on the streets of Brussels in Belgium where he slept and begged until he had enough money to get a train into Germany. The volume of people presented for asylum was high at the time, and the system was under significant pressure to carefully process/reject refugees accordingly. In our early WhatsApp exchanges, his worry was evident:

WhatsApp conversation with Abbas, April 2016

DAN: Abbas what's happening?

ABBAS: Hello my friend. I am very, very sorry because I don't contact with you but every day I wake up at 5am and go to school at 8am in another city after that I take a train to my work because I make a "prakticum" (work experience) in school for kids finally I reach my home at 7pm. And the court will send me back to Spain this month or the next. Please forgive me that I don't call you.

DAN: Its ok... you working now, that's great...is it paid in any way? Will you stay or come to Spain?

ABBAS: They will send me back within the next two months.

FIGURE 25 Abbas and I at the train station (Oelde, 2018).

When Abbas's asylum was denied in Germany, and he was to be sent back to Spain, it caused him severe panic attacks and he was admitted to a mental health institution. There he was given sleeping pills and painkillers for a few weeks and hired a lawyer to represent him to appeal the decision. While his lawyer put in an appeal, he escaped and went into hiding. The police searched for him at the refugee housing centre but had no luck. The small amount of money he had left went on legal costs to challenge his case. His perseverance paid off and he won given the effort he had made to learn the language and get a part-time job. He agreed to repay outstanding to the lawyer on a monthly basis for the duration of the lawyer's time. To this day, he still owes €1,200.

By 2018, Abbas had passed his practicum and had a part-time job in the school (See figure 25). His German improved and the main teacher in the school gave him extra tutorials. Life is almost stable, even if a few of the schoolkids' parents think he is a terrorist and he barely makes enough money each month: his €700 wage after tax, accommodation, electricity and phone leave him with about €150 to survive on or about €5 a day. He is the only refugee in the town with a job and he has nearly been there for three years:

DAN: What do people do if they don't have a job?
ABBAS: People don't want to learn, many want to rest, sleep, do nothing.
DAN: Why are they not interested?

ABBAS: Because they get everything, €1,500 for furniture for a flat, €400 a month for food and things like that. Because I have a job, I have to pay all this myself. This is unfair, they take all the money and I work all the time. No one gives me money for furniture. In the job centres no one can understand us, there are no translators. They get healthcare for free but I pay for mine. So there is no reason to work.

DAN: Do the refugees know that?

ABBAS: Yes, they all know that. It makes no sense for them to work as some will even have less money as there are not enough well paid jobs around like mine. There is a lot of jobs here but they are temporary, the pay is bad.

Back at the border: Melilla revisited

At the border with Morocco, the police in their sunglasses continue to routinely stop the cars and carry out the necessary procedures to allow all this. I walk past the border police and into an open office which is designed for interviewing people seeking asylum: I am to meet Juan, a senior border officer. I am firstly introduced to several young officers who are in the midst of interviewing Syrians who have just arrived to the border; inside the office sits a man by the computer and an interpreter and an elderly Syrian man struggling with answering his questions. Behind me is a family of seven who sit in and around the small bench provided for them while, one by one, each is summoned to the office for their details to be recorded. Their faces are tired and dirty, and as the officers explain, they speak no Spanish or English, hence the necessary translator during the interviews. The officers look me up and down and ask for my identification. I show them my passport; they take it and study it carefully as one of them runs his fingers over the photo to check its authenticity before saying nothing and handing it back to me. While the Syrian family sweat under the pressure, another officer approaches. He leads me to another office and we enter to find a short fat man, typing away very slowly at his keyboard. He looks up at me cautiously as I explain the motive for my request to meet him. Three years ago, I had met his colleague who has since retired. Now he has the helm and is in charge of border crossings:

JUAN: In this misery the divide is money: the poor Syrians can't pay they will try the boats or something. In all societies there are classes, so the higher classes will fly for example or pay their way out somehow. Otherwise they have to pay smugglers. Its not like organised like a pyramid, and there is a big boss: its more fluid. There are small groups who offer the service and if they don't have the money, they take the boats. Many die, many more than we know. It is a business.

Black markets, grey existence, Brussels

Equally for Asim – the man who translated for me in a homeless shelter – things have continued to be difficult. In 2015, such was the volume of applicants at the time that someone like him – a young male with no children – was not a priority. Shortly after our meeting in Belgium, I sent him WhatsApp messages:

WhatsApp conversation with Asim, December 2015

DAN: Asim, I arrived back in Madrid. It was a pleasure to meet you and I hope to keep in contact. Please ask me if I can help you in any way.
ASIM: Ok my friend.. Thank you for the gift ☺ …kiss Nadia [my daughter] for me.
DAN: ☺☀.

Over the next two years, Asim continued to wait for his asylum decision to be made and lingered homeless around the city trying to make money in any way he could. Then in March 2017,

ASIM: Hello Daniel. How are you? I asked new asylum. I'm waiting if they say yes they will send me to centre. I ask for centre only place to sleep. I'm waiting…Also I'm with psychology doctor have appointment I need report. If they give me negative I'll go to Germany.
DAN: Ok so you are safe but still in Belgium. But where do you sleep now then?
ASIM: I'm with friend for the moment. I asked friends to find me job in black market.
DAN: What do you hope to do?
ASIM: Anything I can do. Cleaner, Restaurant, Construction works.
DAN: Is there any of that work available? I would guess other people in your situation are doing the same, working in black. Do you know anyone?
ASIM: Many friends doing the same they living in centre and working.
DAN: But how can it be there is so much work for people who have had their asylum rejected?
ASIM: In black market for example you work in restaurant cleaner in the kitchen start at 2pm until 1am they give €30 or less than €3 per hour. Also they give you food for free.

The exploitation evident and telling of familiar refugee employment conditions around Europe. By the summer 2019, Asim had a more stable job cleaning in an old people's residential home and was living in a small studio. The spare money he was able to save each month after eating basic food was around €200 and this he sent to his family in Iraq. Throughout all this time, he had alluded to the need for some psychological support but said nothing until one evening in the summer of 2019 he declared in some messages:

ASIM: I need help, I take medication for depression.

DAN: Depressed because of what happened in Iraq or because of new life in Belgium?

ASIM: Depression was me since I was 15 years old but I didn't know. I remember it was hard childhood.

DAN: Is it OK to ask what happened? You don't have to tell me if you don't want to it's ok.

ASIM: If I stop medication I remember everything. My father [who worked in the military] was bad.

DAN: Oh. Violent?

ASIM: Yes.

DAN: I am very sorry to hear this. When we talked I don't think you mentioned it but there was no pressure to anyway. Have you seen a therapist or psychologist?

ASIM: Yes but not things changed. I remember I was taken and given to old man I think he was 70 years old I go to his house. He was supposed to be taking care about me but he was taking my clothes off.

DAN: Shit, I'm sorry.

ASIM: I knew it it's something not ok. I am crying now.

DAN: I guess it is something you can only manage but not completely forget.

ASIM: I went to police but they did nothing, it was 2007, I was 17 years old. I smoked drugs last week.

DAN: I can't imagine the Iraq police being very interested. Did the weed help or did it make you paranoid? Sometimes it can relax people or increase their worry and anxiety.

ASIM: No it makes me feel so bad. Every time I smoke I start thinking to go to the train and throw myself under to stop this fucking life but I am scared to do it.

The rock and hard place, Idlib

Additional pressure on Turkey has continued in the light of the persistent conflict in Idlib, a small city in the northeast of Syria which suffered severe droughts in 2008 and 2014. Food and water insecurity plague the city under siege from Assad as he attempts to break the last threshold of the rebel free army. The siege and general conflict in the area have led to the continued refugee exodus into Turkey, which by the close of 2019 was hosting nearly four million refugees. Throughout the book there have been ample signs of the poverty, destitution and exploited labour provided by mostly Syrian refugees in Turkey and this still continues to this day. This is likely part of the reason that in February 2020, the Turkish President Erdogan was quoted to have said in a direct threat to the European Union, "Our gates are open. The refugees will go as far as they can" (Rankin et al., 2020).

Since then, thousands of refugees attempted to storm the land border between Turkey and Greece only to be met with tear gas and shots by the Greek police as well as temporarily suspending their duties to register asylum claims, thus deporting anyone illegally entering (Amnesty International, 2020).

And who would have thought that all this could be further exacerbated by an unknown virus with no apparent cure that has deadly implications for the elderly, vulnerable and/or terminally ill? As country after country ground to a halt, I decided to launch my own survey on the impact of lockdown and perceptions of the coronavirus. In early February 2020, I sent Mukhles to see if he could help me with an Arabic translation of my survey:

DAN: I am uploading your Arabic translation.

MUKHLES: No problem so you can send it to send it to my friends.

DAN: Hope it can capture what is happening in Iraq and Syria. The camps have the virus.

MUKHLES: Yeah I heard about that, it's really bad.

MUKHLES: Sorry I didn't ask you are ok there, because there are a lot of coronavirus cases in Spain.

DAN: I am fine. The media make a lot of panic. In truth we do not know the real risk.

MUKHLES: Yes it is true for Turkey as well.

DAN: Worse there?

MUKHLES: About 30 thousand cases here and the streets almost empty.

DAN: It is ready, I just uploaded it. Please do the survey and send it literally as many people you can in the region. Turkey Syria Iraq, anywhere.

MUKHLES: Ok Prof Daniel I will do my best.

MUKHLES: 👍

11

REVELATIONS

In Exodus, ten plagues were cast upon the Pharaoh and his people before freedom was sought in the land of milk and honey. In Revelation, however, the plagues return with greater force and significance. John, believed to be one of Jesus's 12 apostles, is asked to deliver Jesus message about the end of days or the apocalypse. A voice calls to him, "I will show you what is to take place in the future" (4:1) before, in his visions, angels from the Old Testament appear and lighting and thunder rage. The visions encompass the release of war, intense heat, famine and disease upon the earth. When the survivors of all this continue to behave "immorally," further havoc, chaos and destruction are inflicted on the planet. As with Exodus, there are parallels with our current circumstances. Having failed to learn from previous warnings about climate change, onward marches immoral neoliberal capitalism and further climate punishment is inflicted upon us by more harmful measure. A vision of the future comes true and my book is testament to how war, climate change, famine and disease are now firmly beset upon us: the irony is that, despite this, still we continue along the same systemic suicidal pathway. That is unless there is a significant jolt to the global system which can encourage politics and social life to do things differently.

After being detected in December 2019, the rapid spread of the Covid-19 coronavirus meant that by March 2020 most countries had been locked down: borders closed, movement stopped and economies halted as the world ground to a standstill. The rich elegantly retreated to their secret islands while the poor knuckled down and got ready for the onslaught. Everyone else was pretty much sent home and told to keep away from each other while millions were left in the margins. Throughout March and April 2020, researchers, NGOs and volunteers worked tirelessly to get equipment, supplies and resources to the world's most impoverished refugee camps in the hope of supporting some of the 70 million displaced people (Subbaraman, 2020). These people, almost all of whom live in poverty, have poor housing, poor health and limited access to medicine, are almost immediately disadvantaged and this wrath has the potential to intensify their precariousness.

More business of misery or new businesses in misery?

The fact that nine in ten people across the world are living in countries with travel restrictions because of coronavirus and one in two people of the global population is living under lockdown (Reidy, 2020; Connor, 2020) does not remove the motivation refugees have for leaving their war-torn and socially unstable home countries in favour of a new life somewhere else. Yet they seek this safety in a time when the drawbridge which had started to be pulled up is now fully closed. Many countries, including Hungary, the United States, Mexico and Canada, used the virus as a way of arguing for tighter border controls in an effort to curb further contamination of their populations: the irony is that scheduled flights continued to operate and go from these very countries. The United States, in particular, is one such country who upped deportation of "illegal aliens" back to Central and South America – even if the right to asylum cannot be completely suspended (UNHCR, 2020) – the majority of whom allegedly tested positive for coronavirus (Al Jazeera, 2020a).

In Europe, countries have postponed asylum hearings and decision making (Wallis, 2020) while despairing tactics were used by governments to shunt refugees and migrants into makeshift housing in an effort to halt the spread of the virus. In Greece, refugees were in quarantine at the already "at-limit" camps such as Elonas on the mainland and on the islands (Al Jazeera, 2020b). In Bosnia, thousands of refugees were transferred to a remote camp in Lipa, near the Croatian border, where access to water, heat and power was minimal (Tondo, 2020). In France, in the camps where I had visited at Calais and Dunkirk in this research study, cases were on the increase among the already-festering conditions of overcrowding, poor sanitation and substandard health (Kelly, 2020) – all the while supermarkets turning down refugees and they were increasingly subject to police brutality (DW, 2020a). Across all these camps among many others, the virus caused interruption to child protection systems rendering children even more vulnerable to exploitation (World Vision, 2020) even when many refugees fear more basic and present threats such as starvation more significant than the advent of the coronavirus (DW, 2020b).

Unfairly targeted, refugees across Europe – either about to embark or already in transit – were subject to further stigmatization under this new confinement. There were even woefully irresponsible reports linking new "illegal sea crossings" from France to the United Kingdom by desperate refugees with the potential for risky transmission of coronavirus: anything to take the focus away from the mismanagement of protecting the elderly and vulnerable, the lengthy period in lockdown and the inevitable political and economic fallout in the UK and replace it with a story of a boatful of desperate people seeking a fate worse than trying again. In the Facebook forums, the indignation was rampant as some British people moaned from their moral high ground. But in such times, there is no rest for the entrepreneurs working in the business of misery or, better still, the new businesses of misery emerging from the inevitable economic fallout.

For example, in Italy, as the lockdown eases and work restrictions are lifted, there are fears that the mafia may exploit migrant workers such as refugees in the agricultural sector – an industry worth €24.5 billion (InfoMigrants, 2020). Mafia exploitation known as "caporalato" sees workers slaving for long hours and also subject to violence. However, Italy, much like Spain, has long relied on such undocumented migrant work to support domestic agricultural economies to generate handsome profits. The economic instability ahead will drive up the prices as the queue of desperate hopefuls trying to get somewhere never diminishes. With the increasing difficulty of getting to places like Germany coupled with the closing of their economies, maybe this explains the rekindled interest in getting to Spain. Only now it is more expensive than ever. In April 2020, 100 Moroccans paid around €5,000 each to try and reach the Spanish mainland (Martín, 2020), some €4,000 above what it was during the period 2015 and 2018.

Coronavirus: the dress rehearsal for climate change

Perhaps it won't just be the refugees who are clambering to Europe for the advent of global warming is expected to significantly increase the evolution of new viruses and their transmission (Wu et al., 2016). Increasing global temperatures shorten winter seasons, which enables animals and insects (as well as people) to migrate north to other regions like Europe. For example, Gale et al. (2010) consulted a panel of experts in a "risk assessment" to estimate future risks to the European Union from particular "vector-borne" viruses. They found that while the increase of exposure to risk was prevalent among numerous viruses, in particular, their research suggested that African horse sickness virus, Crimean-Congo hemorrhagic fever virus, and West Nile virus were those which posed the greatest risk. New viruses will flourish and perhaps even old ones will return. There is even concern that the melting of the ice caps will unravel previous diseases and viruses that have not circulated for millions of years and that our immune systems will be unable to cope with them (Wallace Wells, 2020).

Evidence shows that extreme weather changes, droughts, floods and the like are ideal breeding grounds for viruses to evolve and mutate (WHO, 2007). When temperatures change, so to do habitats, ecosystems and environments which impact animal movement arthropod distribution patterns (Gould, 2009), and this is how we rewrite the rules that have thus far governed all life on the planet (Wallace Wells, 2020). Moreover, as the world's population increases and land is cleared for agriculture, habits like rainforests will shrink and this increases the risk of the transmission of more deadly viruses and diseases (Gustin, 2020). Other man-made damage to the planet is found to produce similar risks. Pollution, for example, has also been found to impact the outbreak of viruses. Take the 2002

Severe Acute Respiratory Syndrome or SARS outbreak in China which disproportionately killed more people in urban areas where air quality was dirty and
polluted (Cui et al., 2003).

Could this have been the case for COVID-19 aka coronavirus which was
reportedly transmitted from bats sold for consumption at a Chinese live animal
markets in Wuhan? In 2009, the United States Agency for International Development (USAID) launched a programme to monitor zoonotic viruses – those
which pass from animals to humans – in an effort to curb the potential for a pandemic. While the USAID, which is one of the largest global initiatives to assist
with health matters in foreign countries, has continued to be funded well, it has
not managed to predict nor prevent the outbreak of the new coronavirus. Indeed,
over the course of its 15-year existence, the Agency discovered 2,000 new viruses in 30 different countries in Africa and Asia only for their funding to be cut
by the Trump administration in 2019 – just before the onset of the coronavirus
pandemic (Gustin, 2020). Keesing et al. (2010: 650) note that

> The connection [between climate change] with disease is: The species that
> thrive when biodiversity declines are the species that are best at transmit-
> ting diseases.

Species like rats and bats, the latter which is said to have been the cause for the
latest coronavirus transmission, breed rapidly when their habits are reduced, and
their population spills over into new environments, closer to urban areas (Schvoerer et al., 2008). For millions of people across the world, living in comparative
comfort and far from the front-line impact of the climate change, the advent of
the virus was like a shock to the system – probably because aspects of the third
world came to the first. Irrespective of the severity of risk coronavirus carries to
the global population, its arrival has ruptured the comfortable consumer bubble
in which many people in the West experience as a personal freedom to engage in
the wonders of shopping, dining out and posting the experiences on Instagram as
evidence of their "happy" and "successful" participation in society.

Revelations: the picture from privilege

Yet a few months in lockdown seemed to be a potential turning point for some
of these people. From 30th March to 8th May 2020, I made an online survey
accessible and collected 985 responses from 59 different countries. The research
aimed at looking at how lockdown was experienced by individuals, partners and
families in different countries, their perceptions on strategies such as social distancing and self-isolation and how this affected individuals and general everyday
life. There were other questions relating to the media, government management
and what this outbreak may mean for the future, particularly given our current problems such as war, inequality, climate change and people displacement.
Health workers from the United Kingdom, supermarket staff from Spain, IT

admin from the United States, lecturers from Germany, kitchen assistants from Chile and NGO volunteers from South Africa all completed the survey which did what it could to get responses regular posts on Facebook and LinkedIn. It was hoped that the survey might reach some of the poorest of the world's population as this man recognised from Honduras:

> There is a need to compare our middle class lockdown and its impacts with those who are in real poverty, without access to space, internet, food, water, remote work and healthcare. This virus is shown in some social media as a lovely street party creator but also is creating huge inequality and risk for those who are not so fortunate and it is to these people we should focus our efforts on helping.

But the advent of the coronavirus and subsequent lockdown had certainly provoked people to think differently like this woman from Sweden:

> I think we've become way too disconnected from ourselves, spending our lives in a constant state of stress and rarely making time for just taking things slow and reflecting over our lives and ourselves. Because of lockdown a lot of people are now pretty much forced to slow down and confront themselves, which I suppose is a good thing. For some it may be a wakeup call, as they may realize they've been spending their time focusing on the wrong things. In that way the coronavirus crisis can be the catalyst someone needed to turn their life around.

The lockdown experience took people out of their everyday circumstances of work, family and routine and imposed on them a new set of norms and conditions which, in turn, started to reshape how they organised their lives. In the UK for example, a slow governmental response combined with conflicting stances on when a lockdown should take place and under what conditions, and sudden vulnerability of millions of people, many communities showed solidarity and started working together for each other. This woman from the UK noticed that

> Communities are coming together more, people are volunteering more to help one another and hopefully that will continue, people are learning to appreciate the simple things in life, people are getting their priorities straight, everyone is having to slow down and become more aware of their own mortality and that of people they love.

In fact, when the UK government realised they couldn't do it alone nor had the resources to cope with putting lockdown measures in place while assisting the vulnerable, they endorsed public support by asking people to "clap for them" and put out a call for volunteers. More than half a million people put themselves forward to assist in supporting the health services – which had been dilapidated in the face of years of cuts and austerity politics (Murphy, 2020). Still this had other people feeling doubtful about, even in the face of such "solidarity," that this could translate to "change" like these people from the United States, Austria and Hungary, respectively:

> I am fascinated with the "we are all in this together" but are we really? Are we really still divided by economic/class? Hollywood, athletes, media personalities, upper class have the means to get tested but what about how this is compared to the poor?
>
> *(USA)*

> There is the potential to rethink our current system which is just waiting for the next crisis to come (e.g. climate collapse) or the kind of work we value, but I'm pessimistic about that actually going to lead to change.
>
> *(Austria)*

> I think things will either sooner or later will go back to how they were, because this is how we are. I very much hope it is not going to be how things become, but I do think we will end up in the same mess from where we started. Maybe the scientific community will have better cooperation among themselves, maybe more people will continue to cook for themselves, but in general, most people will continue to get back to the way things were. I hope not, but I think so.
>
> *(Hungary)*

For some people, the advent of the coronavirus exposed the system, its inequality yet provoked this feeling of skepticism about change. This dichotomy between "solidarity" and "fragility" was recognised by some people – the former tending to be seen as a temporary feature while the latter to exacerbate poverty and social suffering as these three quotes from people from Turkey, Brazil and Portugal wrote:

> Everything has a benefit... as the virus now shows how important it is to unite all groups of society and all state institutions.
>
> *(Turkey)*

> Maybe it can expose the contradictions of the capitalism, make people more aware of how the rich are just trying to screw us up. Then, maybe we could start some new solidarity networks. I just joined one to help!
>
> *(Brazil)*

> Well, I think that by now... those benefits exist only in a "potential form" – we would need some strong reflection work during and after the crisis to actually create benefits out of this. Of course, the pollution

dropped and some solidarity has been shown, but for how long will they last after this is over? On the other hand, I fear that the social unbalance will be even stronger, and the poorer will be left with even less resources. I think this could be a great opportunity for one to reflect on the way we are living, but we are really billions of people around the word and it's kind of impossible to reflect globally, so I'm very skeptical about this. Not such a bad case scenario, but I think we will continue as before.

(Portugal)

Note the kind of "macro epiphany" the Portuguese man seems to have as he is writing the text: how, in fact, it's one thing to want and think about social change but another thing to redesign a whole global social system to incorporate those ambitions. So the virus, its risk and a sudden rupture in the status quo in everyday life prompted many people to rethink their current situations and reflect on the state of the world in the face of a virus which they perceived to be here for medium-to-long term for nearly three-quarters of my sample (71%, $n =$ 672) expected the virus to return in some form. The uncertainty around these renewed "waves" of infection as well as a reliable and widely available vaccine coupled with the accumulating debt as governments throw money at science and prop up millions of people in their respective economies creates collective insecurity and major doubt about the future. This was certainly evident in these three quotes from people from Chile, the United Kingdom and Morocco:

I don't know, I think that in a few months we will be able to see benefits or destruction because everything depends on what happens in the impact of the world economy.

(Chile)

I have concerns about those living in cramped, challenging and abusive conditions and the impact on global economy and forgotten issues – migration, war, poverty, other diseases and the impact on mental health for those who are alone etc.

(UK)

There are no benefits at all. Rather, on the contrary, society is tired and people feel anxious and constantly afraid of the unknown, and there is no longer hope for humans to do anything.

(Morocco)

What the future holds, however, we cannot say or know. What seems quite clear though is that people see the future as different: 57% ($n = 539$) people said there was now "an opportunity to think differently about society," while 32% ($n = 306$) felt "the future had already drastically been changed because of the coronavirus." This was reflected in how participants felt about their professional futures, or that of their families, in the context of work/education for over one-third of the sample felt that "coronavirus had placed many doubts in their mind about the future" as this woman from the United States wrote:

> My biggest stressor right now is the economy. There are already more people unemployed and more to come. I'm worried about my husband losing his career even as things start to bounce back. He's a pilot and 9/11 saw a 12 year furlough for many. That's terrifying. I'm also worried about the mental health of people, I know our local hospital has already seen a spike in demand. Being alone and stressed isn't a good combination for anyone, let alone someone with a history of depression and anxiety.

Perhaps we now feel a little bit more professionally redundant as nurses, supermarket cashiers, waste workers and the like continued working during the lockdown despite the potential high risk of infection. In the end, it was these people in these forgotten and burnt-out public service industries which enabled the world to continue to function at its most basic level as this man from France commented:

> Rethinking our way of living, consuming, moving around. At the political level, understand that we have gone too far in our capitalist Western societies where only money counts. Today, which jobs are still essential on which people still move around? Education and health. These are underpaid and very little valued jobs, even though they are the most important ones.

For a short time, these 'heroes' were clapped but that was soon forgotten. Time will tell about whether there be investment in these areas to ensure we are able to deal with future pandemics. Perhaps there won't be any money in any case as nation states are already speculating about the economic and social fallout of the coronavirus which has inadvertently drawn the world to a standstill: – the only certainty it the inevitability. In a situation where mass debt could prompt governments to be more scrupulous about spending may dent our newfound "social consciousness" for supporting everyone in a global society. Now will climate change be reconsidered as a priority on the global agenda?

Revelations: the picture from poverty

The picture from privilege is of concern and doubt while the picture from poverty is of perpetual anxiety and suffering. In a world where war, famine and, in the context of Covid-19, disease and viruses become ever more prevalent, it's difficult to ignore the fact that John's revelations feel somewhat closer to reality. Sam, a young unemployed man from a poor township of Pietermaritzburg, completed my survey. He comes from a small city in South Africa where, as he described it, "the people already suffer from lack of food and water, there is rarely electricity" (see Moyo et al., 2012; Mapisa, 2017). It is normal to see high levels of urban poverty and inequality in Pietermaritzburg and as Hlahla and Hill (2018) show, the city already experiences drought, heat waves, cold spells, hailstorms, floods, disease outbreaks, and veld fires. Yet with the advent of the coronavirus, poverty has increased, vital volunteer aid doesn't get through and there are violent disputes over food aid. He wrote:

> "The government promised to give food parcels during lockdown what they did they gave people old food with fungi and insects in it. Rotten food. So people cannot stand for that enough is enough we need no promises no nothing we will do things on our own. We overthrowing government slowly some people don't even vote now including me I don't vote for any president because they not helping with anything."

The coronavirus is rife in his community because "poor people like us cannot afford masks" he says. For Sam, life looks significantly more complex now. The "future is hard" he summarises as he reflects on how his friend committed suicide when he was tested positive for Covid-19 and his neighbour was beaten to death by the police for disobeying the strict lockdown curfew.

In Cameroon – the East African country which sits below the climate-ravaged Sahel belt (Chapter 1) – Wilson, a young journalist, wrote to me describing how the advent of the coronavirus was adding further social pressure to already tense relations between people in the country because of sharpened inequality and climate-change related problems of crop failure and drought (Gaymard et al., 2015). He said:

> Many people work cash in hand in the informal sector of agriculture. Most are farmers but people are not trading or buying in Cameroon. All the borders are closed with Equatorial Guinea, Chad, Nigeria but due to Covid, all borders are closed. There is a big economic impact. More discontent. People are not buying food, no one can afford to travel to buy as the prices are expensive now and there is none of these markets taking place. A woman I know even committed suicide because she got into debt with the bank after borrowing money to start a small agricultural business. No one bought her produce, she was already in debt.

The coronavirus pandemic has the potential to ratchet up pressure on such communities already suffering at the hands of inequality and climate change and evidence beyond my new study highlights this. For example, research shows that increased droughts caused by climate change in the Nile regions perpetuate West Nile virus epidemics and forecasts indicate that more prolonged droughts could triple the number of cases in the regions (Paull et al., 2017). Undoubtedly, this puts people under direct risk in already pressured circumstances as it did in Brazil with the advent of the mosquito which transmits the Zika virus – a virus considered dangerous when transmitted to pregnant women because of the birth defects for unborn babies (Noor and Ahmed, 2018). Exceptional climatic conditions created by El Niño in 2015 were said to have led to a "record warmest" over the eastern part of South America. Such temperatures, as Paz and Semenza (2016: 745) suggest, provoke droughts and thus expand the mosquito's geographic range and "increase the frequency of the female mosquito biting rate." What originated in South America has since spread to Africa, Asia and Australasia and even cases were reported in Portugal and Germany. In a review of the socioeconomic and health impact of Zika in Latin American and Caribbean countries, it was found to disproportionately affect "the poorest and most vulnerable groups, especially poor women in peri-urban communities" (UNDP, 2017: 9).

Climate change is expanding the tropics at rate of 30 miles a decade which means changes to tropical ecosystems (Parenti, 2011). Indeed, for some generations, Yellow Fever was attributed to the Amazon Basin where the Haemagogus and Sabethes mosquitos flourished. However, by 2016, the mosquitos were found to have moved from the rainforest across the country to the poor favelas of São Paulo and Rio de Janeiro where around 30 million people living in poverty braced themselves against a disease that has a mortality rate of between 3% and 8% (Wallace Wells, 2020). Similarly, unusually heavy rainfalls late in 2019 provided ideal conditions for locusts in East Africa. Already tens of millions of people have lost their livelihoods and communities in Kenya, Ethiopia and Uganda to plagues of locusts which have ravaged their crops. It is estimated that already this year in 2020 around 192 billion locusts, which is 8,000 times the normal amount, are destroying the food supplies of 35,000 people a day: truly biblical proportions of destruction directly attributed to "scrambled weather patterns" (Gramer, 2020):

> …Even more reason to leave,
> Even more reason to come,
> Their country to the thief,
> Resources they retrieve,
> No time to stay or grieve,
> Across the sea in storm,
> Their country got too warm,
> A fate worse to try again,
> Where the motivation from,
> The news it writes them wrong,
> A future gamble when,
> Europe failed them long,
> The stigma and the hate,
> Is the changed climate,
> …Yet at the border's gate…
> In the ranks they wait,
> Or the moment gone,
> Before the moment late.

FIGURE 26   Young refugees studying the boat arrival and departure times as well as security.

The old city of Melilla has several enclaved beaches where young boys meet to board boats in the port for mainland Spain. They mostly hide in cars or vans, in seek refuge in some nook or cranny on the boats. Most of the city walls rest high on cliffs, but there are a few places to descend to the rocky beaches and walk around into the port. This said, it's not easy; there are several Civil Guard controls as well as boat surveillance. On the beaches and rocks, the young men rest during the day and start to gather as evening comes. Some risk boarding boats during the day, others the night, while others tend to study like these two young boys I find at the top of the old city barracks, engaged in a long process of observing when the boats come, where the security is and when is the right time to go (Figure 26). While the remnants of war now sit rusting nearby, they look for a new opportunity to reach Europe - the promised land – a place where inequality is rising, discontent rages in the urban peripheries and sweltering heatwaves, extreme storms and unpredictable flooding break records each year.

REFERENCES

Abel, G., Brottrager, M., Cuaresma, J., and Muttarak, R. (2019) 'Climate, conflict and forced migration' in *Global Environmental Change*, Vol 54: 239–249.

Adamo, N., Al-Ansari, N., Sissakian, V., Knutsson, S., and Laue, J. (2018) 'Climate change: Consequences on Iraq's environment' in *Journal of Earth Sciences and Geotechnical Engineering*, Vol 8 (3): 43–58.

Adams, J. (2007, May 3) 'Rising sea levels threaten small Pacific island nations' Retrieved June 18, 2020, from *The New York Times*: http://www.nytimes.com/2007/05/03/world/asia/03ihtpacific.2.5548184.html?pagewanted=all

Afouxenidis, A. (2015) 'Neoliberalism and democracy' in J. K. Dubrow (Ed.), *Political Inequality in an Age of Democracy,* London and New York: Palgrave MacMillan. (pp. 40–48).

AFP. (2016) 'Denmark is to start taking refugees" possessions to pay for their stay' in *The Journal*, 21st January 2016, cited online on 28th May 2020 at https://www.thejournal.ie/denmark-refugee-plan-2559299-Jan2016/

Aich, V., Ahmad, N., Knuerr, A., Khoshbneen, A., Hattermann, F., Paeth, H., Scanlon, A., and Paton, E. (2017) 'Climate change in Afghanistan deduced from reanalysis and coordinated regional climate downscaling experiment (CORDEX)-South Asia simulations', in *Climate*, Vol 5 (38): 1–25.

Aizebeokhai, A. (2009) 'Global warming and climate change: realities, uncertainties and measures' in *International Journal of Physical Sciences*, Vol 4 (13): 868–879.

al-Shayeji, A. (1997) 'Dangerous perceptions: Gulf views of the U.S. role in the region' in *Middle East Policy Council*, Vol 5 (3) archive cited online on https://mepc.org/node/4696.

Alisic, E., and Letschert, M. (2016) 'Fresh eyes on the European refugee crisis' in *European Journal of Psychotraumatology*, Vol 7 (1): 1–4.

Al Jazeera. (2020a) 'Guatemala: US deportations driving up country's coronavirus cases' in *Al Jazeera*, 15th April 2020, cited online on 27th May 2020 at https://www.aljazeera.com/news/2020/04/guatemala-deportations-driving-country-coronavirus-cases-200415161233540.html

Al Jazeera. (2020b) 'Greece to start setting up closed migrant camps' in *Al Jazeera*, 10th February 2020, cited online on 27th March 2020 at https://www.aljazeera.com/news/2020/02/greece-start-setting-closed-migrant-camps-200210205413986.html

Allsopp, J., and Chase, E. (2017) 'Best interests, durable solutions and belonging: Policy discourses shaping the futures of unaccompanied migrant and refugee minors coming of age in Europe', in *Journal of Ethnic and Migration Studies*, Vol 45 (2): 1–19.

Alnasrawi, A. (2000) 'Iraq: Economic embargo and predatory rule' in E.W. Nafziger, F. Stewart and R.Väyrynen (Eds) *War, Hunger, and Displacement: The Origins of Humanitarian Emergencies*, Vol 2, Oxford: Oxford University Press. (pp. 89–119).

Al-Quraishi, A., and Negm, A. (2019) *Environmental Remote Sensing and GIS in Iraq*, Geneva: Springer Nature.

Alvaredo, F., Chancel, L., Piketty, T., Saez, E., and Zucman, G. (2018) *World Inequality Report 2018*, New York: World Inequality Lab.

Amnesty International. (2013) *Communities shattered by arms proliferation and abuse in Cote d'Ivoire*, London: Amnesty International.

Amnesty International. (2020) *Greece/Turkey: Asylum-seekers and migrants killed and abused at borders*, London: Amnesty International.

Andersson, R. (2014) *Illegality, Inc: Clandestine Migration and the Business of Bordering Europe*, San José: University of California Press.

Angelovski, I., Patrucic, M., and Marzouk, L. (2016) 'Revealed: The £1bn of weapons flowing from Europe to Middle East' in *The Guardian*, 27th July 2016, cited online on 27th May 2020 at https://www.theguardian.com/world/2016/jul/27/weapons-flowing-eastern-europe-middle-east-revealed-arms-trade-syria

Artur, L., and Hilhorst, D. (2012) 'Everyday realities of climate change in Mozambique' in *Global Environmental Change*, Vol 22 (2): 529–536.

Askew, A. (1987) 'Climate change and water resources' in The Influence of Climate Change and Climatic Variability on the Hydrologie Regime and Water Resources (Proceedings of the Vancouver Symposium, August, no. 168, 1987).

Assaffron. (2017) 'Grounded theory and ethnography in the study of transit-mobilities of refugees in border zones. Challenges from fieldworks (Italy/Greece) with people fleeing Syria', in *Revista Internacional de Estudios Migratorios*, Vol 7 (3): 131–152.

Azooz, A., and Talal, S. (2015) 'Evidence of climate change in Iraq' in *Journal of Environment Protection and Sustainable Development*, Vol 1 (2): 66–73.

Baines, E. (2016) *Vulnerable Bodies: Gender in a Global/Local World*, London: Routledge.

BAMF (2019) *Wanderungsmonitoring: Bildungs- und Erwerbsmigration nach*, Berlin: Forschungszentrum Deutschland.

Barbelescu, R. (2017) 'Still a Beacon of human rights? Considerations on the EU response to the refugee crisis in the mediterranean', in *Mediterranean Politics*, Vol 22 (2): 301–308.

Bansak, K., Hainmueller, J., and Hangartner, D. (2016) 'How economic, humanitarian, and religious concerns shape European attitudes toward asylum seekers' in *Science*, doi:10.1126/science.aag2147.

Barbier, E., and Hochard, J. (2017) 'Poverty, rural population distribiution and climate change' in *Environmental and Developmental Economics*, Vol 23 (3): 234–256.

Barima, Y., Kouakou, A., Bamba, I., Sange, Y., Godron, M., Andrieu, J., and Bogaert, J. (2016) 'Cocoa crops are destroying the forest reserves of the classified forest of Haut-Sassandra (Ivory Coast)' in *Global Ecology and Conservation*, Vol 8: 85–98.

Barslund, M., Di Salvo, M., and Laurentsyeva, N. (2018) *The Impact of Refugees on the Labour Market: A Big Splash in a Small Pond?* Brussels: CEPS.

Bartolome, L. (1994) 'Beyong the methods fetish: towards a humanising pedagogy' in *Harvard Educational Review*, Vol 64 (2): 173–194.

Bauböck, R. (2017) 'Refugee Protection and Burden-sharing in the European Union' in *Journal of Common Market Studies*. doi:10.1111/jcms.12638. Online first, October 2017.

Bauman, Z. (2003) *Wasted Lives: Modernity and Its Outcasts*, London: Polity Press.

Bauman, Z. (2016) *Strangers at the Door*, London: Polity Press.

BBC. (2015) 'Desperate migrants try to swim to Britain from France' in *BBC*, 20th July 2015, cited online on 29th May 2020 at https://www.bbc.com/news/uk-33584706

BBC. (2018) 'Trump on climate change report: 'I don't believe it' in *BBC*, 26th November 2018, cited online on 27th May 2020 at https://www.bbc.com/news/world-us-canada-46351940

BBC. (2020a) 'Climate change: more than 3bn could live in extreme heat by 2070' in *BBC*, 5th May 2020, cited online on 27th May 2020 at https://www.bbc.com/news/science-environment-52543589

BBC. (2020b) 'Germany shooting: 'far-right extremist' carried out shisha bars attacks' in *BBC*, 20th February 2020, cited online on 27th May 2020 at https://www.bbc.com/news/world-europe-51567971

Bingsheng, K., and Yijun, H. (2007) *Poultry Sector in China: Structural Changes During the Past Decade and Future Trends*, Beijing: Research Center for Rural Economy, Ministry of Agriculture, China.

Black, R. (2001) 'Fifty years of refugee studies: From theory to policy' in *International Migration Review*, Vol 35 (1): 57–78.

Bogic, M., Ajdkovic, D., Bremner, S., and Franciskovic, T. (2012) 'Factors associated with mental disorders in long-settled war refugees: Refugees from the former Yugoslavia in Germany, Italy and the UK' in *British Journal of Psychiatry*, Vol 200 (3): 216–223.

Bonan, G. (2008) 'Forests and climate change: forcings, feedbacks and the climate benefits of forests' in *Science*, Vol 320 (13): 1444–1449.

Bonomolo, A., and Kirchgaessner, S. (2015) 'UN says 800 migrants dead in boat disaster as Italy launches rescue of two more vessels' in The Guardian, 20th April 2015 cited online at https://www.theguardian.com/world/2015/apr/20/italy-pm-matteo-renzi-migrant-shipwreck-crisis-srebrenica-massacre

Bordignon, M. and Moriconi, S. (2017) 'The case for a common European refugee policy' in *Bruegel Policy Contribution*, No. 2017/8, Bruegel, Brussels.

Borrill, J., Burnett, R., Atkins, R., Miller, S., Briggs, D., Weaver, T., and Madden, A. (2003) 'Patterns of self harm and attempted suicide among white, black and mixed race female prisoners' in *Criminal Behaviour and Mental Health*, Vol 13 (4): 229–240.

Botfield, J., Zwi, A., and Newman, C. E., (2016) 'Young migrants and sexual and reproductive health care', in F. Thomas (Ed.) *Handbook of Migration and Health*, Cheltenham: Eldward Elgar Publishing. (pp. 438–458).

Bou Dib, J. Alamsyah, Z., and Qaim, M. (2018) 'Land-use change and income inequality in rural Indonesia' in *Forest Policy and Economics*, Vol 94 (1): 55–66.

Boukli, A., and Kotzé, J. (2018) *Zemiology: Reconnecting Crime and Social Harm*, London: Palgrave MacMillan.

Bourdieu, P. (1984) *Distinction: A Social Critique of the Judgment of Taste*, Cambridge: Harvard University Press.

Bourgois, P., and Schonberg, J. (2009) *Righteous Dopefiend*, San Francisco: Berkeley University Press.

Bowen, S. (2003) 'No more adhocracies: reforming the management of stabilisation and reconstruction operations' in *Prism*, Vol 3 (2): 3–18.

Brekke, J.P. and Brochman, G. (2014) 'Stuck in transit: secondary migration of asylum seekers in Europe, national differences, and the Dublin regulation' in *Journal of Refugee Studies*, Vol 28 (2): 145–162.

Briggs, D. (2008) 'Robbery careers and desistance attempts' in Safer Communities, Vol 7, (3): 27–34.

Briggs, D., Rhodes, T., Marks, D., Kimber, J., Holloway, G., and Jones, S. (2009) 'Injecting drug use, unstable housing, and the scope for structural interventions' in *Drugs, Education, Prevention and Policy*, Vol 15 (5): 436–450.

Briggs, D. (2010) 'True stories on bare times on road: Developing empowerment, identity and social capital among urban minority ethnic young people in North London' in *Journal of Racial and Ethnic Studies*, Vol 33 (5): 851–871.

Briggs, D. (2012) *Crack Cocaine Users: High Society and Low Life*, London: Routledge.

Briggs, D., and Dobre, D. (2014) *Culture and Immigration in Context: An Ethnography with Romanian Migrant Workers in London*, London: Palgrave MacMillan.

Briggs, D. (2017) 'Lost hope from a lost land': ethnographic reflections on the Syrian refugee crisis' in *Discovery Society*, Issue 41 and available online at http://discoversociety.org/2017/02/01/lost-hope-from-a-lost-land-ethnographic-reflections-on-the-syrian-refugee-crisis/

Briggs, D., and Monge Gamero, R. (2017) *Dead End Lives: Drugs and Violence in the City Shadows*, Bristol: Policy Press.

Briggs, D., and Cordero, R. (2018) 'Young refugees, youth work and a call for political energy: Notes from an unfunded ethnographic study', in M. Pisani., T, Basarab., B. Giovanna Bello, and S. Laine (Eds) *Between Insecurity and Hope Reflections on Youth Work with Young Refugees*, Brussels: Council of Europe and European Commission. (pp. 25–45).

Briggs, D., Pérez Suárez, J., and Cordero Verdugo, R. (2018) 'From crime science to the crime of science', *Safer Communities*, Vol 17 (1): 22–32.

Brodie, N., and Sabrine, I. (2018) 'The illegal excavation and trade of Syrian cultural objects: a view from the ground' in *Journal of Field Archaeology*, Vol 43 (1): 74–84.

Burke, M., Dykema, J., Lobell, D., Miguel, D., and Satyanath, S. (2014) 'Incorporating climate uncertainty into estimates of climate change impacts' in *Review of Economics and Statistics*, Vol 97 (2): 1–39.

C-Adapt. (2016) *Climate Change in Afghanistan: What Does It Mean for Rural Livelihoods and Food Security*, Gothenburg: C-Adapt.

Cardoso, P., Erdinc, I., Horemans, J., and Lavery, S. (2014) *Precarious Employment in Europe*, Brussels: RennerInstitut.

Carlon, D., Downs, A., and Wert-Gray, S. (2006) 'Statistics as fetishes the case of financial performance measures and executive compensation' in *Organisational Research Methods*, Vol 9 (4): 475–490.

Carr, M. (2015) *Fortress Europe: Inside the War against Immigration*, London: Hurst Publishers.

Carrera, S. and Vankova, Z. (2019) *Human Rights Aspects of Immigrant and Refugee Integration Policies*, Brussels: Council of Europe.

Carrington, D. (2017) 'Farms hit by labour shortage as migrant workers shun 'racist' UK' in *The Guardian*, 22nd June 2017, cited online on 27th May 2020 at https://www.theguardian.com/environment/2017/jun/22/farms-hit-by-labour-shortage-as-migrant-workers-shun-racist-uk

CEAR (Comisión Española de Ayuda de Refugiado). (2016) *Informe 2016: Las personas refugiadas en España y Europa*, Madrid: CEAR.

Chellaney, B. (2014, February 20) 'The battle for water. Retrieved June 19, 2020', from The Hindu: http://www.thehindu.com/opinion/lead/the-battle-for-water/article5707274.ece

Chimni, B. (1998) 'The geopolitics of refugee studies: a view from the South' in *Journal of Refugee Studies,* Vol 11 (4): 350–374.

Chirisa, I., Bandauko, E., Mazhindu, E., Kwangwama, N., and Chikowore, G. (2016) 'Building resilient infrastructure in the face of climate change in African cities: Scope, potentiality and challenges' in *Development Southern Africa,* Vol 33 (1): 113–127.

Colchester, M., and Chao, S. (2014) *The oil palm sector at the crossroads,* Jakarta: Sawit Watch and TUK INDONESIA.

Connolly, K. (2015) 'Killing of Eritrean refugee in Dresden exposes racial tensions in Germany' in *The Guardian,* 15th January 2015, cited online on 27th May 2020 at https://www.theguardian.com/world/2015/jan/15/pegida-dresden-eritrean-refugee-murder-far-right-germany

Connor, P. (2020) 'More than nine-in-ten people worldwide live in countries with travel restrictions amid COVID-19' in *Pew Research Centre,* 1st April 2020, cited online on 27th May 2020 https://www.pewresearch.org/fact-tank/2020/04/01/more-than-nine-in-ten-people-worldwide-live-in-countries-with-travel-restrictions-amid-covid-19/

Cornish, P. (2019) 'The men making a fortune from Syria's war' in *Financial Times,* 2nd October 2019, cited online on 27th May 2020 at https://www.ft.com/content/525ec4e4-e4a3-11e9-9743-db5a370481bc

Crary, J., (2013) 24/7: *Late Capitalism and the Ends of Sleep,* London; New York: Verso.

Crawford, N. (2013) *Civilian Death and Injury in the Iraq War, 2003–2013,* Costs of War, Boston University Publication.

Crawley, H., Duvell, F., Jones, K., McMahon, S., and Sigona, N. (2016) *Unravelling Europe's Migrant Crisis: Journeys Over Land and Sea,* Bristol: Policy Press.Cui, Y., Zhang, Z., Froines, J., Zhao, J., Wang, H., Yu, S., and Detels, R. (2003) 'Air pollution and case fatality of SARS in the People's Republic of China: an ecologic study' in *Environmental Health,* Vol 2 (15): 2–15.

Cummings, C., Pacitto, J., Louro, D., and Foresti, M. (2015) *Why People Move: Understanding the Drivers and Trends of Migration to Europe,* London: Overseas Development Institute.

Daoud, A., Halleröd, B., and Guha-Sapir, D. (2016) 'What is the association between absolute child poverty, poor governance, and natural disasters? A global comparison of some of the realities of climate change', in *PLOS ONE,* Vol 11 (4): 1–20.

Daponte, B. (1993) 'A case study in estimating causalities from War and its Aftermath: The 1991 Persian Gulf War', in *Physicians for Social Responsibility Quarterly,* Vol 3: 57–66.

Dekker, R., Engbersen, G., and Faber, M. (2015) *The Use of Online Media in Migration Networks,* Popul. Space Place in Population, Space and Place, Vol 22: 539–551.

Desiderio, M. (2017) *Integrating Refugees into Host Country Labor Markets: Challenges and Policy Options,* Washington: Migration Policy Institute.

Despretz, P. (2019) *2019 Update on Deforestation in South West Cote d'Ivoire,* London: Vivid Economics.

Dick, S. (2019) 'The Arms Trade and Syria' in *Georgetown Journal of International Affairs,* 2nd September 2019, cited online on 27th May 2020 at https://www.georgetownjournalofinternationalaffairs.org/online-edition/2019/9/2/the-arms-trade-and-syria

Dimitrov, A., and Angelov, G. (2017) 'Refugee integration in the EU: challenges and economic impact' in *Economic Alternatives,* 4: 584–600.

Diwakar, V., Lovell, E., Opitz-Stapleton, S., Shephert, A., and Twigg, J. (2019) *Child Poverty, Disasters and Climate Change,* London: Chronic Poverty Advisory Network.

Donahue, B. (2016) 'Meet the Two Brothers Making Millions Off the Refugee Crisis in Scandinavia' in *Bloomberg,* 6th January 2016, cited online on 28th May 2020 at https://www.bloomberg.com/features/2016-norway-refugee-crisis-profiteers/

Donchyts, G., Baart, F., Winsemius, H., Gorelick, N., Kwadijk, J., van de Giesen. (2016) 'Earth's surface water change over the past 30 years' in *Nature Climate Change*, Vol 6: 810–813.

Doomernik, J., and Ardon, D. (2018) 'The city as an agent of refugee integration' in *Urban Planning*, Vol 3 (4): 91–100.

Doward, J. (2017) 'Iraqi invasion of Kuwait in 1990 used by UK to boost weapon sales', in *The Guardian*, 12th August 2017, cited online on 26th May 2020 at https://www.theguardian.com/world/2017/aug/12/arms-trade-margaret-thatcher-kuwait-saddam-hussein.

Dubus, N. (2018) 'Integration or building resilience: What should the goal be in refugee resettlement?' in *Journal of Immigrant & Refugee Studies*, Vol 16 (4): 413–429.

Dummett, M. (2016) *"This Is What We Die for": Human Rights Abuses in the Democratic Republic of Congo Power the Global Trade in Cobalt*, London: Amnesty International.

Dunlap, A. (2019) 'Wind, coal, and copper: the politics of land grabbing, counterinsurgency, and the social engineering of extraction' in *Globalisations*, doi:10.1080/14747731.2019.1682789.

Dunlap, R., McCright, A., and Yarosh, J. (2016) 'The political divide on climate change: partisan polarization widens in the U.S' in *Environment: Science and Policy for Sustainable Development*, Vol 58 (5): 4–23.

DW. (2019a) 'Germany needs 260,000 immigrants a year to meet labor demand' in *DW*, 12th February 2019, cited online on 27th May 2020 at https://www.dw.com/en/study-germany-needs-260000-immigrants-a-year-to-meet-labor-demand/a-47470731

DW. (2019b) 'EU asylum applications fall to pre-2015 levels' in *DW*, 14th March 2019, cited online on 27th May 2020 at https://www.dw.com/en/eu-asylum-applications-fall-to-pre-2015-levels/a-47921935

DW. (2020a) 'Fears of mafia exploitation as Italy opens labor market to farm workers' in *DW*, 4th April 2020, cited online on 27th May 2020 at https://www.infomigrants.net/en/post/24288/fears-of-mafia-exploitation-as-italy-opens-labor-market-to-farm-workers

DW. (2020b) 'Syrian refugees in Lebanon more scared of starvation than COVID-19' in *DW*, 7th May 2020, cited online on 27th May 2020 at https://www.infomigrants.net/en/post/24580/syrian-refugees-in-lebanon-more-scared-of-starvation-than-covid-19

Eckstein, D., Künzel, V., Schäfer, L., and Winges, M. (2020) *Global Climate Risk Index 2020 Briefing Paper*, Bonn: Germanwatch.

Enticott, J., Shawyer, F., Vasi, S., Buck, K., Cheng, H., Russell, G., Kakuma, R., Minas, H., and Meadows, G. (2018) 'A systematic review of studies with a representative sample of refugees and asylum seekers living in the community for participation in mental health research' in *BMC Medical Research Methodology*, Vol 37 (17): 1–16.

Entorf, H., and Lange, M. (2018) *Refugees Welcome? Understanding the Regional Heterogeneity of Anti-Foreigner Hate Crimes in Germany*, ZEW Discussion Papers, No. 19-005, ZEW - Leibniz-Zentrum für Europäische Wirtschaftsforschung, Mannheim.

EPA. (2016) *What Climate Change Means for Guam*, Washington: EPA.

EUAFR (European Union Agency for Fundamental Human Rights). (2016) *Current Migrant Situation in the EU: Hate Crime*, Vienna: EUAFR.

European Commission. (2016) *Research on Migration: Facing Realities and Maximising Opportunities*, Brussels: European Commission.

EWGCSR. (2018) *Iraq: Climate-Related Security Risk Assessment*, Stockholm: Stockholm International Peace Research Institute.

EY. (2016) *Managing the EU Migration Crisis*, London: EY.

FAOSTAT (2016) *The State of Food Agriculture: Climate Change, Agriculture and Food Security*, Rome: FAO.

Farina, E., Green, C.P., and McVicar, D. (2019) *Zero Hour Contracts and Their Growth*, Belfast: Institute of Labour Economics.

Fekete, L. (2018) 'Migrants, borders and the criminalisation of solidarity in the EU' in *Race and Class*, Vol 59 (4): 65–83.

Fisher, M. (2009) *Capitalist Realism: Is There No Alternative?* London: Zero Books.

Fletcher, R. (2012) 'Capitalising on Chaos: Climate Change and Disaster Capitalism' in *Theory and Politics in Organisation*, Vol 12 (1/2): 97–112.

Fontanari, E. (2019) *Lives in Transit. An Ethnographic Study of Refugees' Subjectivity across European Borders*, New York: Routledge.

Fox, A., Khan, L., Briggs, D., Rees-Jones, N., Thompson, Z., and Owens, J. (2005) *Throughcare and Aftercare: Promising Practice in Service Delivery for Clients Released from Prison or Leaving Residential Rehabilitation*, London: Home Office, Online Report 01/05.

Funk, N. (2016) 'A spectre in Germany: refugees, a 'welcome culture' and an 'integration politics'' in *Journal of Global Ethics*, Vol 12 (3): 289–299.

Gale, P., Brouwer, A., Ramnial, V., Kelly, L., Kosmider, R., Fooks, A., and Snary, E. (2010) 'Assessing the impact of climate change on vector-borne viruses in the EU through the elicitation of expert opinion' in *Epidemiological Infections*, Vol 138, 214–225.

Garcés, Y. (2015) *Europa ante la crisis de los refugiados 10 efectos colaterales*, Barcelona: CIDOB.

Gaymard, S., Kay, N., and Etoundi, J. (2015) 'Climate Change and Beliefs in Cameroon: A Qualitative Study Among Farmers in the Equatorial and Sudano-Sahelian Zones' in *Canadian Social Science*, Vol 11 (7): 53–64.

Gazdar, H. (2002) 'Pre-modern, modern and post-modern famine in Iraq' in *IDS Bulletin* Vol 33 (2002) archived in https://core.ac.uk/download/pdf/43539711.pdfGhaziri, N., Blaser, J., Darwiche, J., S, J.C., Zozaya, J., Marion-Veyron, R., Spini, D., and Bodenmann, P. (2019) 'Protocol of a longitudinal study on the specific needs of Syrian refugee families in Switzerland' in *BMC International Health and Human Right*, Vol 32 (19): 1–7.

Ghulami, M. (2017) *Assessment of Climate Change Impacts on Water Resources and Agriculture in Data-Scarce Kabul Basin, Afghanistan*, Cannes: Université Côte d'Azur.

Gleick, P. (2014) 'Water drought, climate change and conflict in Syria' in *American Meteorology Society*, Vol 6 (3): 331–340.

Glorius, B., and Doomernik, J. (2020) *Geographies of Asylum in Europe and the Role of the European Localities*, Chemnitz: IMiScoe.

Gould, E. (2009) 'Emerging viruses and the significance of climate change' in *Clinical Micro Biological Infections*, Vol 15 (6): 503.

GRAIN. (2011) *The Great Food Robbery: How Corporations Control Food, Grab Land and Destroy the Climate*, Barcelona: Grain.

Gramer, R. (2020) 'Top U.S. aid chief warns of locust devastation in East Africa' in *Foreign Policy*, 26th February 2020, cited online on 27th May 2020 at https://foreignpolicy.com/2020/02/26/usaid-mark-green-locust-swarms-east-africa/

Greenpeace. (2019a) *Palm Oil's New Frontier: How Industrial Expansion Threatens Africa's Rainforests,* Amsterdam: Greenpeace.

Greenpeace. (2019b) *Burning Down the House: How Unilever and Other Global Brands Continue to Fuel Indonesia's Fires,* Amsterdam: Greenpeace.

Gunerlap, B., Gunerlap, I., and Liu, Y. (2015) 'Changing global patterns of urban exposure to flood and drought hazards' in *Global Environmental Change*, Vol 31 (2): 217–225.

Günşen, T., Sever, H., and Sever, M. (2015) 'A Survey Study on the Profile of Human Smugglers in Turkey' in *Advances in Applied Sociology*, Vol 5 (1): 1–22.

Gustin, G. (2020) 'Our growing food demands will lead to more corona-like viruses' in *Climate News*, 24th March 2020, cited online on 27th May 2020 at https://insideclimatenews.org/news/23032020/coronavirus-zoonotic-diseases-climate-change-agriculture

Haase, N., and Somaskanda, N. (2017) 'Why Germany's far-right flourishes in Dresden' in *DW*, 16th June 2017, cited online on 27th May 2020 at https://www.dw.com/en/why-germanys-far-right-flourishes-in-dresden/a-39076094

Haferlach, L., and Kurban, D. (2017) 'Lessons learnt from the EU-Turkey refugee agreement in guiding EU migration partnerships with origin and transit countries' in *Global Policy*, Vol 8 (4): 85–93.

Hall, C.M., Amelung, B., Cohen, S., Eijgelaar, E., Gössling, S., Higham, J., Leemans, R., Peeters, P., Ram, Y., and Scott, D. (2015) 'On climate change skepticism and denial in tourism' in *Journal of Sustainable Tourism*, Vol 23 (1): 4–25.

Hall, R. (2019) 'In the future, only the rich will be able to escape the unbearable heat from climate change. In Iraq, it's already happening' in *The Independent*, 10th August 2019, cited online on 26th May 2020 at https://www.independent.co.uk/news/world/middle-east/climate-change-apartheid-poor-iraq-effects-heatwave-a9049206.html

Hall, S., Winlow, S., and Ancrum, C. (2008) *Criminal Identities and Consumer Culture: Crime, Exclusion and the New Culture of Narcissism*, Devon: Willan Publishing.

Hall, S. (2012) *Theorizing Crime and Deviance: A New Perspective*, London: Sage.

Hall, S., and Winlow, S. (2018) 'Big trouble or little evils: the ideological struggle over the concept of harm' in T. Rayman and O. Smith (Eds.) *The Deviant Leisure Perspective: A Theoretical Introduction*, London: Palgrave MacMillan. (pp. 107–126).

Hall, S., Kuldova, T., and Horsley, M. (2020) *Crime, Harm and Consumerism*, London: Routledge.

Hallegatte, S., Bangalore, M., Bonzingo, L., Fay, M., Kane, T., Narloch, U., Rozenburg, J., Treguer, D., and Vogt-Schilb, A. (2015) *Shockwaves: Managing the Impacts of Climate Change on Poverty*, Washington: World Bank Group.

Hameso, S. (2017) 'Farmers and policy-makers' perceptions of climate change in Ethiopia, Climate and Development' in *Climate and Development*, Vol 10 (4): 347–359.

Hansen, R., and Randeira, S. (2016) 'Tensions of refugee politics in Europe' in *Science*, Vol 353 (6303): 994–995.

Hassanyar, M., Tsutsumi, J., and Najamatsu, R. (2019) 'Farmers' perceptions of climate change and adaptive responses; evidence from Kunduz River Basin, Afghanistan' in *Transylvanian Review*, Vol XXVII (44): 1–14.

Hegghammer, T. (2006) 'Global jihadism after the Iraq war' in *Middle East Journal*, Vol 60 (1): 11–32.

von Hein, M. (2020) 'Crises are fuelling the global arms trade: SIPRI report' in *DW*, 9th March 2020, cited online on 27th May 2020 at https://www.dw.com/en/crises-are-fueling-the-global-arms-trade-sipri-report/a-52688298

Heldt, E. (2018) *European Policy Failure During the Refugee Crisis: Partial Empowerment, Reluctant Agents, a Cacophony of Voices, and Unilateral Action*, EUI Working Paper RSCAS 2018/36.

Herbert, M. (2014) 'Partisans, profiteers, and criminals: Syria's illicit economy' in *The Fletcher Forum of World Affairs*, Vol 38 (Winter): 1.

Hernandez, M. (2009) 'Psychological theories of immigration' in *Journal of Human Behaviour in the Social Environment*, Vol 19 (6): 713–726.

Hillyard, P., and Tombs, S. (2007) 'From crime to social harm?' in *Crime, Law and Social Change*, Vol 48 (9): 9–25.

Hinnebusch, R. (2007) 'The US invasion of Iraq: explanations and implications', in *Critique: Critical Middle Eastern Studies*, Vol 16 (3): 209–228.

Hlahla, S., and Hill, T. (2018) 'Responses to climate variability in urban poor communities in Pietermaritzburg, KwaZulu-Natal, South Africa' in *Sage Open*, Vol 8 (3): 1–16.

Hoffman, D., and Tyler, P. (1990) 'Bush denounces Saddam as threat to Arabs, West' in *Washington Post*, 16th August 1990, cited online on 24th March 2020 at https://www.washingtonpost.com/archive/politics/1990/08/16/bush-denounces-saddam-as-threat-to-arabs-west/f3ba4a06-7aba-4c94-91c6-8191738be667/

Holden, E. (2019) 'Trump begins year-long process to formally exit Paris climate agreement' in *The Guardian*, 5th November 2019, cited online on 27th May 2020 at https://www.theguardian.com/us-news/2019/nov/04/donald-trump-climate-crisis-exit-paris-agreement.

Holley, P. (2015) 'The tiny pill fuelling Syria's war and turning fighters into superhuman soldiers' in *The Washington Post*, 19 November, https://www. washingtonpost.com/news/worldviews/

Holtom, P., Bromley, M., Wezeman, P., and Wezeman, S. (2013) *Trends in International Arms Transfers*, 2013, Stockholm: SPIRI.

Hoste, R. (2015) 'Romania: half of EU pug farms' in *Agrifuture*, Summer: 20–21.

Hulme M. (2019) 'Is it too late (to stop dangerous climate change)? An editorial' in *WIREs Climate Change*, e619. doi:10.1002/wcc.619

Human Rights Watch. (2017) *World report 2017*, New York: Human Rights Watch.

Human Rights Watch. (2019) *Syria: Events of 2018*' in *World Report 2018*, New York: Human Rights Watch.

Hussein, H., Natta, A., Yehya, A., and Hamadna, B. (2020) 'Syrian refugees, water scarcity, and dynamic policies: how do the new refugee discourses impact water governance debates in Lebanon and Jordan?' in *Water*, Vol 12 (2): 324–332.

İçduygu, A., and Millet, E. (2016) *Syrian Refugees in Turkey: Insecure Lives in an Environment of Pseudo-Integration, Working Paper 13*, Istanbul: Koç University.

International Labour Organisation (ILO). (2019) *World Employment Social Outlook*, Geneva: International Labour Office.

International Organisation of Migration (IOM). (2014) *Fatal Journeys: Tracking Lives Lost During Migration*, Geneva: International Organisation of Migration.

IPCC. (2013) *Bio-Brief 2: Climate Change*, Singapore: Asian Development Bank.

IPCC. (2019) *Summary for Policymakers, In: IPCC Special Report on the Ocean and Cryosphere in a Changing Climate [H.-O. Pörtner, D.C. Roberts, V. Masson-Delmotte, P. Zhai, M. Tignor, E. Poloczanska, K. Mintenbeck, A. Alegría, M. Nicolai, A. Okem, J. Petzold, B. Rama, N.M. Weyer (eds.)]*, Singapore: Asian Development Bank.

Jackson, C. (2017) 'The inequalities of climate change and poverty: impact analysis and potential solutions' in *Inquiries Journal*, Vol 9 (3): 1–3.

Jacobsen, K., and L. Landau. (2003) 'The dual imperative in refugee research: Some methodological and ethical considerations in social science research on forced migration' in *Disasters*, Vol 27 (3): 185–206.

Jones, R. (2016) *Violent Borders: Refugees and the Right to Move*, London: Verso.

Jones, L., and Cunliffe, P. (2020) *Saving Britain's Universities: Academic freedom, Democracy and Renewal*, CIEO: Canterbury.

Kancs, d'A., and Lecca, P. (2018) 'Long-term social, economic and fiscal effects of immigration into the EU: the role of the integration policy' in *World Economy*, Vol 41: 2599–2630.

Kampanyasi, T. (2019) *Syrian Refugees: Abuse & Exploitation in Turkish Garment Factories*, London: Business and Human Rights Resource Centre.

Kearns A., and Whitely, E. (2015) 'Getting there? The effects of functional factors, time and place on the social integration of migrants' in *Journal of Ethnic and Migration Studies*, Vol 41(13): 2105–2129.

Karak, M. (2019) 'Climate change and Syria's civil war' in *JSTOR Daily*, 12th September 2019, cited online on 27th May 2020 at https://daily.jstor.org/climate-change-and-syrias-civil-war/

Kedem, S. (2018) 'The global weapons trade is booming due to wars in Syria and Yemen' in *Verdict*, 10th May 2018, cited online on 27th May 2020 at https://www.verdict.co.uk/middle-east-violence-drives-103-rise-in-regional-arms-imports/

Keegan, J. (2010) *The Iraq War*, London: Vintage Books.

Keesing, F., Belden, L., Daszak, P., Dobson, A., Harvell, C., Holt, R., Hudson, P., Jolles, A., Jones, K., Mitchell, C., Myers, S., Bogich, T., and Ostfeld, R. (2010) 'Impacts of biodiversity on the emergence and transmission of infectious diseases' in *Nature*, Vol 468 (December): 647–652.

Kelley, C., Modtadi, S., Cane, M., Seager, R., and Kushnir, Y. (2015) 'Climate change in the Fertile Crescent and implications of the recent Syrian drought' in *Proceedings of the National Academy of Sciences of the United States of America (PNAS)*, Vol 112 (11): 3241–3246.

Kelly, A. (2020) 'Covid-19 spreading quickly through refugee camps, warn Calais aid groups' in *The Guardian*, 9th April 2020, cited online on 27th April 2020 at https://www.theguardian.com/global-development/2020/apr/09/covid-19-spreading-quickly-though-refugee-camps-warn-calais-aid-groups#maincontent

Klikauer, T. (2018) 'German government investigates anti-Semitism' in *Ethnic and Racial Studies* Vol 41 (13): 2337–2343.

King, D., Browne, J., Layard, R., O'Donnell, G., Rees, M., Stern, N., and Turner, A. (2015) *A Global Apollo Programme to Combat Climate Change*, London: London School of Economics.

King, N. (2016) *No Borders: The Politics of Immigration Control and Resistance*, London: Zed Books.

Kingsley, P. (2017) *The New Odyssey: The Story of the Twenty-First-Century Refugee Crisis*, New York: Liveright Publishing.

Klare, M. (2011) 'The public health implications of resource wars' in *American Journal of Public Health*, Vol 101 (9): 1615–1619.

Klein, N. (2007) *The Shock Doctrine: The Rise of Disaster Capitalism*, New York: MacMillan USA.

Knippertz, P., Evans, M., and Field, P. (2015) 'The possible role of local air pollution in climate change in West Africa' in *Nature Climate Change*, Vol 5 (9): 815–822.

Kostiner, J. (2009) 'Between the Gulf Wars: restrained conflict' In J. Kostiner (Ed.) *Conflict and Cooperation in the Gulf Region*. Wiesbaden: VS Verlag für Sozialwissenschaften. (pp. 141–200).

Krestenitis, Y., Androulidakis, Y., Makris, C., Kobiadou, K., Baltikas, V., and Diamanti, P. (2016) 'Evolution of storm surge extreme events in Greek Seas under climate change scenario' Paper presented at the 11th Panhellenic Symposium on Oceanography and Fisheries, At Mytilene, Lesvos island, Greece, 2nd May 2015.

Kulp, S., and Strauss, H. (2019) 'New elevation data triple estimates of global vulnerability to sea-level rise and coastal flooding' in *Nature Communications*, Vol 10: 1–12.

Kuns, B., and Visser, O. (2016) 'Towards an agroholding typology: differentiating large farm companies in Russia and Ukraine', Discussion Paper prepared for presentation at the 90th Annual Conference of the Agricultural Economics Society, University of Warwick, England 4–6th April 2016.

Lakhani, S. (2013) *Extractive Industries and Peacebuilding in Afghanistan the Role of Social Accountability*, Washington: US Institute of Peace.

Latour, B. (2018) *Down to Earth: Politics in the New Climate Regime*, London: Polity Press.

Lawson, F. (2017) 'Egypt versus Ethiopia: The Conflict over the Nile Metastasizes' in *The International Spectator: Italian Journal of International Affairs*, Vol 52 (4): 129–144.

Lederer, E. (2014) 'UN: ISIS got up to $45 m in ransoms' in *Daily Star*, 25 November, http://www.dailystar.com.lb/News/Middle-East/2014/ Nov-25/278829-un-isis-got-up-to-45min-ransoms.ashx

Lee, C. (2009) 'Sociological theories of immigration pathways to integration for U.S. immigrants' in *Journal of Human Behaviour in the Social Environment*, Vol 19 (6): 730–743.

Lister, C. (2015) 'Assessing Syria's jihad' in *Survival*, Vol 56 (6): 87–112.

Loewenstein, A. (2015) 'How private companies are exploiting the refugee crisis for profit' in *The Independent*, 23rd October 2015, cited online on 29th May 2020 at https://www.independent.co.uk/voices/how-companies-have-been-exploiting-the-refugee-crisis-for-profit-a6706587.html

Loewenstein, A. (2019) 'Peace in Afghanistan? Maybe—but a minerals rush is already underway' in *The Nation*, 30th January 2019, cited online on 26th May 2020 at https://www.thenation.com/article/archive/afghanistan-war-peace-talks-minerals/

Le Billion, P. (2018) *Non-State War Economies*, New York: Cornell University Press.

Lichtenstein, G., and Puma, J. (2018) 'The refugee integration survey and evaluation (RISE): results from a four-year longitudinal study' in *Journal of Refugee Studies*, 1–20. doi:10.1093/jrs/fey034.

Lindgren, S. (2019) 'Hacking social for the age of Datafication' in *Journal of Digital Social Research*, Vol 1 (1): 1–9.

LLC. (2019) Palm Oil Market [By Product Type (Palm Kernel Oil & Cake, Crude Palm Oil and Others); By Application Type (Biofuels, Personal Care, Edible Oil, Lubricants and Others); By Regions]: Market size & Forecast, 2017–2026, LLC: New York.

Lloyd, A. (2018) *The Harms of Work*, Bristol: Policy Press.

Lund, A. (2018) *The Factory: A Glimpse into Syria's War Economy*, Stockholm: The Century Foundation.

Mahdi, K. (2012) *Oil and Oil Policy in Iraq: Past and Present*, London: Polity Press.

Masipa, T. (2017) 'The impact of climate change on food security in South Africa: Current realities and challenges ahead' in *Jàmbá – Journal of Disaster Risk Studie*, Vol 9 (1): a411. https:// doi.org/10.4102/jamba. v9i1.411

Matthews, R., Easton, H., Briggs, D., and Pease, K. (2007) *Assessment of the Outcomes of Anti-Social Behaviour Orders*, Bristol: Policy Press.

Matthews, R., and Briggs, D. (2008) 'Lost in translation: Interpreting and implementing anti-social behaviour strategies' in P. Squires (Ed) *ASBO Nation: The Criminalisation of Nuisance*, Bristol: Policy Press. (pp. 87–100).

Monterescu, D., and Rajaram, P. (2016) 'Immobilizing Mobility: Border Ethnography, Illiberal Democracy and the Politics of the Refugee Crisis in Hungary' in *American Ethnologist*, Vol 43 (1): 1–12.

Moris, D. and Kousoulis, A. (2018) 'Refugee crisis in Greece: healthcare and integration as current challenges' in *Perspectives in Public Health*, Vol 137 (6): 309–310.

Noor, R., and Ahmed, T. (2018) 'Zika virus: epidemiological study and its association with public health risk' in *Journal of Infection and Public Health*, Vol 11 (5): 611–616.

Oduntan, O., and Ruthven, I. (2017) 'Investigating the information gaps in refugee integration' in *Computer Science*, Vol 54 (1): 1–10.

Onghena, Y. (2015) *Europa ante la crisis de los refugiados 10 efectos colaterales*, Barcelona: CIDOB.

Oosterveld, W., and Bloem, W. (2017) *The Rise and Fall of ISIS: From Evitability to Inevitability*, The Hague: Hague Centre for Strategic Studies.

Oxfam. (2020) *Time to Care: Unpaid and Underpaid Care Work and the Global Inequality Crisis*, Oxford: Oxfam.

Makki, D. (2018) 'Syria's War Economy Exacerbates the Divide between the Rich and the Poor' published online by the *Middle East Institute* and cited online on 24th March 2020 at https://www.mei.edu/publications/syrias-war-economy-exacerbates-divide-between-rich-and-poor

Mapisa, T. (2017) 'The impact of climate change on food security in South Africa: current realities and challenges ahead' in *Journal of Disaster Risk Studies*, Vol 9 (1): 1–7.

Marbach, M., Hainmueller, J., and Hangartner, D. (2018) 'The long-term impact of employment bands on economic integration of refugees' in *Science Advances*, Vol 4 (9): 1–6.

Martín, M. (2020) 'Más de 5.000 Euro por escapar de España en patera' in *El País*, 24th April 2020, cited online on 27th May 2020 at https://elpais.com/espana/2020-04-23/mas-de-5000-Europor-escapar-de-espana-en-patera.html

Martínez, J., and Eng, B. (2016) 'The unintended consequences of emergency food aid: Neutrality, sovereignty and politics in the Syrian civil war, 2012–15' in *International Affairs*, Vol 92 (1): 153–173.

Maxwell, N. (2017) 'Can universities save us from disaster?' in *The Horizon*, Vol 25 (2): 115–130.

McDonald-Gibson, C. (2017) *Castaway: Stories of Survival from Europe's Refugee Crisis*, London: Granta.

McLoughlin, P. (2020) 'Hard economic times test the patience of Assad loyalists' in *The New Arab*, 25th January 2020, cited online on 27th May 2020 at https://english.alaraby.co.uk/english/indepth/2020/1/25/syria-weekly-hard-times-test-assad-loyalists-patience

McMichael, P. (2012) 'The land grab and corporate food regime restructuring' in *Journal of Peasant Studies*, 39 (3–4): 681–701.

McNaugher, T. (1990) 'Ballistic missiles and chemical weapons: The legacy of the Iran-Iraq War' in *International Security*, Vol 15 (2): 5–34.

Miller, T. (2018) *Storming the Wall: Climate Change, Migration and Homeland Security*, San Francisco: City Lights Publishers.

Moyo, A., Rennkamp, B., Grottera, C., and Wills, W. (2012) *Reducing Inequality and Poverty While Mitigating Climate Change, MAPS Researfch Paper*, Rio de Janeiro, Cape Town, LIMA/COPPE/UCT MAPS.

NCA. (2018) *Fourth National Climate Assessment*, Washington: NCA.

Newell, P., and Paterson, M. (2010) *Climate Capitalism: Global Warming and the Transformation of the Global Economy*, Cambridge: Cambridge University Press.

Niemann, A. and Zaun, N. (2018) 'EU refugee policies and politics in times of crisis: theoretical and empirical perspectives', in *Journal of Common Market Studies*, Vol. 56 (1): pp. 3–22.

NPR. (2019) 'Transcript: Greta Thunberg's speech at the U.N. climate action summit', cited online on 2nd April 2020 at https://www.npr.org/2019/09/23/763452863/transcript-greta-thunbergs-speech-at-the-u-n-climate-action-summit?t=1585836912892

Painter, J., and Gavin, N. (2015) 'Climate skepticism in British Newspapers, 2007–2011' in *Environmental Communication*, doi:10.1080/17524032.2014.995193.

Palmer, T. (2014) 'Record-breaking winters and global climate change' in *Atmospheric Science*, Vol 344 (6186): 803–804.

Parenti, C. (2011) *Tropic of Chaos: Climate Change and the New Geography of Violence*, New York: Bold Type Books.

Parry, M. (1990) *Climate Change and World Agriculture*, London: Earthscan Publications Limited.

Paull, S., Horton, D., Asfaq, M., Rastogi, M., Kramer, L., Diffenbaugh, N., and Kilpatrick, A. (2017) 'Drought and immunity determine the intensity of West Nile virus epidemics and climate change impacts' in *Proceedings B Research*, Vol 284: 1–10.

Paz, S., and Semenza, J. (2017) 'El niño and climate change-contributing factors in the dispersal of Zika virus in the Americas?' in *The Lancet*, Vol 387 (February): 745.

Peace, T., and Meer, N. (2019) *Refugee Integration in Europe since the 'Crisis'*, EUI Working Paper RSCAS 2019/31.

Petrenko, C., Paltseva, J., and Searle, S. (2016) *Ecological Impacts of Palm Oil Expansion in Indonesia*, Washington: ICCT.

della Porta, D. (2018) *Solidarity Mobilizations in the 'Refugee Crisis': Contentious Moves*, London: Palgrave MacMillan.

Porter, M., and Haslam, N. (2005) 'Predisplacement and postdisplacement factors associated with mental health of refugees and internally displaced persons: A meta-analysis' in *Journal of the American Medical Association*, Vol 294 (5): 602–612.

Priest, D. (2005) "Iraq new terror breeding ground," in *Washington Post*, January 14, 2005.

Price, R. (2018) *Environmental Risks in Iraq. K4D Helpdesk Report.* Brighton: Institute of Development Studies.

Purnomo, H., Okarda, B., Dermawan, A., Illham, Q., Pacheco, P., Nurfratriani, F., and Suhendang, E. (2020) 'Reconciling oil palm economic development and environmental conservation in Indonesia: A value chain dynamic approach' in *Forest Policy and Economics,* Vol 111. doi: 10.1016/j.forpol.2020.102089

Rankin, J., Smith, H., Connolly, K., and McKernan, B. (2020) 'Refugees told 'Europe is closed' as tensions rise at Greece-Turkey border' in *The Guardian,* 6th March 2020, cited online on 27th May 2020 at https://www.theguardian.com/world/2020/mar/06/refugees-europe-closed-tensions-greece-turkey-border

Rayman, T. (2019) 'The enigma of social harm and the barrier of liberalism: why zemiology needs a theory of the good' in *Justice, Power and Resistance: The Journal of the European Group for the Study of Deviance and Social Control*, Vol 3 (1): 1–30.

Reale, E., Avramov, D., Canhial, K., Donovan, C., Flecha, R., Holm, P., Larkin, C., Lepori, B., Mosoni-Fried, J., Oliver, E., Primeri, E., Luigvert, L., Scharnhorst, A., Schubert, A., Soler, M., Soos, S., Sorte, T., Travis, C., and Van Horik, R. (2018) 'A review of literature on evaluating the scientific, social and political impact of social sciences and humanities research' in *Research Evaluation*, Vol 27 (4): 298–308.

Reay, D., Smith, P., van Amstel, A. (2010) *Methane and climate change*, London: Earthscane Publications Limited.

Reidy, E. (2020) 'The COVID-19 excuse? How migration policies are hardening around the globe' in *The New Humanitarian*, 17th April 2020, cited online on 27th May 2020 at https://www.thenewhumanitarian.org/analysis/2020/04/17/coronavirus-global-migration-policies-exploited

Renzaho, A., Polonsky, M., Mellor, D., and Cyril, S. (2016) 'Addressing migration-related social and health inequalities in Australia: call for research funding priorities to recognise the needs of migrant populations' in *Australian Health Review,* Vol 40 (3): 3–10.

Romei, T. (2018) 'Why Italy's economy is stagnating' in *Financial Times*, 12th November 2018, cited online on 27th May 2020 at https://www.ft.com/content/b3c85b34-e10a-11e8-a6e5-792428919cee

Roy, M., Guy, S., Hulme, D., and Jahan, F. (2011) *Poverty and Climate Change in Urban Bangladesh (CLIMURB): An Analytical Framework*, Manchester: Brooks World Poverty Institute.

Roy, O. (2002) *Islamic Radicalism in Afghanistan and Pakistan*, Geneva: UNHCR.

Rueff, H., and Middleton, N. (2015) 'Contraction of the Gobi Desert, 2000–2012' in *Remote Sensing* Vol 7 (2): 1346–1358.

Sadowski, Y. (2010) *Scuds or butter? The political economy of arms control in the Middle East*, Washington: The Brookings Institute.

Sainsbury, N., Genner, M., Saville, G., Pinnegar, J., O'Neill, C., Simpson, S., and Turner, R. (2018) Changing storminess and global capture fisheries' in *Nature Climate Change*, Vol 8 (June): 655–659.

Salvage, J. (2002) *Collateral Damage: The Health and Environmental Costs of War on Iraq*, London: Medact.

Samaha, N. (2016) 'The black market kings of Damascus', *The Atlantic*, 3rd October 2016, cited online on 27th May 2020 at https://www.theatlantic.com/international/archive/2016/10/syria-war-economy-damascus-assad/502304/

Savage, M. (2019) 'NHS winter crisis fears grow after thousands of EU staff quit', in *The Guardian*, 24th November 2019, cited online on 27th May 2020 at https://www.theguardian.com/society/2019/nov/24/nhs-winter-crisis-thousands-eu-staff-quit

Savage, M., Doughterty, B., Hamza, M., Butterfield, R., and Bharwani, S. (2009) *Socio-economic impacts of climate change in Afghanistan*, Stockholm: Stockholm Environmental Institute.

Scardigno, F. (2019) 'The cultural integration of young refugees: an experience within the Italian academic context' in *Italian Journal of Sociology of Education*, Vol 11 (3): 283–303.

Schellnhuber, H. (2006) *Avoiding Dangerous Climate Change*, Cambridge: Cambridge University Press.

Schvoerer, E., Massue, J., Gut, J., and Stoll-Keller, F. (2008) 'Climate change: impact on viral disease' in *The Open Epidemiology Journal*, Vol 1 (January): 53–56.

Schweitzer, R., Consterdine, E., and Collyer, M. (2018) *A Review and Analysis of the Recent Literature on the Common European Asylum System*, Chemnitz: CEASEVAL.

Selby, J., Dahi, O., Frolich, C., and Hulme, M. (2017) 'Climate change and the Syrian civil war revisited' in *Political Geography*, Vol 60 (September): 232–244.

Senesi, S., Daziano, M., Chaddad, F., and Palau, H. (2016) 'Ownership versus management: the role of farming networks in Argentina' in *International Food and Agribusiness Management* Review, Vol 20 (2) 221–239.

Shani, A., and Arad, B. (2014) 'Climate change and tourism: time for environmental scepticism' in *Tourism Management*, Vol 44 (October): 82–84.

Siddique, A. (2012) *Sources of Tension in Afghanistan and Pakistan: A Regional Perspective Afghanistan's Ethnic Divides*, Barcelona: Centre for International Affairs.

Simatele, D., and Simatele, M. (2015) 'Climate variability and urban food security in sub-Saharan Africa: lessons from Zambia using an asset based adaptation framework' in *South African Geographical Journal*, Vol 97 (3): 243–263.

Smiatek, G., Kaspar, S., and Kuntsmann, H. (2013) 'Hydrological climate change impact analysis for the Figeh Spring near Damascus, Syria' in *Journal of Hydrometeorology*, Vol 14 (2): 577–593.

Springer, S. (2008) 'The nonillusory effects of neoliberalisation: linking geographies of poverty, inequality and violence' in *Geoforum*, Vol 39 (4): 1520–1525.

Sriver, R. (2011) Man-made cyclones' in *Nature*, Vol 479 (November): 50–51.

Standing, G. (2011) *The Precariat: The New Dangerous Class*, New York: Bloomsbury Academic.

Steenkamp, C. (2017) 'The crime-conflict nexus and the civil war in Syria' in *Stability: International Journal of Security & Development*, Vol 6 (1): 1–18.

Sternberg, T., Rueff, H., and Middleton, N. (2015) 'Contraction of the Gobi Desert, 2000–2012' in *Remote Sens*, Vol 7: 1346–1358.

Stevens, D. (2017) 'Asylum, refugee protection and the European response to Syrian migration' in *Journal of Human Rights Practice*, Vol 9 (2): 184–189.

Strang, A., and Quinn, N. (2019) 'Integration or isolation? Refugees' social connections and wellbeing' in *Journal of Refugee Studies*, fez040. doi:10.1093/jrs/fez040.

Subbaraman, N. (2020) ''Distancing is impossible': refugee camps race to avert coronavirus catastrophe' in *Nature*, 24th April 2020, cited online on 27th May 2020 at https://www.nature.com/articles/d41586-020-01219-6

Supran, G., and Oreskes, N. (2017) 'Assessing ExxonMobil's climate change communications (1977–2014)', in *Environmental Research Letters*, Vol 12 (8): 1–18.

Tassinari, F. (2016) 'The renationalisation of European politics: evidence from the refugee crisis' in *Dossier: Mobility and Refugee Crisis in the Mediterranean*: IE Mediterranean Yearbook 2016: 127–131.

Taylor, G. (2017) 'Steep rise in 'hate crimes' with a racist motive reported in Oslo' in *Norway Today,* 20th April 2017, cited online on 27th May 2020 at https://norwaytoday.info/news/steep-rise-hate-crimes-racist-motive-reported-oslo/.

Terink, W., Immerzeel, W., and Droogers, P. (2013) 'Climate change projections of precipitation and reference evapotranspiration for the Middle East and Northern Africa until 2050' in *International Journal of Climatology*, Vol 33 (14): 3055–3072.

Thomas Cameron, B. (2014) 'Reflections on refugee studies and the study of refugees: implications for policy analysts' in *Journal of Management and Public Policy,* Vol 6 (1): 4–13.

Tifft, L., and. Sullivan, S. (2001) 'A needs-based, social harms definition of crime' In in S. Henry and M. Lanier (Eds) *What Is Crime? Controversies over the Nature of Crime and What to Do About It*, Lanham: Rowman and Littlefield. (pp. 179–203).

Tombs, S. (2018) 'For pragmatism and politics: Crime, social harm and zemiology' in T. Rayman and O. Smith (Eds) *The Deviant Leisure Perspective: A Theoretical Introduction*, London: Palgrave MacMillan. (pp. 11–32).

Tondo, L. (2019) 'Nearly 900,000 asylum seekers living in limbo in EU, figures show' in *The Guardian*, 25th August 2019, cited online on 27th May 2020 at https://www.theguardian.com/world/2019/aug/25/asylum-seekers-limbo-eu-countries

Tondo, L. (2020) 'Bosnia crams thousands of migrants into tent camp to 'halt Covid-19 spread' in *The Guardian*, 27th March 2020, cited online on 27th March 2020 at https://www.theguardian.com/global-development/2020/mar/27/bosnia-crams-thousands-of-migrants-into-tent-camp-to-halt-covid-19-spread

Trilling, D. (2018) *Lights in the Distance: Exile and Refuge at the Borders of Europe*, London: Picador.

Tyson, A., Varkkey, H., and Al Banna, S. (2018) 'Deconstructing the palm oil industry narrative in Indonesia: evidence from Riau province' in *Contemporary Southeast Asia*, Vol 40 (3): 422–448.

UCCRN. (2018) *The Future We Don't Want: How Climate Change Could Impact the World's Greatest Cities*, New York: UCCRN.

Ulloa, S. (2018) 'Climate change as a cause of violence in Iraq', in *FUF*, 19th December 2018, cited online on 26th May 2020 at https://fuf.se/climate-change-as-a-cause-of-violence-in-iraq/

UNDESA. (2020) *Inequality in a Rapidly Changing World*, Geneva: United Nations.

UNDP. (2017) *A Socio-Economic Impact Assessment of the Zika Virus in Latin America and the Caribbean: With a Focus on Brazil, Colombia and Suriname*, New York: UNDP.

UNEP. (2017) *Afghanistan's Climate Stories in Dari Language*, Geneva: UNEP.

UNHCR. (2015) *The Sea Route to Europe: The Mediterranean Passage in the Age of Refugees*, Geneva: UNHCR.

UNHCR. (2016a) *Global Tendencies: Forced Displacement 2016*, Geneva: UNHCR.

UNHCR. (2016b) *Out of Sight, Out of Mind: Deaths in Detention in the Syrian Arab Republic*, Geneva: UNHCR.

UNHCR. (2018a) *"I Lost My Dignity": Sexual and Gender-Based Violence in the Syrian Arab Republic*, Geneva: UNHCR.

UNHCR. (2018b) *Siege as a Weapon of War: Encircle, Starve, Surrender, Evacuate*, Geneva: UNHCR.

UNHCR. (2018c) *Stateless in Europe: Ordinary People in Extraordinary Circumstances*, Geneva: UNHCR.

UNHCR. (2019a) *Turkey Factsheet July 2019*, Geneva: UNHCR.

UNHCR. (2019b) *Refugee and Migrant Arrivals to Europe in 2019 (Mediterranean)*, Geneva: UNHCR.

UNHCR. (2020) *Advisory Opinion on the Extraterritorial Application of Non-Refoulement Obligations under the 1951 Convention Relating to the Status of Refugees and Its 1967 Protocol*, Geneva: UNHCR.

UNICEF. (2018) *Children's Rights in the Cocoa-Growing Communities of Cote d'Ivoire*, Geneva: United Nations.

United Nations. (2017) *Abuse, Exploitation and Trafficking 'Stark Reality' for Migrant Children Trying to Reach Europe*, Geneva: United Nations.

United Nations. (2020) *"They Have Erased the Dreams of My Children": Children's Rights in the Syrian Arab Republic*, Geneva: United Nations.

United Nations Office on Drugs and Crime (UNODC) (2011) *Smuggling of Migrants: A Global Review and Annotated Bibliography of Recent Publications*. New York: United Nations.

United Nations Office of Drugs and Crime (UNODC) (2018) *Global Study on Smuggling of Migrants 2018*, New York: United Nations.

UPR Working Group. (2016) *Human Rights Violations against Women and Girls in Syria*, Presented at the 26th Session of the UPR Working Group of the Human Rights Council, 25th July 2016.

USDS. (2018) *Trafficking in Persons Report – Syria, 28 June 2018*, Washington: USDS.

Vandevoordt, R., and Verschraegen, G. (2019) 'The European Refugee Controversy: Civil Solidarity, Cultural Imaginaries and Political Change' in *Social Inclusion*, Vol 7 (2): 48–52.

Vorosmarty, C., Green, P., Salisbury, J., and Lammers, R. (2000) 'Global Water Resources: Vulnerability from Climate Change and Population Growth' in *Science*, Vol 289 (7): 284–287.

Voutsina, K. (2019) *Living for Years in a Transitory Home*, Athens: Feinstein International Centre.

Wallace-Wells, D. (2020) 'The Coronavirus Is a Preview of Our Climate-Change Future' in *Intelligencer*, 8th April 2020, cited online on 27th May 2020 at https://nymag.com/intelligencer/2020/04/the-coronavirus-is-a-preview-of-our-climate-change-future.html

Wallis, E. (2020) 'Which migrant services in Europe are suspended or reduced due to COVID-19?' in *Info Migrants*, 3rd March 2018, cited online on 27th March 2020 at https://www.infomigrants.net/en/post/23524/which-migrant-services-in-europe-are-suspended-or-reduced-due-to-covid-19

Wacquant, L. (2009) *Punishing the Poor: The Neoliberal Government of Social Insecurity*, Durham: Duke University Press.Wezeman, P., Fleurant, A., Kuimova, A., Da Silva, D., Tian, N., and Wezeman, S. (2019) *Trends in International Arms Transfers, 2019*, Stockholm: SPIRI.

Wilkins, C. (2018) 'Refugees Still Sleeping Rough in Paris Despite Macron's Promises' in *France24*, 7th January 2018, cited online on 27th May 2020 at https://www.france24.com/en/20180106-refugees-still-sleeping-rough-paris-despite-macron-promises

WILPF. (2016) *Violations against Women in Syria against the Disproportionate Impact of the Conflict on Them*, Geneva: WILPF.

Windle, J. (2016) *Suppressing Illicit Opium Production in Asia and the Middle East: Successful Intervention and National Drug Policies*, London: I.B. Taurus.

Winlow, S., and Hall, S. (2012) 'What Is an Ethics Committee? Academic Governance in an Epoch of Belief and Incredulity' in *British Journal of Criminology*, Vol 52 (2): 400–416.

Winlow, S. Hall, S., Treadwell, J., and Briggs, D. (2015) *Riots and Political Protest: Notes from the Post-political Present*, London: Routledge.

Winlow, S., Hall, S., and Treadwell, J. (2017) *The Rise of the Right. English Nationalism and the Transformation of Working-Class Politics*, Bristol: Policy Press.

Wolf, M., and Ossewaarde, M. (2018) 'The Political Vision of Europe During the 'Refugee Crisis': Missing Common Ground for Integration', *Journal of European Integration*, 40 (1): 33–50.

World Bank Group. (2016) *The Cost of Fire: An Economic Analysis of Indonesia's Fire Crisis*, Jakarta: World Bank Group.

World Bank Group. (2018) *Piecing Together the Poverty Puzzle: Overview*, Washington: World Bank Group.

World Economic Forum. (2019) *World Economic Forum Meeting 2018*, Geneva: World Economic Forum.

World Health Organisation (WHO). (2007) *The World Health Report 2007: A Safer Future*, Geneva: WHO.

World Health Organisation (WHO). (2018) *Report on the Health of Refugees and Migrants in the WHO European Region: No Public Health without Refugee and Migrant Health*, Geneva: WHO.

World Poverty Report. (2019) *World Poverty Statistics that Everyone Should Know: Global Poverty Report*, Lifewater: San Luis Obispo.

World Vision. (2019) *Climate Change Adaptation and Mitigation*, London: World Vision.

World Vision. (2020) 'COVID-19 increases risk of child abuse and exploitation for refugee and internally displaced children - World Vision' in *World Vision*, 27th March 2020, cited online on 27th May 2020 at https://www.wvi.org/newsroom/coronavirus-health-crisis/covid-19-increases-risk-child-abuse-and-exploitation-refugee

World Vision. (2019) *Climate Change, Adaptation and Mitigation*, Kabul: World Vision Afghanistan.

Wright Mills, C. (1959) *The Sociological Imagination*, New York: University Open Press.

Wright, C., and Nyberg, D. (2015) *Climate Change, Capitalism and Corporations: Processes of Creative Self Destruction*, Cambridge: Cambridge University Press.

Wu, X., Yongmei, L., Zhou, S., Chen, L., and Xu, B. (2016) 'Impact of climate change on human infectious diseases: empirical evidence and human adaptation' in *Environmental International*, Vol 86 (1): 14–23.

Young, J. (2007) *The Vertigo of Late Modernity*, London: Sage.

Zaun, N. (2017) 'States as gatekeepers in EU asylum politics: explaining the non-adoption of a refugee quota system' in *Journal of Common Market Studies*, Vol 56 (1): 1–25.

Zetter, R. (1988) 'Refugees and refugee studies – a label and an agenda' in *Journal of Refugee Studies*, 1 (1): 1–6.

Zikra, M., and Lukijanto, S. (2015) 'Climate change impacts on Indonesian coastal areas' in *Procedia Earth and Planetary Science*, Vol 14: 57–63.

Zimmerman, K. (2016) 'Refugee and migrant labor market integration: Europe in need of a new policy agenda' Paper presented at the EUI Conference on the Integration of Migrants and Refugees, 29–30 September 2016.

Zion Market Research. (2018) *Global Report: Palm Oil Market Analysis by Derivative*, Zion Market Research: New York.

Žižek, S. (2016) *Against the Double Blackmail: Refugees, Terror and Other Problems with the Neighbours*, London: Allen Lane.

INDEX

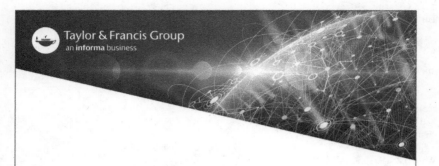